T0229894

Component-Oriented Development and Assembly

Paradigm, Principles, and Practice Using Java

In an initiative to promote authorship across the globe, Infosys Press and CRC Press have entered into a collaboration to develop titles on leading edge topics in IT.

Infosys Press seeks to develop and publish a series of pragmatic books on software engineering and information technologies, both current and emerging. Leveraging Infosys' extensive global experience helping clients to implement those technologies successfully, each book contains critical lessons learned and shows how to apply them in a real-world, enterprise setting. This open-ended and broad-ranging series aims to brings readers practical insight, specific guidance, and unique, informative examples not readily available elsewhere.

Component-Oriented Development and Assembly

Paradigm, Principles, and Practice Using Java

Piram Manickam
S. Sangeetha
S. V. Subrahmanya

CRC Press
Taylor & Francis Group
Boca Raton   London   New York

CRC Press is an imprint of the
Taylor & Francis Group, an **informa** business

AN AUERBACH BOOK

Infosys® Press

CRC Press
Taylor & Francis Group
6000 Broken Sound Parkway NW, Suite 300
Boca Raton, FL 33487-2742

© 2014 by Taylor & Francis Group, LLC
CRC Press is an imprint of Taylor & Francis Group, an Informa business

No claim to original U.S. Government works

Version Date: 20130925

International Standard Book Number-13: 978-1-4665-8099-2 (Hardback)

Library of Congress Cataloging-in-Publication Data

Manickam, Piram.
  Component-oriented development and assembly : paradigm, principles, and practice using Java / Piram Manickam, S. Sangeetha, S. V. Subrahmanya.
     pages cm
  Includes bibliographical references and index.
  ISBN 978-1-4665-8099-2 (hardcover : alk. paper)
  1. Component software. 2. Java (Computer program language) I. Sangeetha, S. II. Subrahmanya., S. V. III. Title.

QA76.76.C66M36 2014
005.3--dc23   2013037853

Visit the Taylor & Francis Web site at
http://www.taylorandfrancis.com

and the CRC Press Web site at
http://www.crcpress.com

This book is dedicated to our mentor Mr. Kris S. Gopalakrishnan,
Vice Chairman of Infosys Limited

Contents

Foreword

Modern software systems are large, distributed, increasingly decentralized, and complex beyond the ability of a single architect, designer, engineer, or project manager to comprehend. Modeling, development, integration, deployment, maintenance, and the evolution of modern software systems is a problem that, on the one hand, has been attacked with a multitude of methods, techniques, and tools, but on the other hand, is still considered "unsolved" and remains compelling to software engineering researchers and practitioners. The past couple of decades has seen a proliferation of attempts to conquer this challenge. There are a number of examples, ranging from the very successful and widely used object-oriented development methodology, to much shorter lived and ultimately less widely used subject-oriented and aspect-oriented development, to the more recent emergence of service-oriented development.

Each of these attempts has introduced its own set of concepts, constructs, and abstractions. However, they all share the goal of breaking up a system into a set of meaningful constituent components, each of which solves a part of the overall problem, that is reasonably insulated from the remainder of the system, and is sufficiently small enough to be understood, designed, implemented, and maintained by a single engineer or a small team of engineers. These components are then composed and interact to solve the larger problem. This is a very simple but powerful concept that has worked wonderfully in many other domains, from the playful compositions of Lego® blocks, to furniture construction, to the construction of buildings, to the engineering of highly complex automotive and avionics systems, and incredibly complex biological systems.

This recognition that component-based development is a way to conquer the complexity of modern software systems has been followed by the emergence of a growing ecosystem of component-based models, frameworks, tools, and platforms. However, without a proper understanding of this landscape, anyone trying to enter it will ultimately risk leaving without success and in frustration. It is for this very reason that *Component-Oriented Development and Assembly* is a timely collection of observations, insights, and understandings that provides the appropriate structure and sheds the needed light on this important topic. The authors provide a carefully thought out treatment of software components and component-oriented development. They do so in a manner that is, at the same time, rigorous and accessible to a spectrum of readers: from those who are generally knowledgeable in software engineering but do not have a background in component-oriented development, to those who have significant prior exposure but are looking to shore up their knowledge and develop expertise in the state-of-the-art. Simply put, *Component-Oriented Development and Assembly* will be a valuable addition to any software engineer's bookshelf!

Professor Nenad Medvidović

Professor and Associate Chair for Ph.D. Affairs

Computer Science Department

University of Southern California

Author of the Book—Software Architecture: Foundations, Theory, and Practice

Preface

Component-oriented software development inherently supports the reuse of artifacts. Component-based software engineering (CBSE) has been a research field for quite some time, especially in academic circles, but it has taken a considerable amount of lead time for it to be adopted by the industry. For some time now, the industry has been leveraging the advancements of component-oriented development and assembly (CODA) technology. There is no single book that provides a comprehensive overview of the multiple technologies that support CODA for students and practitioners. This book is an effort in that direction, while restricting the scope to the Java platform to illustrate CODA principles.

The book is organized into three parts covering the principles, practice, and paradigm of Component-Oriented Development and Assembly:

- Part I—Principles: Concepts in CODA
- Part II—Practice: Hands-On CODA Using Various Java Component Models
- Part III—Paradigm: Component Testing, Business Application Case Study, and Tools

Part I provides the conceptual foundation for component-oriented software. Concepts of an interface, the composition of components through provided and required interfaces, component models, and component frameworks are introduced. The concepts are explained with the help of Java as a development platform. Components have to be stitched together using glue code in the absence of a component model. A homegrown component model and a supporting component framework are used to explain the concepts and to illustrate the core concepts on which most of the standard Java component frameworks are built. A brief overview of various standard Java component models is presented.

Part II focuses on educating readers with various standard Java component models and describing how to develop a component-oriented system using these component models. The second part opens with a chapter on the design and architecture of component-oriented software. This is followed by chapters that cover various Java component models such as OSGi, SCA, Java EE, Spring, and Enterprise OSGi in depth. Each technology is explained with the help of implementation. All of the chapters make use of the same application scenario to elaborate on component-oriented solutions. This makes it easy to follow the example implementations in different chapters as well as helps the reader to compare and contrast the differences across implementations in different component models. OSGi and SCA are authoritative organizations that define guidelines for the component world. This book adheres to the guidelines set up by them.

Part III presents various aspects of the component-oriented development paradigm. The first chapter in this part deals with testing and quality assurance aspects of component-oriented software. The next chapter provides an end-to-end case study of a real-life business problem that is solved using the CODA approach. The last chapter provides input on how the use of tools can bolster the CODA approach. In this chapter, a fictitious component workbench is presented, and the software components from the case study are assembled using this tool.

Overall, the book provides enough information for anyone to start practicing CODA. We believe this book is appropriate for:

- Practicing software engineers to learn component-oriented technologies and programming
- Practicing software architects to get a concise view of various component-oriented technologies available in Java along with hands-on examples
- Academic students studying software development for understanding the benefits of component-oriented software development and assembly, for learning the concepts, and for gaining hands-on programming knowledge in various component models in Java

The book has a companion Web site (http://www.codabook.com) on which all the source code used in the book are hosted. The source code for the CODA implementation of the end-to-end case study presented in Chapter 11 using various Java component models are also hosted on the Web site. The Web site will also serve as a technical forum for further discussions of the topic, and for any updates such as errata.

Acknowledgments

We would like to acknowledge and immensely thank Infosys Limited for supporting and encouraging this book project. We would like to especially thank S. Gopalakrishnan, our mentor, and Vice Chairman, Infosys Limited, for his constant guidance, support, and encouragement during the execution of the project and for generating interest on this topic. We would like to thank Professor Nenad Medvidović, Professor and Associate Chair for Ph.D. Affairs, Computer Science Department, University of Southern California, for writing the Foreword.

We would like to thank Professor Y. Narahari, Chairman, Department of Computer Science and Automation, Indian Institute of Science (IISc), Bangalore, for his valuable technical review input on the book. We also thank Ravindra Babu Tallamraju, Principal Researcher, Infosys Limited, for helping with a detailed technical review of the book. Special thanks are due to Srikantan (Tan) Moorthy, SVP, Group Head of HR, former Global Head of Education and Research, and Nandita Gurjar, Global Head of Education and Research, for their constant support and encouragement.

Our sincere thanks to our colleagues Soumya Bardhan, Shikhar Johari, Vishal Vijay Verma, Rohit Jain, Vaasavi Lakshmi Jammalamadaka, Karthika K. Ravigopal Nair, Vibhuti Mahendra Pithwa, and Navdeep Kumar, for their help in software development, documentation, and testing of the companion code and the workbench tool to demonstrate the concepts and principles. Special thanks are due to Soumya Bardhan and Shikhar Johari for their contribution of creating all the figures used in this book.

Special thanks are due to T.S. Mohan for his help. We would like to extend our special thanks to Deepa Jagdish, John Wyzalek, Jessica Vakili, and Linda Leggio at Taylor & Francis for their support throughout the project. Last but not the least, the authors would like to acknowledge and thank their beloved families for their patience during this project.

Trademark

All the registered trademarks used in this book are the properties of their respective owners/companies. The authors have no rights to these trademarks. Example organizations, products, domain names, e-mail addresses, logos, people, places, and events depicted in this book are fictitious and no association with any real organization, product, domain name, e-mail address, logo, person, place, or event is intended or should be inferred.

Companion Web Site

The book has a companion Web site (http://www.codabook.com) on which all the source code used in the book are hosted. The Web site will also serve as a technical forum for further discussions of the topic, and for any updates such as errata.

The Authors

Piram Manickam is an ardent technologist. During the past two decades he has worked with many software development teams and built a number of systems using various development platforms. He has a special interest in object-oriented design. He has authored many technical articles. He has been practicing and teaching component-oriented development and assembly (CODA) for the last few years. He is a technical consultant and architect on many software component–based projects at Infosys. He is a graduate of electronics and communication engineering from Regional Engineering College (currently NIT) in Tiruchirapalli, India. He is currently pursuing a master of science in computer engineering from the Illinois Institute of Technology, Chicago.

S. Sangeetha is a senior technical architect at Infosys. She has been working on Java, Java EE–related technologies, for more than 14 years. She is involved in the design and development of prototypes and POCs on several enterprise application solutions. She is also involved in grooming architects at Infosys through the program Connect Architecture. She has been practicing and teaching component-oriented development and assembly (CODA) for the last few years. Sangeetha has authored many technical articles and coauthored a book titled *J2EE Architecture* (Tata McGraw-Hill, 2005). She has a bachelor's degree in engineering (electronics communication engineering) from Madras University (India).

S. V. Subrahmanya (also known as SVS) has more than 25 years of experience in the information technology industry and academics. SVS is currently working at Infosys Limited as vice president and is a research fellow at Infosys. He heads the E-Commerce Research Labs. He is also responsible for competency development of employees across the technical spectrum including new upcoming areas of technology at Infosys. SVS has published many papers in reputed journals and international conferences. He has coauthored books titled *Discrete Structures, Web Services: An Introduction* (Tata McGraw-Hill, 2004), *J2EE Architecture* (Tata McGraw-Hill, 2005), and *Enterprise IT Architecture* (Wiley India, 2006).

PART I
PRINCIPLES
Concepts in CODA

1

INTRODUCTION TO COMPONENT-ORIENTED DEVELOPMENT AND ASSEMBLY (CODA)

1.1 Introduction

Component-Oriented Development and Assembly (CODA) has lots of benefits. Product building in the modern industrial age has revolved around assembling end products from components rather than building from scratch. Although this is true for most modern-day products in many disciplines, the majority of software engineers prefer to build software products from the ground up, save alone the reuse of application frameworks, design patterns, and coding idioms. The objective of component-oriented software development and assembly is to reduce the development effort as much as possible and encourage the reuse of existing components to assemble new applications. When implemented successfully, this approach can bring down costs, reduce cycle time, and improve overall product quality. In this chapter, we introduce the concepts of component-oriented development and assembly.

This chapter introduces readers to the component paradigm. It introduces software components along with concepts of interfaces, composition, component models, and component frameworks. At the end of the chapter, readers are expected to have gained an understanding of the component-oriented paradigm and how this paradigm can be practiced in software development.

1.2 Motivation for Software Components

When we compare the software industry with other mature industries, it seems to be in its early stages of evolution. This is because other industries have advanced to automated mass production capabilities from primeval practices of individual craftsmanship-based production, and the majority of software is hand-built one line at a time by individual craftsmen (programmers) even now. The component-based software development paradigm is expected to help evolve the software industry from micro-level line-by-line building practice to a macro-level mass production practice.

Software products and services vendors are always under pressure to deliver better-quality products at lower cost and shorter time frames. Most of the time the software engineering team buckles under this pressure. What are the challenges that software engineers face in achieving these goals, and how do they overcome the challenges?

The biggest challenge is that the requirements for newer systems are getting more complex than ever before, and software development techniques have not adapted rapidly to the changing demands. Because of this, software developers are perennially looking forward to newer techniques that can bridge the gap between business demands and state-of-the-art software development methodologies.

Divide and conquer is a time-tested technique to effectively manage a complex problem. The technique involves breaking the larger problem into smaller, more manageable problems. After the smaller solutions are obtained, they can be combined to get the larger solution. CODA uses the divide and conquer technique to solve the problem of complexity.

1.3 Components—An Ice Breaker

Component as a concept stems from two root concepts: composition and decomposition. Composition is the act of assembling a system from individual parts. Decomposition is the act of dismantling parts from a system. The parts participating in the acts of composition and decomposition are known as the components of the system. Put another way, a component is part of a whole (system) which it can be attached with or detached from.

A common example of a component-based system is Lego®, in which building blocks are assembled to a toy structure or dismantled. A more sophisticated example could be an electronic product (e.g., a stereo system), which is assembled from basic components such as resistors, transistors, and advanced components such as integrated circuits (ICs).

Any product, be it software or otherwise, can be built in many different ways. For example, a kitchen cabinet can be completely custom built from raw materials, or it can be assembled from standard modular kitchen parts available from market, or it can be built from a mix of modular kitchen parts and custom-made parts. Similarly, software products can be completely custom built, or they can be built by integrating off-the-shelf software products available from market, or they can be built using a mix of both. The key difference between both of these examples is that while modular kitchen parts can be *assembled* to arrive at the final product, off-the-shelf software products need to be *integrated* to arrive at the final product. The reason for this difference is that the modular kitchen parts were designed and manufactured to be compatible with one another, while the software products were not.

Components are parts of a product that are meant to be assembled together. The basic component principle is to design and build parts that are meant to work together rather than work in isolation. Parts of a modular kitchen follow this principle, while disparate software products do not. The result is easy assembly of kitchen components and tough integration of software products. Some software products that follow the component design principle do exist. For example, Eclipse IDE is made of components, and it is easy to acquire new plugin components for the IDE and literally plug them to the core of the Eclipse product.

1.4 Component Characteristics

Apart from the basic characteristics of being part of a whole, components exhibit many other characteristics pertaining to composition and decomposition operations. We discuss the common characteristics of components in the next few subsections. We describe these common characteristics of components with examples of nonsoftware components. We use these characteristics later to extract an ideal candidate from among a variety of common software constructs that could potentially play the role of a software component.

1.4.1 Part of a Whole

Components can be composed to and decomposed from a system. Composition of an appropriate set of components should yield a complete functional system; decomposition of a complete system should yield the set of constituent components. This is a fundamental characteristic of a component.

1.4.2 Component Ecosystem

By virtue of their basic characteristic of participating in composition and decomposition, components are designed to be used in a compositional way together with other components. For example, in mechanical components, a nut does not serve any purpose in isolation from a bolt.

In other words, a component is not normally designed in isolation, but as part of a collection of collaborating components. The collaborating components work in the context of a component framework governed by a component model. The collaborating components, the component framework, and the component model together form a component ecosystem.

1.4.3 Component Framework

The component framework provides a common fabric or environment over which the components may be composed. For example, in electronic components, the printed circuit board (PCB) serves as the fabric over which the electronic components can be assembled; in mechanical components, the car skeleton or an equivalent mechanical core structure serves as the framework over which mechanical components are assembled.

1.4.4 Component Model

A component model defines what components are, how they can be constructed, how they can be composed, and how they can be deployed. The component model also defines the component framework. For example, a component model for electronics components is defined by the Electronics Industries Alliance (EIA).

1.4.5 Component Interfaces

Each component specifies one or more interfaces through which other components can be composed with it. The interfaces adhere to the composition standards defined in the component model. For example, the interface of a nut is a hollow cylinder with a threaded inner surface and a specified diameter. The interface of a bolt is a solid cylinder with a threaded outer surface and a specified diameter.

1.4.6 Provided and Required Interfaces

Interfaces specified by a component are of two types. One type of interface is meant for other components to compose with this component and make use of the functionality provided by this component. This type of interface is called a *provided interface*. Another type of interface is meant for other components to compose with this component and provide some functionality to this component. This type of interface is called a *required interface*. A component's interface specifications include both the provided and required interfaces.

As an example for provided and required interfaces, consider the case of a nut and bolt, which are to provide the functionality of fastening two mechanical components together. The bolt provides a solid cylinder with a threaded outer surface as the interface for composition. The nut provides a hollow cylinder with a threaded inner surface as the interface for composition. If the diameters of the nut and bolt match, they can compose together and fasten other mechanical parts.

Note that the nut's provided interface (a hollow cylinder with threaded inner surface) is the same as the bolt's required interface, and the bolt's provided interface (a solid cylinder with threaded outer surface) is the same as the nut's required interface.

1.4.7 Component Compatibility

Two components that coexist in a component ecosystem can be composed together only if they are compatible with each other. Two components are said to be compatible if they have complementing interfaces (i.e., the provided interface of one component should be the same as the required interface of the other). For example, a nut of 2 cm diameter cannot be fastened over a bolt of 3 cm diameter. Likewise, a nut cannot be fastened over any nail irrespective of its diameter. If there is a nut and a bolt with an equal diameter specification, then they have complementing interfaces, which makes them compatible.

1.4.8 Implementation Independence

Two compatible components (which have complementing interface specifications, by definition of compatibility) can always be composed, irrespective of the manner in which their interfaces are implemented. The composition operation concerns only the interfaces of the components and is immune to varying implementations. For example, a nut made of copper can be fastened together with a bolt made of iron, as long as they both have compatible diameters. The implementation independency leads to two other important properties—exchangeability and producer-consumer independence.

1.4.9 Producer–Consumer Independence

A component may be produced and consumed by different commercial entities, as long as the producer and consumer have a common interface definition for the component in context. This property of the component is a derivative of implementation independence. For example, the nut can be produced by company A, and the bolt can be produced by company B, and both of them can be consumed by company C as parts of a composite product. This is possible because all three companies would have fixed the interface specification (diameter of the nut and bolt) as part of the material supply contract.

1.4.10 Active and Passive Component

During the composition process that composes components together, some of the participating components may be actively performing the composition, whereas the others may be passively participating in the composition process. For example, when a gear and a shaft are being fastened by a nut and a bolt, the gear and the shaft are passive participants of the fastening process, and the nut and the bolt are the active components performing the fastening. Note that this notion of active and passive components is limited to the composition process; it does not imply that the passive components will continue to play a passive functional role in the resultant composite product. For example, in the resultant gear assembly from the previous example, the shaft and gear are active functional components during mechanical operations, even though they were passive components during composition.

1.5 Historical Perspective of Software Components

Early software systems developed in the 1950s used machine languages and assembly languages that did not have any software components. With the introduction of Fortran-I in the mid-1950s, software systems could be developed in a higher-level programming language than assembly language. However, code reuse was still limited in Fortran-I.

Fortran-I-based software systems developed in the 1950s could not use any software component, not even in the source code form for this reason. When Fortran II was introduced in 1958, the concept of a subprogram was introduced. The subprogram could be either a function or a subroutine. Subprograms are reused by many main programs through function or subroutine invocations. Thus, Fortran II-based software systems employed subprogram-based source code components. Fortran II also provided support for independent compilation of a subprogram. Therefore, the subprogram could be used as a static binary component as well.

In 1960, Algol-60 was released, which introduced the block structure concept. The block structure allowed programmers to localize parts of programs with new data environments or scopes. These code blocks could be reused across programs by means of a rudimentary reuse process that copies blocks of code from one program to another. Even though the code blocks are not scalable source code components, they are an important concept in source code components.

In 1967, the Simula-67 programming language was born, and it brought with it the concept of classes. At that time, the concept of data abstraction and abstract data type did not exist, and the connection of Simula-67 classes to these concepts was not found until 1972. Simula-67 also introduced inheritance.

Thus, class as a component in the object-oriented paradigm was born.

In 1971, the Pascal programming language was introduced. Pascal implementations support separate compilation. Each unit includes both interface and implementation. Interface of one compilation unit can be imported to another compilation unit with a *uses* statement. This feature promoted static binary components in Pascal implementations.

In 1978, C was born. It promoted the reuse of function libraries as static binary components. Header files served as interfaces between components.

Smalltalk, which was born in 1972, and reborn in 1980, treated everything as an object, a concept that has been borrowed in modern-day programming languages. The difference between a subprogram component and an object component is that the subprogram is just a method call that does not maintain data, whereas an object maintains and encapsulates data apart from providing a method call form of interaction.

With the birth of C++ in 1984, and subsequently Java in the 1990s, and .NET in 2000, object-oriented programming and class libraries occupied the center stage of components in the form of static binary components and dynamic binary components. Distributed dynamic components became prevalent in the 1990s, with the introduction of Java Beans, CORBA, COM, DCOM, JEE, and other similar technologies. See Figure 1.1 for a historical overview of software components.

1.6 Defining Software Components

Extending the definition of the generic component from Section 1.4, software components are units of composition and decomposition in a software system. Composition of an appropriate collection of software components should yield a complete software

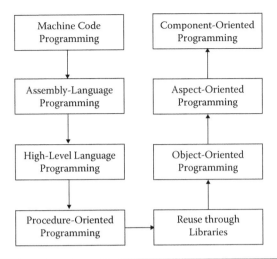

Figure 1.1 Historical perspective of software components.

system; decomposition of a software system should yield the constituent components that make up the software system.

Software components are parts of a software system which can be individually identified, stored, retrieved, assembled, and disassembled. There are two different approaches possible in the definition of software components. One approach is to use the existing software abstractions such as functions and objects as software components. Another approach is to perceive a software component as an idea or abstraction above the level of functions and objects. We follow the latter approach.

A software component provides functionality through an interface. Any other component that requires this functionality composes with this component through the exposed interface. The implementation is kept encapsulated and is not reachable from the consuming component. For example, in Java, an interface declares an interface, whereas a class provides its implementation. The component interface and implementation are similar to this concept. The assembly of components into applications should ideally not involve any recompiling or relinking. The development life cycle of one component should not depend on another component, and the application assembly should be totally decoupled from the development life cycles of individual components.

When we build software systems using components, the component is the fundamental unit of design, implementation, and maintenance. The component offers a piece of functionality which is used by other components. Functionality provided by the component is exposed through interfaces. A component should be an independent unit of development, storage, and distribution.

Functions and objects are popular design abstractions in software. Function is a sequence of operations, abstracted as a unit in order to avoid duplication of the same sequence of code. Functions help to break a long program into smaller manageable units. An object is an encapsulation of data and associated operations. A type defines a group of objects that provide the same set of operations. A class serves as a template for the creation of multiple objects of the same type. Alternatively, a prototypical object can be used to create many other objects of the same type. An individual function or object lacks the ability to encapsulate complex functionality. A collection of functions or objects can encapsulate complex functionality. Such collections are good candidates to serve as software components, provided they can expose easy-to-use interfaces and hide complex internal implementations.

1.6.1 Function Libraries as Software Components

When a collection of functions are packaged together, they form a function library. Together these functions implement complex functionality. However, to access the complex functionality, one need not invoke each of these functions. It is sufficient to invoke certain entry point functions that in turn invoke other functions. The entry point functions are known as an API (application programming interface) of the function library. The function library makes only the API functions visible from outside the library and hides the complexity of other functions. When function libraries are used as software components, one component composes with another component by invoking the API functions exposed by the latter.

There are certain limitations associated with the use of function libraries as software components. The API of a component can be invoked by another component only through a common programming language. The composition of two components happens from the source code of one component which invokes the API function call of the other component. Because the wiring between the two components is hardcoded in the source code, the composition is not amenable to rewiring during runtime. In addition to these limitations, function libraries tend to make use of global variables, which obscure the exposed API and provides backdoor entry to internal functions.

1.6.2 Object Libraries as Software Components

Instead of functions, when we package a collection of objects, we get an object library (like a Java ARchive [JAR] file in Java). Together all the objects implement a complex functionality. However, to access the functionality, it is not necessary to access all the objects in the library. It is sufficient to access a few entry point objects, and they in turn access other internal objects. The object library makes only the entry point objects visible from outside the library and hides the complexity of other objects. Type definition of the exposed objects is known as interface type.

When we use object libraries as software components, they compose through the exposed objects of the component. One component exposes the interface type objects, and the other component consumes them by invoking operations on them.

The consuming component is provided with the interface type object only during runtime. In the source code, the consuming component refers to an object of interface type, but the object is not instantiated until runtime. This breaks the hardwiring constraint associated with function library software components. Object library software components can be easily rewired during runtime. We discuss this feature in detail in the next chapter.

To facilitate reuse, we should be able to store and retrieve software components from a repository. A function library or an object library can be stored in the form of source code or binary code. A software component distributed as source code can get modified before reuse, which is not encouraged. If a software component needs some changes before it can be reused, these changes should be tracked, and the modified component should be stored in the repository as a new component. So a software component repository stores each component as a binary code in primary storage. A secondary storage can store the component as source code, but this storage is restricted to users with an obligation by them to submit a new derived component into the repository. This is discussed in detail with examples in the next chapter. In the rest of this book, we concentrate on software components made of object libraries and not of function libraries. (See Figure 1.2.)

1.7 Elements of a Software Component

A software component has the following major elements:

- Component specifications
- Component interfaces
- Component implementation(s)
- Component model that prescribes the following:
  - Composition mechanism
  - Component storage and distribution mechanism
- Runtime framework specification and standard services

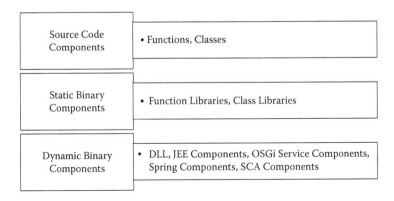

Figure 1.2 Candidate software components.

1.7.1 Component Specification

A software component provides a piece of functionality. The component specification documents the piece of functionality implemented by the component. Apart from the functional specifications, the component specification also includes details of the interfaces through which the component functionality can be accessed. The interface specification is typically in the form of signatures of all the operations exposed through it. In addition to syntactic specification of the operations, the interface specifications can include some semantics such as the preconditions and postconditions associated with each operation.

The specification of the component should include the list of interfaces that it provides and the list of interfaces that it requires. The provided interface exposes the component's functionality. The specification can also include the quality (nonfunctional) attributes of the component. One of the important characteristics of a software component is that it must support black–box reuse. Knowing only the specification details of the component, one must be able to make use of the component without any knowledge about its internal implementation.

1.7.2 Component Interfaces

Components are meant to work together. As discussed earlier, the interactions between components happen only through interfaces. The component interface defines a set of accessible operations. An interface can be considered as contract between two components. One component offers the interface, and another component consumes the interface. A component may offer and consume more than one interface.

An interface is merely a list of operations with their syntax and semantics and does not specify any implementation. Because of this, a component in a component assembly can be replaced with another component with different implementation, but which offers the same interface. The replacing component can also provide a richer interface than the original component. Such a replacement enriches the overall functionality offered by the system. Through an iterative replacement of components by richer components, gradual system evolution can be well managed.

Typically, an interface specification is only syntactic in which the signatures of various operations of the interface are specified. A semantic specification needs to specify the effect of invoking the operations on the interface. Such a specification also requires a domain and data model that explains the semantics. A less formal semantic specification can include the preconditions and postconditions associated with each operation defined in the interface. Semantic specification provides a stronger contract between the components than syntactic specifications.

It is important to notice that as components evolve and provide richer interfaces, a versioning mechanism is required to track the differences between evolving interface specifications. A providing component and a consuming component are unknown to each other prior to assembly. The only common premise on which both operate is the common interface specification. Hence, any mismatch between the providing and requiring sides can result in catastrophic consequences during runtime.

In addition to the above, an interface specification can include global constraints and invariants maintained across operation invocations. This can be useful in understanding the semantics of the component in conjunction with the preconditions and postconditions associated with each operation. An interface specification serves as a contract between the component providing the interface and the component consuming the interface.

Apart from the functional specifications of an interface, it is important to consider the quality attributes (extra-functional or nonfunctional attributes) of the component. This can be specified by means of service level guarantees such as latency, reliability, accuracy, availability, mean time between failures, mean time to repair, capacity, and so forth.

Apart from the programming interface, a component can have a data interface and a user interface. The data interface defines data structures used in the programming interface specifications. The data interface also specifies persistence functionality provided by the component. The user interface provides user interaction mechanisms.

1.7.3 Component Implementation

A component specification can be implemented by one or more component implementations. Multiple implementations of the same specification are interchangeable in a final system after the deployment. The implementations conform to the component specifications. Although the component specification defines the functionality provided by the component and the interface contracts, it does not define implementation specifications. There may be some implementation constraints mentioned as part of the specifications, but not the complete implementation specifications. Thus, different implementations can be of different programming languages or different algorithms.

Component implementation must be packaged in a binary code format as prescribed by the component model. It can include a validation code that verifies if the required interfaces of the component are satisfied in a deployed environment. The implementation package can be accompanied by requirements, specifications, design details, and test cases.

1.7.4 Component Model

A component model is a component standard that specifies the common component fabric with sockets on which components with standard plugs can be deployed. The component model defines a standard socket to be implemented by the component framework, and a standard plug to be implemented by components. Apart from the common socket and plug for the component fabric, the component model also standardizes the mechanism by which one component can expose the interface through a socket and another component can consume that interface using a plug. This is called the composition standard specification in the component model.

Apart from the standardization of the composition mechanism among the components and between the components and the common fabric, the component model defines how a component must be packaged, stored, and distributed. Typically, the component model is supported by a runtime component framework onto which components are deployed. The component framework serves as the fabric containing sockets onto which the deployed components plugin. Examples of component models are EJB, .NET, CORBA, Spring, SCA, and OSGi. These component models define a component framework, structure of the component that can be deployed onto the framework, and a composition mechanism between the components. Some of the component models also define a mechanism using components which can publish their provided interfaces. Other components can search for an interface that they require. Some component models also define an auto discovery mechanism, in which the framework performs the lookup on behalf of the requiring component. More details about the component model and frameworks are discussed in Chapter 3.

1.8 Component-Based Software Engineering

Traditional software development involves design and development for specific requirements. The classic waterfall life cycle model assumes that requirements are frozen before design is carried out. After the design is frozen, developers typically look for pieces of implementation from other systems which can be reused in the implementation of the current system.

In the component-based software engineering approach, reuse starts at the system design stage (Figure 1.3). The component-based system design makes use of all the available components to come up with the design of the system. If some required components are not available, then they are built from scratch. Unlike traditional software development, component-oriented development has different life cycle phases.

1.8.1 Requirements

During this phase, the requirements of the system as a whole are captured and the requirements' specifications are created.

Figure 1.3   Stages in component-based software engineering.

1.8.2 Component Specifications

During this phase, the requirements are analyzed and the architect in consultation with the existing software assets repository identifies architectural elements of the system. From the architectural specification, individual component specification is derived. Many of these identified components may already have specifications as part of the existing asset repository. Component architecture and component design documents are the artifacts created during this phase. The component model to be used for the system is also identified during this phase.

1.8.3 Component Provisioning

Many of the components may be sourced from the existing asset repository. Those components that are not readily available are created and developed during this phase as per the component specifications. Typically, components are developed according to a standard component model chosen during the architectural phase. The end result would be the source code and binary code representation of the components created.

1.8.4 Component Assembly

The newly developed components and existing components are assembled to create the software application. The assembly of the components is done with the help of a component framework that supports the identified component model.

1.8.5 Testing

Integration and system testing are carried out to validate that the system meets all of the requirements' specifications. System test cases and integration test cases are created. The system is tested against the test cases. If required, the components and the system will go through a defect fixing phase.

1.8.6 Deployment

The assembled components are packaged as per the packaging mechanism specified by the component model. For example, Java-based components are packaged in JAR files. The packaged components are deployed in the environment that supports the component framework.

1.8.7 Component-Based Life Cycle Artifacts

There are several artifacts involved during the component development and deployment cycle, and they are graphically represented in Figure 1.4. The business executive defines the functionality of the system, which is captured as a business domain

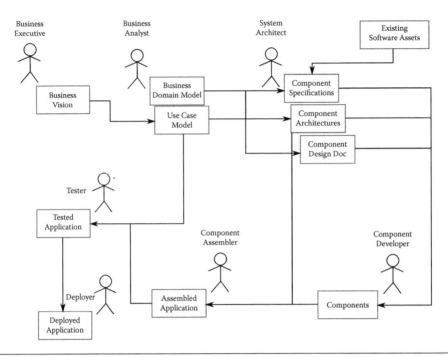

Figure 1.4   Component-based life cycle.

model and use case model by the business analyst. The system architect who is specialized in component engineering creates component specifications from the business domain model and the use case model. The architect is responsible for creating component architecture and the design document by referring to the existing software asset repository. At the end of this activity, the architect would have identified existing components and the components to be built. The design document is handed over to the component developer who develops the component adhering to the specification using a standard component model identified by the architect. The assembler assembles the software application with the existing components and the newly built components. The tester tests the components as per the test cases, and the deployer is responsible for deploying the assembled and packaged application to the deployment environment supporting the component framework.

1.9 Advantages of Component-Based Software Engineering

Traditional software engineering works on the premise that requirements for a system are completely specified before the system is designed and built. In practicality, the requirements always evolve over time. Component-based system engineering is fully aligned to this evolving requirements scenario. A component assembled into the system under construction can be replaced by another component without affecting the rest of the system. This provides an efficient and controlled system evolution path, in which one can enrich the functionalities of individual components and replace them to gradually evolve the system.

Components also aid in faster system build turnaround time because the system is built from available components. In case some of the required components are not available, parallel development of the required components can reduce cycle time. Components are used in multiple contexts in different products. Hence, they become less error prone and more rugged as they get widely deployed in many products over a period of time.

There are many other advantages in using components to build software. These advantages are summarized below:

- Increased productivity
- Contained complexity
- Reduced cycle time
- Improved quality
- Parallel and distributed development teams
- Reduced maintenance cost

There are many advantages to building a system from components than otherwise (for instance, as a monolith). Software product firms such as Microsoft®, Oracle®, or IBM® can reuse software components designed and developed as part of one product in another product, either as is or with variations to the original. If we consider custom software development firms such as Infosys® or Accenture®, each software system made by them is custom made for the clients. These firms can reuse software components designed and developed as part of one custom software system in other software systems, reducing effort and increasing quality as we elaborate below.

1.9.1 Reusability

Components promote reuse. A component designed and developed as part of one product can be applied in the composition of multiple other products. Reuse of readily available components in turn reduces the overall cycle time for development of a software system.

1.9.2 Parallel Development

If a system is designed as a composition of multiple components (some of which may already exist and others may be new), then each of the new components can be developed by different teams concurrently. This is possible due to the producer-consumer independence characteristic of components, which was presented earlier. Parallel development in turn can reduce overall time to market.

1.9.3 Easy Maintainability

Maintenance of a component-based software system is easier than that of a monolithic software system. This is due to the fact that fault isolation and correction can be localized to a single or a set of components, which can be modified without affecting the overall system. In a monolithic system one is faced with the challenge of managing unknown effects that can occur in other parts and in the overall system when a maintenance effort is carried out at one part of the system.

1.9.4 System Evolution

Evolution is the longest and most expensive phase of the software product life cycle. Component-based software systems are more open to evolution, as the composition of the system can go through gradual changes over a course of time without a big bang effect on the overall system. In other words, when a first wave of evolution happens on a software system, a set of constituent components may get exchanged with a newer set of components that cater to the requirements of evolution. The overall system is not affected during this exchange of components. After some time, when a second wave of evolution happens, another set of components may get exchanged with newer components, and so on. Thus, at the end of some Nth evolution wave, the software system may have a completely new set of components compared with the original composition structure it had before the first evolution wave. Such a smooth and gradual evolution is not easily achieved in a monolith system.

1.9.5 Single Point of Maintenance

When a component is applied in the composition of multiple software systems, apart from reusability, an additional benefit that is easily obtained is that software contained within this component is maintained only once. Defects need not be fixed redundantly in each system; any defect reported in one system would cause the component to be modified to fix the defect, and the defect fix is automatically propagated to all the other systems that employ the same component. Additionally, documentation of the component is maintained in one place.

1.9.6 Increased Quality

The more a component is reused, the more defects would get exposed. Thus, with appropriate central defect fixes and propagation of fixes to all systems, the overall quality of software systems would improve.

1.9.7 Rapid Prototyping Support

Reusable components can provide an effective basis for quickly building a prototype of a software system. This provides an opportunity to present mock systems during bidding, or to get feedback from the stakeholders during the early stages of development.

1.10 Summary

In this chapter, we were introduced to the component paradigm. We understood how components can reduce complexity. This chapter introduced software components along with concepts of interfaces—required interfaces and provided interfaces, component composition, component models, and component frameworks.

There are many advantages to building a system from components like increased productivity, reduced cycle time, improved quality, and reduced cost. We learned about the characteristics and elements of a software component. The component specification describes the functionality implemented by the component, and the component implementation implements the functionality. A component model is used as a component standard for building components. We also discussed the various phases of the CODA software engineering process and the artifacts used.

Review Questions

1. What is a software component?
2. What are the benefits of components?
3. What is provided interface?
4. What is required interface?
5. What is a component model?
6. What is a component framework?
7. What are the elements of a software component?

2

COMPONENT THINKING IN JAVA

2.1 Introduction

In this chapter, we present an introduction to software components using the Java platform with hands-on examples. We present various component constructs available in Java. We build an example application using the basic component constructs available out of the box in the Java Standard Edition (Java SE) platform. We discuss the pros and cons associated with using out-of-the-box component constructs in Java. We enhance the example application and demonstrate ways of improving the basic component constructs. We show that the use of a component model and component framework makes the job of the component developer and assembler easy.

2.2 Component Constructs in Java SE

The Java platform, Standard Edition (Java SE) consists of the following elements:

- Java Programming Language
- Java Software Development Kit (JDK)
- Java SE Application Programming Interface (API)
- Java Runtime Environment (JRE)

As application developers, we write object-oriented programs using Java classes. The Java classes that we define can refer to other Java classes within the application's code. In addition, the Java classes can refer to classes external to our application's code after certain configurations are carried out. For example, we refer to Java SE API to invoke prebuilt platform provided features. When we invoke any class defined in the Java SE API, we are referring to classes external to our application's code. Where does this external code come from? The Java SE API specifications are implemented and packaged inside the JRE runtime library called `rt.jar`.[*] We get visibility and access to this external code from within our source code by including the `rt.jar` file in the build path (during development time) and in the class path (during runtime). As an example consider the application source code shown below:

```
package codabook.helloworld;
public class HelloWorld {
        public static void main(String[] args) {
```

---

[*] ***rt.jar*** is the file name in Microsoft Windows platforms; in MacOS the file name is ***classes.jar***.

```
        System.out.println("Hello");
    }
}
```

In this example, we defined a `HelloWorld` Java class inside a Java package `codabook.helloworld`. The class refers to the `System` class which is part of another Java package `java.lang`. The `System` class is not part of our application, but it is part of the `rt.jar` file that is included in our build path. Usually, to refer to classes outside of the Java package that the source code belongs to, we need to refer to the external class with a fully qualified name such as `java.lang.System` or we need to import the class using an import statement like `import java.lang.System`, after which we can use the simple class name such as `System` across our source code. We did not have to do it in this example because all the classes in `java.lang` are imported implicitly by the Java compiler. Consider another example whose source code is shown below:

```
package codabook.greeting;
import java.util.Scanner;
public class Greeting {
        public static void main(String[] args) {
                System.out.println("Hello, What is your name?");
                Scanner scanner = new Scanner(System.in);
                String name = scanner.nextLine();
                System.out.println("Greetings, " + name + "!");
        }
}
```

In this example, we have written a `Greeting` class inside `codabook.greeting` Java package. The `Greeting` class has referred to the `System` external class similar to the last example. In addition, it refers to the `Scanner` external class, which is part of the `java.util` package provided by the `rt.jar` file. Because the `java.util` package is not imported implicitly by the Java compiler, we explicitly defined an `import java.util.Scanner` statement in our source code. Alternatively, we can refer to the `Scanner` class using its fully qualified name `java.util.Scanner`. The source code below illustrates this.

```
package codabook.greeting;
public class Greeting {
        public static void main(String[] args) {
                System.out.println("Hello, What is your name?");
                java.util.Scanner scanner =
                        new java.util.Scanner(System.in);
                String name = scanner.nextLine();
                System.out.println("Greetings, " + name + "!");
        }
}
```

In all the example programs we presented, the rt.jar file has packaged reusable Java classes. Similar to the rt.jar file, a developer can package custom code into a JAR file for distribution and use with other applications. Thus, JAR files provide a good mechanism for storing and distributing physical software components in Java.

While the JAR file provides a physical component boundary, the Java package construct provides a logical component boundary across components. For example, the rt.jar file includes many packages such as java.lang, java.util, and so forth. This helps the same physical component to carry multiple logical components.

There is an additional advantage in using packages as a logical boundary for components. It helps us to reuse simple class names across multiple components. For example, we had used the Scanner class in the example programs presented so far. This class was provided by the physical component rt.jar and the logical component java. util package. Suppose we had to define another Scanner class as part of another software component, say, a credit card processing component. If this new component has a logical boundary different from java.util, say, codabook.creditcard, the two Scanner classes have unique fully qualified names though they share a common simple name. In the next section, we show how to build software components using the package as a logical boundary and the JAR file as a physical boundary.

2.3 Java Software Components Using JAR and Package

Any Java code implementing a piece of functionality can be turned into a component by defining logical and physical component boundaries around it. For example, consider a Java class that calculates the age of a person given her date of birth. The source code of the AgeCalculator class is given below:

```
package codabook.agecalculator01;
import java.util.Calendar;
import java.util.GregorianCalendar;
public class AgeCalculator {
        public int calculateAge(Calendar dateOfBirth) {

                //...some code omitted for brevity

                if (isCurrentYearBdayPassed)
                     age = currentYear - birthYear;
                else
                     age = currentYear - 1 - birthYear;

                return age;
        }
}
```

The AgeCalculator class is within a logical boundary as defined by the package codabook.agecalculator01. We can create a physical package by compiling this package into the `AgeCalculator01.jar` file. Any developer who needs age calculation logic as part of an application that is being developed can reuse the age calculator component, by including the `AgeCalculator01.jar` file in the build path and importing the `codabook.agecalculator01.AgeCalculator` class into the source code. Let us build one such application. The application would collect the date of birth details from the user, make use of the age calculator component to calculate the age, and display the age back to the user. The application's source code is shown below:

```
package codabook.agecalculator01.app;
import java.util.*;
import codabook.agecalculator01.AgeCalculator;
public class AgeCalculatorApp {
        public static void main(String[] args) {

                AgeCalculator ageCalculator =
                            new AgeCalculator();

                //...some code omitted for brevity

                int age = ageCalculator.
                        calculateAge(dateOfBirth);
                System.out.println("Your age is" + age);
        }
}
```

The age calculator application makes use of the age calculator component as boldfaced in the source code. This is made possible by including `AgeCalculator01.jar` in the build path during the build time and in the class path during runtime. The build time and runtime dependency are illustrated in Figure 2.1. The outer box signifies the physical component boundary, and the inner package box signifies the logical component boundary. Internals of the components are housed within the logical boundary.

The simple JAR and package-based components worked well in the creation of the age calculator application. However, there is one drawback in this schema. In component-oriented development and assembly, we want to source components from independent third-party vendors. This means the vendors and the components that they develop

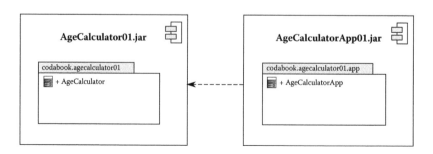

Figure 2.1   Age calculator component dependency.

are unknown to other vendors and components that they develop. Hence, independent vendors should be able to fabricate their components without any dependency on other vendors. The components are brought together only at the time of application assembly.

When we developed our example components, the age calculator component was developed without any dependency other than the Java SE API. However, when we developed the age calculator application, it had a dependency on the age calculator component, and we had to include `AgeCalculator01.jar` in our build path. This means that the application component could not be developed in isolation from the business component. This is an impediment to independent component fabrication. To solve the build time dependency problem, we can make use of Java interface construct. The next section elaborates this approach.

2.4 Java Interfaces to the Rescue of Build Time Tight Coupling

A Java interface declares a set of operations. A component can declare all the functionality that it provides through one or more Java interface definitions. These interface definitions are known as *provided interfaces* of the component. Similarly, a component can declare all the functionality it requires from other components through one or more Java interface definitions. These interface definitions are known as *required interfaces* of the component. The use of interfaces eliminates the tight coupling between components during the build time.

Let us define an interface that specifies the age calculation operation. The Java code for the interface is given below:

```
package codabook.agecalculator02.ifce;
import java.util.Calendar;
public interface AgeCalculatorIfce {
        public int calculateAge(Calendar dateOfBirth);
}
```

We package the .`class` file of this interface definition into its own JAR file called `AgeCalculatorIfce02.jar`. We modify the source code of the age calculator component presented in Section 2.3 to make use of the interface and create a new component `AgeCalculator02.jar`. The source code of this component is presented below:

```
package codabook.agecalculator02;
//...some code omitted for brevity
import codabook.agecalculator02.ifce.AgeCalculatorIfce;
public class AgeCalculator implements AgeCalculatorIfce {
      public int calculateAge(Calendar dateOfBirth) {
            //...some code omitted for brevity
}
}
```

The component requires the `AgeCalculatorIfce02.jar` file in the build path. The `AgeCalculator` class implements the `codabook.agecalculator02.ifce. AgeCalculatorIfce`. Dependency of the `AgeCalculator02.jar` component is illustrated in Figure 2.2.

Next, we modify the application component presented in Section 2.3 so that it makes use of the interface. The resultant `AgeCalculatorApp02.jar` has a source code as below:

```
package codabook.agecalculator02.app;
//...some code omitted for brevity
import codabook.agecalculator02.ifce.AgeCalculatorIfce;
public class AgeCalculatorApp {
        private static AgeCalculatorIfce ageCalculator;
        public static void main(String[] args) {
                //...some code omitted for brevity
                int age = ageCalculator.
                        calculateAge (dateOfBirth);
                System.out.println("Your age is" + age);
        }
}
```

The `AgeCalculatorApp` class is programmed to use the `AgeCalculatorIfce` interface. Hence, it refers to the `AgeCalculatorIfce02.jar` library alone and not the `AgeCalculator02.jar` component. This is illustrated in Figure 2.3.

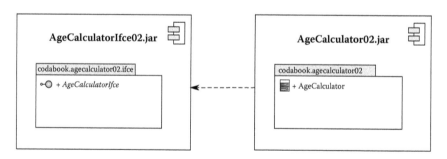

Figure 2.2   Age calculator component along with age calculator interface.

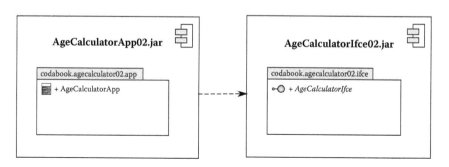

Figure 2.3   Age calculator application component along with age calculator interface.

Figure 2.4 Using interface to break build time dependency.

We have broken the build time dependency between the application and business components using the interface as illustrated in Figure 2.4. But what have we done with the runtime dependency? We discuss runtime dependency in the next section.

2.5 Runtime Dependencies While Using Interfaces

Having broken the build dependency and independently built the components, we try to execute the application by deploying all three JAR files. We get a null pointer exception on the ageCalculator variable. Why did this happen? If we inspect the source code of the AgeCalculationApp class, we can see that the ageCalculator variable is declared, but it has never been initialized:

```
private static AgeCalculatorIfce ageCalculator;
```

How do we solve this problem? How about using the code segment below?

```
private static AgeCalculatorIfce
          ageCalculator = new AgeCalculator();
```

This solution would definitely work, but in order to compile this code, we need to include the AgeCalculator02.jar file in the build time path. This brings back the evil of build time dependency. The very reason for introducing the interface was to break the build time dependency. Huh, a chicken-and-egg problem? There are a couple of other ways to initialize the ageCalculator variable without reintroducing build time dependency as presented below:

1. Assemble the providing component and requiring component manually using "glue code."
2. Automate the component assembly using a component model and component framework.

We examine both of these approaches in the next sections.

2.6 Manual Component Assembly Using Glue Code

The crux of the runtime dependency problem that we faced in the last section involves the instantiation of the variable ageCalculator, which is of the interface type. To initialize this variable, we cannot simply invoke the constructor of the AgeCalculator class, because this reintroduces the build time dependency, which we wanted to break in the first place. A manual approach to solve the runtime dependency involves creation of a "glue code" during the components assembly time. The glue code refers to AgeCalculatorIfce02.jar, AgeCalculator02.jar, and AgeCalculatorApp02.jar and provides code that mediates between these and glues the provided interface with the required interface. An example glue code is presented below:

```
package codabook.agecalculator.glue;
import codabook.agecalculator02.AgeCalculator;
import codabook.agecalculator02.app.AgeCalculatorApp;
import codabook.agecalculator02.ifce.AgeCalculatorIfce;
public class AgeCalculatorGlue {

        public static void main(String[] args) {
                AgeCalculatorIfce ageCalculator =
                                    new AgeCalculator();
                AgeCalculationApp.setAgeCalculator
                                    (ageCalculator);});
                AgeCalculationApp.main(null);
        }
}
```

The glue code instantiates the providing component object and passes this object to the requiring component as boldfaced in the source code above. The glue code is built as a component, and this component refers to the other two components and the interface as illustrated by Figure 2.5.

The flip side to the glue code is that it is specific to the components that need to be glued. Custom glue code needs to be written for each group of components that have to be glued. This process can be automated with the help of a component model and component framework, to be discussed in the next section.

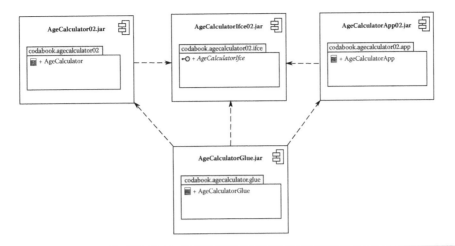

Figure 2.5 Using glue code to break runtime dependency.

2.7 Automated Component Assembly Using Component Framework

The functionality done by the glue code can be automated, provided all the components that participate in the assembly process follow common standards and conventions. Such a set of standards that enables automated component assembly is known as a *component model*. The component model is supported by a *component framework*, which is usually a runtime program that wires the components deployed.

Component models can be divided into two major categories based on how automation of component assembly is achieved:

1. Dependency injection-based component models
2. Publish and consume whiteboard query-based component models

In the dependency injection-based component models, each component declares the set of interfaces provided by it and the set of interfaces required by it. The component framework analyzes this information on all the deployed components and injects the providing component references to requiring components. The dependency injection component model is discussed in detail in Chapter 7.

In the whiteboard query-based component model, each component registers the set of provided interfaces with a whiteboard registry. Any component requiring an interface queries the whiteboard registry to obtain a reference to the providing component. We provide one such component model in the next section.

2.8 Example Component Model

The working mechanism of the whiteboard component model is based on common communication space between components that is provisioned at runtime. The components, which are unknown to one another prior to the assembly, get to know about other components through the common communication facility, and choose a companion component to compose with.

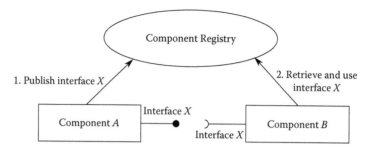

Figure 2.6 Whiteboard component model.

The whiteboard component model is illustrated in Figure 2.6. In this figure, the component registry serves as a common communication facility for all components. Components that provide services through provided interfaces register the provided interface and the service provider object with the component registry. For example, component *A* that provides interface *X* registers the provided interface *X* in step 1, as illustrated in Figure 2.6. The component registry retains a list of provided interfaces and the corresponding provider objects. Components that require services from other components look up to the component registry for the specific interfaces that they require. The component registry consults the list of registered interfaces and supplies the provider object for the interface being looked up. For example, in Figure 2.6, component *B* queries the component registry for anyone who provides interface *X*. The component registry searches through the list of registered interfaces and finds that interface *X* was registered by component *A* in step 1. The component registry retrieves the object registered by component *A* and returns it to component *B*. Thus, component *A* and component *B* are not aware of each other directly, but they use the common whiteboard (the component registry) through which they compose.

Let us define a simple whiteboard component model. In this component model, we stipulate that each component providing service through a provided interface must declare the providing object to be of a type `ComponentInterface`. For example, the age calculator component introduced in previous sections would be modified as below to be conformant with this component model:

```
package codabook.agecalculator03;
//...some code omitted for brevity
import codabook.agecalculator03.ifce.AgeCalculatorIfce;
import codabook.componentmodel.ComponentInterface;

public class AgeCalculator implements AgeCalculatorIfce,
ComponentInterface {

        public int calculateAge(Calendar dateOfBirth) {

                //...some code omitted for brevity
        }
}
```

The AgeCalculator class has been modified to implement ComponentInterface in addition to the AgeCalculatorIfce business interface that it implements. ComponentInterface is just a marker interface (an interface that does not dictate any operation to be implemented but is used for marking a class to be of a certain type). The source code for ComponentInterface is defined in the Component Model.jar library and is presented below:

```
package codabook.componentmodel;
public interface ComponentInterface {
}
```

The ComponentModel.jar library also hosts the ComponentRegistry, whose source code is presented below:

```
package codabook.componentmodel;
import java.util.HashMap;
import java.util.Map;
public class ComponentRegistry {

        static Map<Class<?>, Object> components = new
        HashMap<Class<?>, Object>();

        public static void registerComponent
                        (Class<?> ifceClazz, Object compObject) {
            components.put(ifceClazz, compObject);
        }

        public static Object fetchComponent(Class<?> ifceClazz) {
                return components.get(ifceClazz);
        }
}
```

The registerComponent() static method in the ComponentRegistry is used to register the provided interface of a component in the whiteboard. In our component model, this registering responsibility is entrusted with the component framework. The component framework implementation looks for all the classes that implement ComponentInterface and registers these classes with the ComponentRegistry. A code segment from the component framework implementation is presented below to demonstrate how this happens:

```
package codabook.componentframework;
//...some code omitted for brevity
import codabook.componentmodel.ComponentRegistry;
import codabook.componentmodel.ComponentInterface;
public class ComponentFramework {
        public static void main(String[] args) {
        //...some code omitted for brevity
```

```
    if (clazz.asSubclass(ComponentInterface.class)) {

            Class<?>[] interfaces = clazz.getInterfaces();

            Object compObject = clazz.newInstance();
            for (Class<?> ifceClazz : interfaces) {
                if (ifceClazz ! = ComponentInterface.class)
                        ComponentRegistry.registerComponent
                                    (ifceClazz, compObject);
            }
    }
    //...some code omitted for brevity
    }
}
```

The ComponentFramework scans all the JAR files in a specified deployment folder. Class files inside each JAR file are analyzed, and any class implementing ComponentInterface is identified as implementing a provided interface of the component. An object of this class is instantiated and is registered with the component registry.

A component that requires an interface makes use of the fetchComponent() static method defined in the ComponentRegistry. For example, the AgeCalculatorApp presented in previous sections is modified as below to make use of the component model and framework:

```
package codabook.agecalculator03.app;
//...some code omitted for brevity
import codabook.agecalculator03.ifce.AgeCalculatorIfce;
import codabook.componentmodel.ComponentRegistry;
public class AgeCalculatorApp {
        private static AgeCalculatorIfce ageCalculator;
        public static void main(String[] args) {

            ageCalculator = (AgeCalculatorIfce)
                ComponentRegistry.fetchComponent
                    (AgeCalculatorIfce.class);
            //...some code omitted for brevity
            int age = ageCalculator.calculateAge(dateOfBirth);
            System.out.println("Your age is" + age);
        }
}
```

As shown in the boldfaced code, the age calculator app initializes the ageCalculator variable by querying the component registry for any provider for the interface AgeCalculatorIfce. Because the framework code shown above in the ComponentFramework registered the AgeCalculator class from the

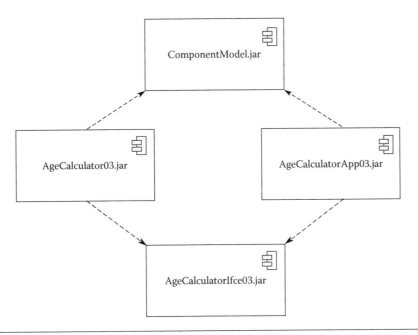

Figure 2.7 Using the component model—age calculator component dependency.

`AgeCalculator03.jar` component against this interface, the query to the component registry returns an object `AgeCalculator` class.

Deployment and running of the components involve copying all the component JAR files shown in Figure 2.7 to a deployment folder and running the `ComponentFramework` from that folder.

2.9 Summary

In this chapter, we presented the component constructs available from Java. We investigated the use of JAR files as physical components and Java packages as logical component boundaries. We discovered that these plain Java constructs demanded tight coupling between components. To alleviate tight coupling, we introduced component interfaces. While component interfaces could solve the tight coupling problem that existed during the build time, we bumped into an instantiation problem due to the decoupling of build dependency. To solve this problem, we introduced manual component assembly using glue code. However, the glue code approach is not scalable as it is specific to the components being assembled. We introduced alternative assembly using component models and frameworks. We discussed two different types of component models and elaborated on the concept with an example whiteboard component model and framework. In the upcoming chapters, we make use of the concepts introduced in this chapter to explain how standard component models and frameworks function.

Review Questions

1. What are the basic component structural constructs in Java SE platform?
2. What are the pros and cons of basic component constructs provided by Java SE platform?
3. Why is a component interface important? What is the primary reason for introducing a component interface?
4. What is glue code? Why is it required?
5. What is the alternative to using glue code?
6. What is a component model?
7. What are the different types of component models?
8. What is the relationship between a component model and a component framework?
9. How are components wired in a whiteboard component framework?
10. Can a component with the provided interface take the responsibility of registering it with a whiteboard component registry? Why or why not?

3
COMPONENT MODELS IN JAVA

3.1 Introduction

A component is a reusable software entity. A component is a deployable piece of software that can be independently developed and maintained. In Chapter 2, we learned the need for componentizing applications to get the benefits of reusability and modularity. We also looked at how the age calculation application can be componentized using a simple component model using a whiteboard query-based component model using a whiteboard pattern and a component repository.

In this chapter, we will try to understand popular component models in Java and briefly compare the features provided by them. Traditionally, to explain component-based software engineering (CBSE) principles, popular component frameworks like CORBA, DCOM, and JavaBeans are used. Instead of this traditional approach, this chapter (and the book) will focus on the latest and widely adopted component models and frameworks specific to the Java platform, like the Enterprise JavaBeans (EJB) component model, OSGi component model (OSGi), Spring component model (Spring), and the component model using Service Component Architecture (SCA).

3.2 Understanding Components

Component-Oriented Development and Assembly is a preferred solution to address the increasing complexity in developing software applications. Component-oriented development has many advantages. Typically, a component is accessed using an interface that is provided by the component. A component can also depend on other interfaces provided by other components for fulfilling the functionality. Components are developed, assembled, and composed with the help of a standardized component model. Each component model has its own standards for development and composition. These component models are accompanied by component frameworks that provide the runtime environment in which components are deployed, assembled, and executed.

Components can be classified into different types depending on where and how they are used. We try to classify the components into the following types based on their usage in N-tier architecture.

- UI Components

  Reusable components created for user interface in applications. These components typically represent UI elements such as form control—text field, radio button, data grid, table, and so forth—used for managing the presentation tier of the application.

- Business Components

  Reusable components that contain the business logic of the application. The components are usually POJO (Plain Old Java Object) based, developed and deployed according to a standardized component model. The model also provides the environment for execution of these components.

- Persistence Components

  Reusable components used in the persistence tier of an enterprise application. These components typically help in managing the persistence between the enterprise application and the data store.

- Application Services Components

  Reusable components that perform services like security, infrastructure management, transaction, and validation for the application. These components are used along with the business components because they provide the application services required for the business components.

The focus of this chapter is on the development of *business components*; let us try to understand how the business components can be developed using the following standardized, matured, and popularly used component models:

- Enterprise JavaBeans (EJB)
- Spring
- OSGi
- Service Component Architecture (SCA)

The objective is to give an introduction of these component models from the perspective of component principles and to understand the features provided by each of them. This chapter does not delve much into the details of each of these component models.

3.3 Enterprise JavaBeans Component Model

Enterprise JavaBeans (EJB) is a component model that is a significant part of Java Platform, Enterprise Edition. This is a standard from JCP (Java Community Process) for representing business components using Java in an N-tier enterprise application.

Enterprise JavaBeans are distributed business components that contain the business logic of the enterprise application. The EJB standard has come a long way from its version 1.0 to the current version 3.2. Since the introduction of the EJB 3.0 specification, EJB has become a truly lightweight, POJO-based component model. We refer to the EJB 3.x specification for our discussion.

The Enterprise JavaBeans component is a combination of an interface referred to as the *business interface* and a class (POJO) containing the implementation for the interface referred to as the *EJB component*.

3.3.1 Business Interface

The business interface of an EJB is a Plain Old Java Interface (POJI). The business interface for the enterprise bean contains the signatures of the business methods. The business interface is the *provided interface* of an EJB component, only this interface is exposed to the clients. The Enterprise JavaBeans model supports both local invocation and distributed invocation. So the component interface (business interface) can be used for local invocation and remote invocation.

3.3.2 EJB Component

The EJB component implements the operations defined in the business interface. The EJB component is available in the following types:

- Stateless Session Bean
- Stateful Session Bean
- Singleton Session Bean
- Message-Driven Bean

A stateless session bean represents the business component that has no conversational state with the client. Stateless session bean components are not shared between clients. They are used for a single method request/response communication between the client and the component.

A stateful session bean is a business component that contains the conversational state for a single client. The conversational state of the component is maintained *only* for a single client.

A singleton session bean is a new type of enterprise bean introduced from EJB 3.2. A single instance of a singleton session bean is shared across multiple clients and allows for concurrent access.

Message-driven beans are business components that are designed to consume messages from messaging systems like Java Message Service (JMS). Message-driven beans enable asynchronous communication, and they get activated upon message arrival.

The type of bean is identified through metadata annotation in the source code of the bean class or through an XML deployment descriptor. The following source code annotations can be used to classify the bean:

- `@Stateless`
- `@Stateful`
- `@Singleton`
- `@MessageDriven`

3.3.3 EJB Container

EJB components are typically deployed into the EJB container, which provides runtime and services for them. The EJB component and the business interface are packaged into a JAR file and deployed in an EJB container. EJB containers manage the life cycle of the EJB components. Typically, clients trying to access the component cannot create an object of the EJB component directly; rather, they get a reference to the object created by the container. Containers are rich in features and provide all the services required for the components. The container also maintains a registry of all the components deployed in it.

3.3.4 Component Reference

Clients accessing enterprise beans (except message-driven beans) can be either remote or local clients. A remote client is one that accesses EJB components using a remote protocol like RMI or IIOP. A local client is one that accesses EJB components from the same JVM in which the component is running.

The EJB components are not instantiated directly using the *new* operator. For accessing EJB components, dependency injection is used for getting a reference to the component deployed in the container. Dependency injection is based on the principle of *Inversion of Control*. The idea is to avoid direct creation of objects using the *new* operator. Dependency injection for EJB components is provided through a metadata annotation `@EJB`. The annotation `@EJB` specifies a reference to the business interface. When this annotation is used, the container will provide a reference of the component to the clients. A local client for EJB simply uses the `@EJB` to get a reference to the component.

A remote client for EJB, where injection is not possible, has an alternative way of accessing EJB components. It can use JNDI (Java Naming and Directory Interface) API for locating the components in the container with a string name usually called JNDI name. For a JNDI lookup, the container responds with the reference of the component which will be used by the clients.

Message-driven beans cannot be accessed by clients directly because they are asynchronous message listeners. This is a type of EJB component that is activated by the arrival of a message in a message destination. Clients cannot directly invoke any of the methods in the message-driven bean.

3.3.5 An Example to Understand the EJB Component Model

The EJB component model discussed above can be understood with a simple example (Figure 3.1). Let us take the example of the *age calculator component* discussed in Chapter 2. As we know, the `AgeCalculator` class has a single method called `calculateAge()`, which takes a `Calendar` parameter to represent the date of birth.

The business interface of the component in the EJB model is a remote interface called `AgeCalculatorBeanRemote`, whose source code is presented below:

```
package codabook.agecalculator.ejb;

import java.util.Calendar;
import javax.ejb.Remote;

@Remote
public interface AgeCalculatorBeanRemote {
  public int calculateAge(Calendar dateOfBirth);
}
```

The business interface is implemented as a stateless session EJB component `AgeCalculatorBean`. The stateless session bean was chosen because the component need not maintain the conversational state across multiple method invocations from the client. Client application using this component invokes the component method and gets the calculated age value:

```
package codabook.agecalculator.ejb;

import java.util.Calendar;
import java.util.GregorianCalendar;
import javax.ejb.Stateless;
```

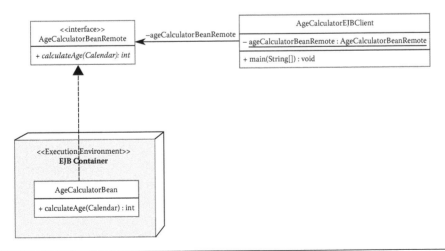

Figure 3.1   The EJB component model—age calculator component example.

```
@Stateless
public class AgeCalculatorBean implements AgeCalculatorBeanRemote
{

    public int calculateAge(Calendar dateOfBirth) {
      Calendar rightNow = new GregorianCalendar();

      int currentYear = rightNow.get(Calendar.YEAR);
      int currentMonth = rightNow.get(Calendar.MONTH);
      int currentDate = rightNow.get(Calendar.DATE);

      int birthYear = dateOfBirth.get(Calendar.YEAR);
      int birthMonth = dateOfBirth.get(Calendar.MONTH);
      int birthDate = dateOfBirth.get(Calendar.DATE);

      int age = 0;

      boolean isCurrentYearBdayPassed =
                (currentMonth > birthMonth)
            || ((currentMonth = = birthMonth)
            && (currentDate > = birthDate));

      if (isCurrentYearBdayPassed) {
        age = currentYear - birthYear;
      } else {
        age = currentYear - 1 - birthYear;
      }

      return age;
    }
}
```

As discussed in Chapter 2, component assembly can be achieved by using either dependency injection provided by the component models or whiteboard publish and consume models. In this model, the instantiation of the component is managed using the dependency injection approach. There is no need to create a glue code for solving the runtime dependency of the component.

The AgeCalculatorBean component provides an interface AgeCalculator BeanRemote, which is registered with the EJB container at the time of deployment. The EJB container provides the component registry, where the component is stored with a global JNDI name. The default JNDI name assigned to a component is the name of the business interface with a lowercase first letter. In this example, when the AgeCalculatorBean component is deployed, the container assigns a default JNDI name ageCalculatorBeanRemote. Optionally, the JNDI name can be specified as part of the @Stateless annotation.

The stateless session bean is accessed by the client using a dependency injection. The annotation @EJB is used on the business interface. In the example code below,

@EJB   annotation is used for a static member variable `ageCalculatorBean Remote`. The client need not create an object of the bean; rather, the container will inject the reference of the bean instance to the client. On seeing this annotation on a reference, the EJB container looks for the bean with the same JNDI name in the registry. Thus, it provides the client with an instance of the *age calculator component*:

```java
package agecalculatorejbclient;

import codabook.agecalculator.ejb.AgeCalculatorBeanRemote;

import java.util.Calendar;
import java.util.GregorianCalendar;
import java.util.Scanner;
import javax.ejb.EJB;

public class AgeCalculatorEJBClient {

  @EJB
  private static AgeCalculatorBeanRemote ageCalculatorBeanRemote;

  public static void main(String[] args) {
    Scanner scanner = new Scanner(System.in);

    System.out.println("What is your year of birth?");
    int year = scanner.nextInt();

    System.out.println("What is your month of birth (1-12)?");
    int month = scanner.nextInt();

    System.out.println("What is your date of birth (1-31)?");
    int date = scanner.nextInt();

    Calendar dateOfBirth = new GregorianCalendar();
    dateOfBirth.clear();
    dateOfBirth.set(year, month - 1, date);

    int age = ageCalculatorBeanRemote.calculateAge(dateOfBirth);

    System.out.println("Your age is " + age);
}
}
```

As shown in the code, the client gets a reference of the business interface by the dependency injection technique provided by the EJB component model. Alternative to the dependency injection, the JNDI API can be used to locate a reference of the business interface.

3.4 Spring Component Model

Spring is the most popular open source framework for building end-to-end enterprise applications in Java. Spring has many positive features such as being lightweight and modular. The Spring framework was initially written by Rod Johnson and was first released in June 2003. Spring components are POJO based, and they do not need heavyweight containers; lightweight Web containers (servlet containers) are sufficient.

Spring is popular because of its support for Inversion of Control (IoC) features in the form of dependency injection. As discussed earlier, dependency injection lets an object obtain a reference of another object without using a *new* operator. Dependency injection is the heart of the Spring framework. Apart from dependency injection, the Spring framework provides support for AOP (aspect-oriented programming) as well. The Spring framework provides the required APIs for development and deployment of the components.

Spring is slightly different from other component models because there is no concept of interface. The component is used directly. The Spring framework is composed of *Spring beans* (the "Component"), which are essentially POJOs deployed in a *Spring container*. The Spring container instantiates the bean components using a configuration mechanism that is usually specified through an *XML file*.

3.4.1 Spring Container

The Spring container is the core of the Spring framework. The container takes the responsibility of instantiating components, configuring properties of components, wiring them together as per dependency injection information specified, and completely managing the life cycle of components from their creation through destruction. The container completely depends on a configuration to decide on which components to instantiate and how to wire.

The Spring container is built on the principle of IoC. The container uses dependency injection to manage the components deployed in them. The components are referred to as *Spring beans*. The Spring container is of two types:

- Spring `BeanFactory` container
- Spring `ApplicationContext` container

The Spring `BeanFactory` container is the simplest container, which is an implementation of the Factory design pattern. The Spring `BeanFactory` container provides basic support for dependency injection. It is defined by an interface called the `BeanFactory` interface in the Spring API. The Spring `ApplicationContext` container is an enhanced container that includes all the functionality provided by the `BeanFactory` container and additionally provides features required for enterprise functionality. Hence, for simple, lightweight applications, the `BeanFactory` container can be used, whereas the `ApplicationContext` container is preferred.

The `ApplicationContext`   container provides several ways to load the bean definitions from the configuration file. It allows loading the XML file from a file system through a class named `FileSystemXmlApplicationContext`, from the CLASSPATH using a class called `ClassPathXmlApplicationContext`, and from a Web application through the class `WebXmlApplicationContext`.

3.4.2 Spring Beans

Spring beans play the role of business components in the Spring framework. They are developed and deployed in the Spring container which manages their life cycles. The instantiation of beans is managed by the container with the help of the configuration file. Spring beans are POJOs and are categorized into two types only at the time of instantiation:

- Singleton
- Prototype

If a Spring bean is singleton, only one single instance of the bean is created per Spring container. The single instance is cached and used for subsequent requests. If a Spring bean is prototype, any number of instances can be created based on the requests. By default, the Spring bean is singleton in nature. The type of bean is specified in the bean definition configuration file.

3.4.3 Spring Configuration

Spring provides three configurations as mentioned below:

- XML-based configuration file
- Annotation-based configuration
- Java-based configuration

The most popular configuration mechanism is through the XML file. This configuration file can have any name but is usually named `Beans.xml` and is critical in managing bean instances. The Spring container loads the XML file and manages the beans defined in the file.

The XML file contains the configuration metadata used by the container for creating a bean instance, managing the bean's life cycle methods, and managing the bean's dependencies. Some of the important metadata that are part of the configuration file are listed below:

- id—id for the bean
- class—Specified the bean class
- name—Alias name for the Id of the bean
- scope—Scope of the bean objects: singleton, prototype

- lazy-init—Bean will be initialized only during the first request
- init-method—Method invoked after initialization of the bean
- destroy-method—Method invoked before the destruction of the bean instance
- constructor-arg—Used for injecting dependencies
- properties—Used for injecting dependencies
- autowire—Used for injecting dependencies

3.4.4 An Example to Understand the Spring Component Model

The Spring component model can be understood with the same *age calculator* example discussed in the EJB component model section (Figure 3.2).

The AgeCalculatorBean is a POJO with the same calculateAge method discussed earlier. The Spring bean need not implement any interfaces:

```
package codabook.agecalculator.spring;

import java.util.Calendar;
import java.util.GregorianCalendar;

public class AgeCalculatorBean {

        public int calculateAge(Calendar dateOfBirth) {
                Calendar rightNow = new GregorianCalendar();

                int currentYear = rightNow.get(Calendar.YEAR);
                int currentMonth = rightNow.get(Calendar.MONTH);
                int currentDate = rightNow.get(Calendar.DATE);

                int birthYear = dateOfBirth.get(Calendar.YEAR);
                int birthMonth = dateOfBirth.get(Calendar.MONTH);
                int birthDate = dateOfBirth.get(Calendar.DATE);

                int age = 0;
```

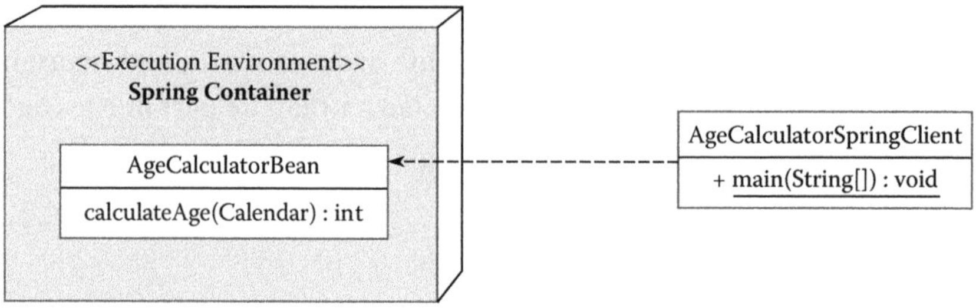

Figure 3.2   Spring component model—age calculator component example.

```
        boolean isCurrentYearBdayPassed =
                (currentMonth > birthMonth)
            || ((currentMonth = = birthMonth)
            && (currentDate > = birthDate));
        if (isCurrentYearBdayPassed) {
                age = currentYear - birthYear;
        } else {
                age = currentYear - 1 - birthYear;
        }
        return age;
    }
}
```

The configuration file is an XML file named Beans.xml. The XML file is placed under the source folder of the project. As mentioned earlier, the XML file is used for uniquely identifying beans and the creation of objects. In the Spring component model, the components get registered with the Spring container through the XML configuration file. When the Spring application is loaded in the memory, the XML file is read first, and the container uses this configuration file to create all the required beans and assigns id as per the tags present in the configuration file. The XML file used in this example is shown below. The AgeCalculatorBean is assigned a unique id ageCalculatorBean in the configuration file. Every bean is identified using the *<bean>* tag in the XML file, and this tag can have child tags like *<property>*:

```
<?xml version = "1.0" encoding = "UTF-8"?>
<beans xmlns = "http://www.springframework.org/schema/beans"
    xmlns:xsi = "http://www.w3.org/2001/XMLSchema-instance"
    xsi:schemaLocation = "http://www.springframework.org/schema/
    beans http://www.springframework.org/schema/beans/spring-
    beans.xsd">

<bean id = "ageCalculatorBean"
    class =
"codabook.agecalculator.spring.AgeCalculatorBean"/>
</beans>
```

To access the AgeCalculatorBean, the id of the bean and the context should be available for client programs. First, the client tries to create an application context appropriately (File or ClassPath or Web). In this example, the client uses the ClassPathXmlApplicationContext API that helps in loading the Beans. xml from the CLASSPATH (the XML file must be available in the CLASSPATH). Based on the information available in the configuration file, the container takes the responsibility of creating and initializing the beans defined in the file. In this case, it is ageCalculatorBean. The context plays an important role to get the reference of the bean because there is no interface. Because there is no interface in the Spring component model, the client obtains a bean reference using the getBean() method of the application context object. The Spring container returns an instance of the bean. The client application uses the reference to invoke the business methods as demonstrated in the client application code below:

```
package agecalculatorspringclient;

import java.util.Calendar;
import java.util.GregorianCalendar;
import java.util.Scanner;

import org.springframework.context.ApplicationContext;
import org.springframework.context.support.
                    ClassPathXmlApplicationContext;
import codabook.agecalculator.spring.AgeCalculatorBean;

public class AgeCalculatorSpringClient {

        public static void main(String[] args) {
                ApplicationContext context =
                        new ClassPathXmlApplicationContext("Beans.xml");

                AgeCalculatorBean ageCalculatorBean =
                        (AgeCalculatorBean) context.getBean
                ("ageCalculatorBean");

        Scanner scanner = new Scanner(System.in);

        System.out.println("What is your year of birth?");
        int year = scanner.nextInt();

        System.out.println("What is your month of birth (1-12)?");
        int month = scanner.nextInt();

        System.out.println("What is your date of birth (1-31)?");
        int date = scanner.nextInt();

        Calendar dateOfBirth = new GregorianCalendar();
        dateOfBirth.clear();
        dateOfBirth.set(year, month - 1, date);

        int age = ageCalculatorBean.calculateAge(dateOfBirth);

        System.out.println("Your age is " + age);
        }
}
```

3.5 OSGi Component Model

OSGi is the latest to join the bandwagon of component models. The OSGi framework is a standards-based platform whose specifications are provided by the OSGi Alliance (www.osgi.org), (formerly OSGi was referred to as the Open Services Gateway

Initiative). The OSGi Alliance is an industry-backed nonprofit organization that was founded in March 1999. The OSGi specification has gone through many releases, and the current major version in use is 4 and version 5 was recently introduced.

The OSGi defines a dynamic module system for Java. This comes as a rescue for Java's modularity problems by giving better control to the code structure, better life cycle management of objects, and a loosely coupled modular architecture.

The OSGi specification consists of two parts:

• OSGi framework
• OSGi standard services

The OSGi framework is the OSGi runtime environment that provides all the functionality as per the specifications. Applications are deployed and executed in the OSGi framework. The OSGi framework provides the API for the development of components. There are a number of framework implementations, and some of the popular ones are *Eclipse Equinox*, *Apache Felix*, and *Knopflerfish*. OSGi standard services define reusable services that should be provided as part of the development platform implementation. There are three conceptual layers in the OSGi framework:

• Module layer—Responsible for packaging and sharing code
• Life cycle layer—Responsible for managing the life cycle of a deployed module during runtime
• Service layer—Responsible for dynamic service publication, searching and binding

3.5.1 OSGi Bundle

An OSGi bundle is a deployment module in the form of a JAR file. A module in OSGi parlance is known as a bundle. Bundles contain class files and resource files, similar to the regular JAR file in Java, but in addition they contain *manifest information* that contains metadata about the bundle. Apart from the regular JAR file's manifest contents, a bundle's manifest file has OSGi specific information such as module name, version number, dependencies, and so forth, thus giving better modularity and easy maintainability. Bundles are more powerful than JAR files in enforcing module boundaries, because a bundle needs to explicitly define what portion of its internal code is externally visible. Similarly, a bundle must explicitly declare any external dependencies that it has with the code exposed by other bundles. A bundle must have a unique identity—bundle name and version.

The OSGi framework matches the exports and imports of deployed bundles to dynamically wire the entire application. This process of bundle resolution ensures consistency among the different bundles in terms of versions and other constraints. An application in OSGi is nothing but a collection of bundles with explicitly defined dependencies. A bundle is deployed in the OSGi framework once it is developed.

3.5.2 OSGi Service Registry

The OSGi service registry promotes service-oriented programming. The service registry provides service publication, service discovery, and service binding. The bundles deployed in the OSGi framework can leverage the service registry for publishing and consuming services. A bundle providing a service publishes the service in the OSGi service registry. A service is defined by a Java interface, which represents a conceptual contract between the provider and consumer. A potential consumer can use the registry to search for providers of a particular service. Once it finds a service provider, it can bind and use the service. Just as bundles can be added and removed in a running application, the services can appear and go dynamically in a runtime application.

3.5.3 OSGi Component

As discussed earlier, a bundle is the deployment unit in an OSGi component model. A bundle is a JAR file that contains:

- Class files
- Resource files
- Manifest files (with additional metadata)

The manifest will have additional metadata as shown below:

```
Manifest-Version: 1.0
Bundle-ManifestVersion: 2
Bundle-Name: com.demo.helloWorld
Bundle-SymbolicName: com.demo.helloWorld
Bundle-Version: 1.0.0.qualifier
Bundle-Activator: com.demo.Activator
Bundle-Vendor: PIRAM
Bundle-RequiredExecutionEnvironment: JavaSE-1.7
Import-Package: org.osgi.framework;version = "1.3.0"
Bundle-ActivationPolicy: lazy
```

The OSGi framework provides an inbuilt API called the `BundleActivator`, which helps the bundle to hook to its own life cycle management. The `BundleActivator` interface has two methods—`start()` and `stop()`—which are invoked when the bundle is started and stopped, respectively. Any bundle can implement this interface to intervene in its own life cycle. The bundle needs to be able to expose certain functionalities as provided interfaces and it needs to consume functionalities as per the required interfaces. Thus, a collection of bundles made into an assembly should be able to work together to form a system. Generally, the provided interface will be created as a separate bundle, and the implementations can be wired dynamically by the OSGi runtime from the implementation bundles. There can be more than one implementation; the wiring happens depending on the runtime.

OSGi bundles are part of the module layer. On top of the module and life cycle layers, the OSGi framework defines the services layer. The services layer defines the OSGi service registry using the components that can publish, look up, and consume services. The OSGi standards also specify an optional declarative services on top of the service layer for the dynamic wiring of components. The declarative services require an XML file named `component.xml`. The `component.xml` defines the component and its provided and required interfaces. The example that follows this section uses declarative services. For more details on declarative services refer to Chapter 5.

3.5.4 An Example to Understand the OSGi Component Model

The OSGi component model can be understood with the same *age calculator* example discussed in the earlier models presented in previous sections (Figure 3.3).

The *age calculator* application used in this example is created with the following bundles for better modularity and maintainability:

1. Interface bundle (`codabook.agecalculator.osgi.ifce`)
2. Implementation bundle (`codabook.agecalculator.osgi.impl`)
3. Client bundle (`codabook.agecalculator.osgi.client`)

The *age calculator component* is composed of the interface bundle and the implementation bundle. The interface bundle (`codabook.agecalculator.osgi.ifce`) defines an interface `IAgeCalculator`. This interface will be used by the implementation bundle to implement the exposed services. The client bundle will use the interface for invoking the required services, which gets bounded to the implementation bundle by the service registry.

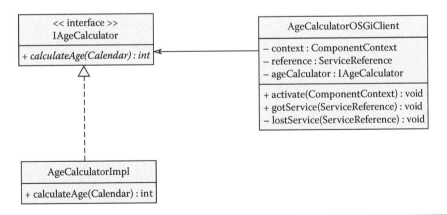

Figure 3.3 OSGi component model—age calculator component example.

3.5.4.1 Interface Bundle The interface bundle contains the interface `IAge Calculator` for the *age calculator component* and is defined as below:

```
package codabook.agecalculator.osgi.ifce;

import java.util.Calendar;

public interface IAgeCalculator {

        public int calculateAge(Calendar dateOfBirth);
}
```

This bundle has *only* the interface, and it exports the `codabook.agecalculator.osgi.ifce` package as shown in the manifest file below:

```
Manifest-Version: 1.0
Bundle-ManifestVersion: 2
Bundle-Name: Ifce
Bundle-SymbolicName: codabook.agecalculator.osgi.ifce
Bundle-Version: 1.0.0.qualifier
Bundle-ActivationPolicy: lazy
Bundle-RequiredExecutionEnvironment: JavaSE-1.6
Import-Package: org.osgi.framework;version = "1.3.0"
Export-Package: codabook.agecalculator.osgi.ifce
```

The contents of the bundle JAR file are illustrated in Figure 3.4.

3.5.4.2 Implementation Bundle The `IAgeCalculator` interface is implemented by the class `AgeCalculatorImpl`, whose code is provided below:

```
package codabook.agecalculator.osgi.impl;

import java.util.Calendar;
```

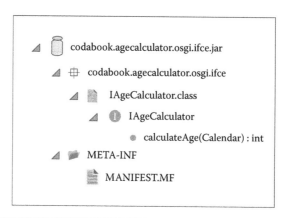

Figure 3.4   Structure of the interface bundle.

```
import java.util.GregorianCalendar;

import codabook.agecalculator.osgi.ifce.IAgeCalculator;

public class AgeCalculatorImpl implements IAgeCalculator {

        public int calculateAge(Calendar dateOfBirth) {
                Calendar rightNow = new GregorianCalendar();

                int currentYear = rightNow.get(Calendar.YEAR);
                int currentMonth = rightNow.get(Calendar.MONTH);
                int currentDate = rightNow.get(Calendar.DATE);
                int birthYear = dateOfBirth.get(Calendar.YEAR);
                int birthMonth = dateOfBirth.get(Calendar.MONTH);
                int birthDate = dateOfBirth.get(Calendar.DATE);

                int age = 0;

                boolean isCurrentYearBdayPassed =
                        (currentMonth > birthMonth)
                    || ((currentMonth = = birthMonth)
                    && (currentDate > = birthDate));
                if (isCurrentYearBdayPassed) {
                        age = currentYear - birthYear;
                } else {
                        age = currentYear - 1 - birthYear;
                }
                return age;
        }
}
```

The AgeCalculatorImpl is the class in the implementation bundle that implements the IAgeCalculator interface and provides the IAgeCalculator service implementation. In the implementation bundle, the interface codabook.agecalculator.osgi.ifce.IAgeCalculator is not added to the CLASSPATH but imported by the OSGi framework. This bundle imports the interface bundle as explained in the MANIFEST.MF below:

```
Manifest-Version: 1.0
Bundle-ManifestVersion: 2
Bundle-Name: Impl
Bundle-SymbolicName: codabook.agecalculator.osgi.impl
Bundle-Version: 1.0.0.qualifier
Bundle-ActivationPolicy: lazy
Bundle-RequiredExecutionEnvironment: JavaSE-1.6
Import-Package: codabook.agecalculator.osgi.ifce,
org.osgi.framework;version = "1.3.0"
Service-Component: META-INF/component.xml
```

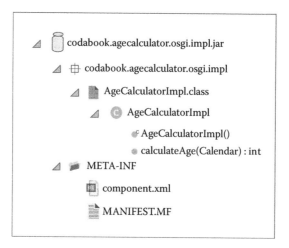

Figure 3.5   Structure of the implementation bundle.

The implementation bundle is exposed as a declarative service component. It is evident from the manifest file, it is evident that the bundle is not exported as a package, but it is exposed as a service with the entry `Service-Component` that this is exposed as a component, and the component description is available in `component.xml`. With the help of such XML files, components declare their provided services. The OSGi framework helps to publish the `AgeCalculatorImpl` as a service in the OSGi service registry. The `component.xml` is as below:

```
<?xml version = "1.0" encoding = "UTF-8"?>
<scr:component xmlns:scr = "http://www.osgi.org/xmlns/scr/v1.1.0"
 name = "codabook.agecalculator.osgi.impl">
 <implementation class = "codabook.agecalculator.
                         osgi.impl.AgeCalculatorImpl"/>
 <service>
 <provide interface = "codabook.agecalculator.
                         osgi.ifce.IAgeCalculator"/>
 </service>
</scr:component>
```

The `IAgeCalculator` is exposed as a service, and the service is implemented by the `AgeCalculatorImpl` implementation class. Looking at the `component.xml`, it is clear that the component provides the `IAgeCalculator` service. The component declares the implementation class and the provided interface. The declarative services in the OSGi framework publish the service at the execution time after the bundle is activated. The contents of the bundle JAR file are illustrated in Figure 3.5.

3.5.4.3 Client Bundle   The client bundle is supposed to consume the services exposed by the `IAgeCalculator` service implementation. The client bundle is another component that imports the `codabook.agecalculator.osgi.ifce` package and consumes the service through the OSGi service registry. The client bundle's manifest is as below:

```
Manifest-Version: 1.0
Bundle-ManifestVersion: 2
Bundle-Name: Client
Bundle-SymbolicName: codabook.agecalculator.osgi.client
Bundle-Version: 1.0.0.qualifier
Bundle-RequiredExecutionEnvironment: JavaSE-1.6
Import-Package: codabook.agecalculator.osgi.ifce,
 org.osgi.framework;version = "1.6.0",
 org.osgi.service.component;version = "1.1.0"
Service-Component: META-INF/component.xml
```

The client is also a component which consumes the services provided by the IAgeCalculator component. The bundle JAR file structure is illustrated in Figure 3.6. The `component.xml` in the client bundle references the `IAgeCalculator` service interface:

```
<?xml version = "1.0" encoding = "UTF-8"?>
<scr:component xmlns:scr =
"http://www.osgi.org/xmlns/scr/v1.1.0"
    name = "codabook.agecalculator.osgi.client">
    <implementation class = "codabook.agecalculator.

      osgi.client.AgeCalculatorOSGiClient"/>
    <reference bind = "gotService" cardinality = "1..1"
            interface = "codabook.agecalculator.
                              osgi.ifce.IAgeCalculator"
            name = "IAgeCalculator"
            policy = "dynamic"
            unbind = "lostService"/>
</scr:component>
```

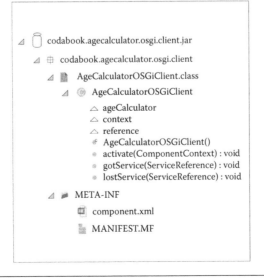

Figure 3.6 Structure of the client bundle.

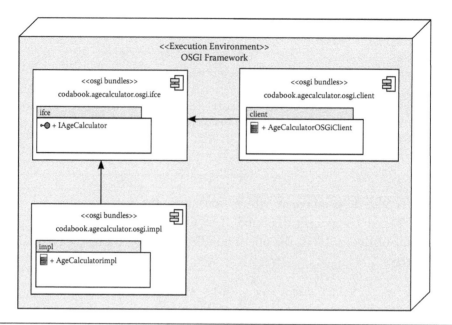

Figure 3.7   Age calculator component bundles deployment in an OSGi container.

Apart from the interface reference, the `component.xml` also refers to some methods called `gotService()` and `lostService()` during the binding and unbinding of service references. These are the methods defined in the client class that will be invoked by the framework for dependency injection. This allows the component to find out the services without retrieving them. The declarative services specifications in the OSGi framework define the methods where the service reference will be injected. The client invokes the `IAgeCalculator` service by looking for the reference of the component in the OSGi service registry using the component context (Figure 3.7). This is explained with the code as follows:

```
package codabook.agecalculator.osgi.client;

import java.util.Calendar;
import java.util.GregorianCalendar;
import java.util.Scanner;

import org.osgi.framework.ServiceReference;
import org.osgi.service.component.ComponentContext;

import codabook.agecalculator.osgi.ifce.IAgeCalculator;

public class AgeCalculatorOSGiClient {

        ComponentContext context;
        ServiceReference reference;
        IAgeCalculator ageCalculator;
```

```
    public void activate(ComponentContext context) {
            System.out.println("Activate Component");

            Scanner scanner = new Scanner(System.in);

            System.out.println("What is your year of birth?");
            int year = scanner.nextInt();

            System.out.println("What is your
                                month of birth (1-12)?");
            int month = scanner.nextInt();

            System.out.println("What is your
                                date of birth (1-31)?");
            int date = scanner.nextInt();

            Calendar dateOfBirth = new GregorianCalendar();
            dateOfBirth.clear();
            dateOfBirth.set(year, month - 1, date);
            if (reference ! = null) {
                    ageCalculator = (IAgeCalculator) context.
                        locateService(
                            "IAgeCalculator", reference);
                int age = ageCalculator.
                  calculateAge(dateOfBirth);
                System.out.println("Your age is " + age);
            }
    }
    public void gotService(ServiceReference reference) {
            System.out.println("Bind Service");
            this.reference = reference;
    }
    public void lostService(ServiceReference reference) {
            System.out.println("unbind Service");
            this.reference = null;
    }
}
```

The client has defined three methods:

- *activate*—Part of declarative services API. This method is invoked when this component is activated. The ComponentContext is used to locate the IAgeCalculator with the injected service reference.
- *gotService*—User-defined method as available in the component.xml, this method is invoked with the service reference (using dependency injection) when the service object is binded.
- *lostService*—User-defined method as mentioned in the client component. xml, this method is invoked with the injected service reference when the service object is unbinded.

In this example, we see that the client is not even aware of the implementation bundle. If there are multiple implementations available for the same service, the service is bounded dynamically by the environment. If there is any change in the implementation, only the implementation bundle will undergo change. A revised bundle can provide additional services that can be consumed by clients. So replacing components is easier and will not affect any other component. This way, OSGi gives good modularity by decoupling components and a pluggable dynamic service model, which are much needed features of a component model.

3.6 Service Component Architecture Model

Service Component Architecture (SCA) is a technology for creating services from components. SCA is a set of OASIS standards, and part of it is developed with the collaboration of vendors from an open source community, referred to as OSOA (Open SOA). SCA helps to build systems as collections of interconnected components. The components created in SCA communicate through the services. The advantage of SCA is its language-neutral component model. It allows services to be built by any language component like Java, C++, BPEL, JavaScript, Ruby, Python, and so forth.

The SCA model is best suited for distributed systems. SCA simplifies the building of systems through the assembling of components. SCA facilitates component assembly in the business tier of an N-tier architecture like other component models discussed in previous sections. SCA has some key elements like services, components, composites, and domains.

In SCA, the functionality provided by the components is exposed as services. Multiple components in the application interact and get bounded by a mechanism called "wire." Components are connected through wire, and their services are exposed through a composite.

Several open source tools/IDEs help to develop SCA application using designer tools. The key elements in SCA are represented through some standard symbols as represented in Figure 3.8.

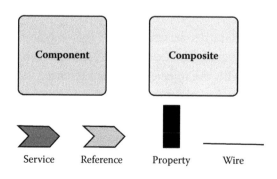

Figure 3.8 SCA key elements.

3.6.1 Services

Services are the functionality provided by the components. They are intended to perform the business function. Services can be implemented in any language like Java, C#, and BPEL. A service has two primary attributes:

- Service contract
- Service address

The service contract defines the methods, input parameters for the methods, and return value. The service contract can be defined in several ways. In Java, the service contract is a simple interface (POJI, Plain Old Java Interface) that exposes the functionality of the components. The service contract in Java is usually an interface that can be used locally as well as remotely. The remote service contract will have SCA annotation @Remotable.

While the service contract exposes the functionality provided by the component, the service address is used by clients to uniquely identify the service. The service address is unique for each service. Reusability is achieved through the service address, because clients connect to the service through the service address.

3.6.2 Component

A component provides one or more services. Components contain the business logic for the functionality exposed by service contracts—interfaces. Components can be implemented in any language supported by runtime like Java, C#, BPEL, Ruby, Python, and so forth. Components are implemented as POJOs in Java. The Java class has to implement the Java interface defined as the service contract. A component will have an associated service and optional references and properties. The service is used for exposing the functionality of the component. A reference is another interface contract provided by some other component. A component's dependency on another component is resolved through reference. A property of a component is a configurable parameter that is used to change the behavior of the component dynamically during runtime (with some of its parameters being changed). In the Java class that represents the component, properties and references are specified through annotation (Figure 3.9).

3.6.3 Composite

A composite is an XML file which is used for configuring components. The association of the component with the service and the reference is all mentioned in the composite. A composite is the main element used for configuring components. Using a composite file, one can define an assembly of components along with wiring details. The XML file is written using a language called SCDL (Service Component Definition Language), which is based on XML. The composite can be written as a set of XML elements or can be created using the composite designer tools provided by IDEs (Figure 3.10).

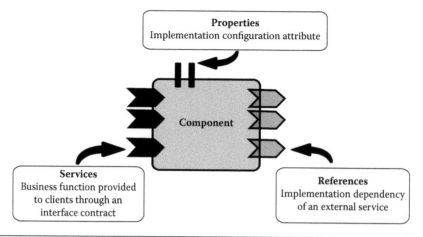

Figure 3.9   Component with services, references, and properties.

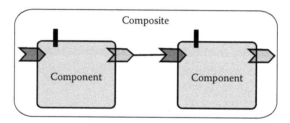

Figure 3.10   Composite.

In the designer tool, first a composite is defined and then components are defined as part of it. The services provided are defined as part of the component definition. A composite is used to configure more than one component.

If a component is dependent on another component, then a reference is defined along with this component. The reference points to the service contract of the other component. Service and reference are connected using "wire." Wire acts as a binding element between the client component and the serving/providing component (Figure 3.11). The wire binding can be defined as a local or remote binding. The wire binding reference is also configured in the composite. In the Java implementation code, the references to other components are referred to using the @Reference annotation. The reference of the target component is obtained using dependency injection. The reference dependency injection can be constructor-based or setter methods–based or field-based injection. However, the field-based injection is concise, which is preferred.

If the component's behavior has to be changed during runtime through a change in the value of the attributes, a property can be defined on the composite.

3.6.4 Domain

The composite is deployed in the SCA runtime environment called "domain." A SCA domain is a collection of SCA runtime instances. SCA runtime instances host

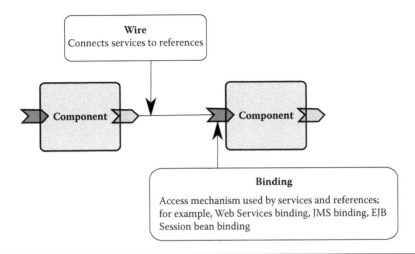

Figure 3.11   Component wiring.

components in containers. An SCA domain allows composites to be deployed as a whole or as individual components. When a composite is deployed in a domain, it is possible that components may get deployed in different runtime instances. The behavior is purely vendor specific. The domain provides required services like resource sharing, communication, and management to the components deployed in it.

3.6.5 An Example to Understand the SCA Component Model

The SCA component model can be understood with the same *age calculator* example discussed in the component models in the earlier sections.

  Here in this example, there is a single component called `AgeCalculatorServiceComponent`, which exposes its functionality through the `AgeCalculatorService` interface, which is the service contract for the `AgeCalculatorServiceComponent`. As a first step, the service contract is defined:

```
package codabook.agecalculator.sca.ifce;
import java.util.Calendar;
public interface AgeCalculatorService {
        public int calculateAge(Calendar dateOfBirth);
}
```

The `AgeCalculatorService` is implemented by the class `AgeCalculatorImpl`, which is a POJO that represents the `AgeCalculatorServiceComponent`:

```
package codabook.agecalculator.sca.impl;

import java.util.Calendar;
import java.util.GregorianCalendar;

import codabook.agecalculator.sca.ifce.AgeCalculatorService;
```

```java
public class AgeCalculatorImpl implements AgeCalculatorService{
      public int calculateAge(Calendar dateOfBirth) {
    Calendar rightNow = new GregorianCalendar();

    int currentYear = rightNow.get(Calendar.YEAR);
    int currentMonth = rightNow.get(Calendar.MONTH);
    int currentDate = rightNow.get(Calendar.DATE);

    int birthYear = dateOfBirth.get(Calendar.YEAR);
    int birthMonth = dateOfBirth.get(Calendar.MONTH);
    int birthDate = dateOfBirth.get(Calendar.DATE);

    int age = 0;

    boolean isCurrentYearBdayPassed = (currentMonth > birthMonth)
      || ((currentMonth = = birthMonth) && (currentDate > =
        birthDate));

    if (isCurrentYearBdayPassed) {
     age = currentYear - birthYear;
    } else {
     age = currentYear - 1 - birthYear;
    }
    return age;
  }
}
```

The service contract and the component are connected using the SCA composite designer tool provided by IDEs like Eclipse. Using the tool, a composite is created named agecalculator.composite. The composite is an XML file that will have an associated agecalculator.composite _ diagram that represents the composite file as a graphical representation. In the agecalculator composite diagram, using the component creation tool, a component is created named AgeCalculatorServiceComponent. A service is added to the composite named AgeCalculatorService. Using the designer tool, the Java interface file is dragged and dropped onto the service defined and the Java implementation class to the AgeCalculatorServiceComponent. The service is promoted using the tool (that is, exposing the service for clients to consume it). Graphical representation of the composite diagram is presented in Figure 3.12.

The composite file contains XML code that describes the component assembly in the composite diagram:

```xml
<?xml version = "1.0" encoding = "UTF-8" standalone = "no"?>
    <sca:composite xmlns:sca = "http://www.osoa.org/xmlns/sca/1.0"
    name = "agecalculator" targetNamespace = "http://eclipse.org/
    AgeCalculatorSCA/src/agecalculator">
  <sca:component name = "AgeCalculatorServiceComponent">
```

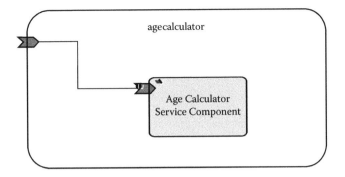

Figure 3.12   SCA component model—age calculator component example.

```
<sca:implementation.java class = "codabook.agecalculator.sca.
    impl.AgeCalculatorImpl"/>
<sca:service name = "AgeCalculatorService">
  <sca:interface.java interface = "codabook.agecalculator.sca.
     ifce.AgeCalculatorService"/>
 </sca:service>
</sca:component>
<sca:service name = "AgeCalculatorService" promote =
    "AgeCalculatorServiceComponent/AgeCalculatorService"/>
</sca:composite>
```

The `AgeCalculatorServiceComponent`   is created and assembled. The component is deployed in the SCADomain as a single component with the id AgeCalculatorService. This is evident from the `<sca:service>` element having an attribute called `promote` in the composite XML file. The SCADomain is the runtime for the SCA components. In this example, Apache Tuscany is the runtime used for deploying the composite. The runtime provides the dependency injection for components and a registry for storing and retrieving component references.

The client for the `AgeCalculatorServiceComponent`   first looks for the composite in the SCADomain where it is deployed. From the domain, the client looks for the service with the service address and the service contract. Once it gets the service reference, the client consumes the methods exposed by the component:

```
package codabook.agecalculator.sca.client;

import java.util.Calendar;
import java.util.GregorianCalendar;
import java.util.Scanner;

import org.apache.tuscany.sca.host.embedded.SCADomain;

import codabook.agecalculator.sca.ifce.AgeCalculatorService;

public class AgeCalculatorSCAClient {
```

```
public static void main(String[] args) {
        SCADomain scaDomain = SCADomain.
          newInstance("agecalculator.composite");
        AgeCalculatorService agecalculatorService =
          scaDomain.getService(AgeCalculatorService.
          class, "AgeCalculatorServiceComponent");

    Scanner scanner = new Scanner(System.in);

    System.out.println("What is your year of birth?");
    int year = scanner.nextInt();

    System.out.println("What is your month of birth (1-12)?");
    int month = scanner.nextInt();

    System.out.println("What is your date of birth (1-31)?");
    int date = scanner.nextInt();

    Calendar dateOfBirth = new GregorianCalendar();
    dateOfBirth.clear();
    dateOfBirth.set(year, month - 1, date);

    int age = agecalculatorService.calculateAge(dateOfBirth);
    System.out.println("Your age is " + age);
    }
}
```

Thus, the SCA component model provides easy steps for creating and assembling components. Assembling components is made easy by graphically linking the reference to the service of the target components.

3.7 Snapshot of Features of the Component Models—EJB, Spring, OSGi, and SCA

As we have seen in this chapter, componentization provides several advantages. The component models play an important role in developing, deploying, and assembling components for an application. We see that component models provide a simpler way for component reference and lookup. Each of the component models has its own implementation of component registry and techniques for dynamic lookup like dependency injection and context-based lookup.

We summarize the features of the component models discussed in the previous section in Table 3.1.

3.8 Summary

In this chapter, we briefly discussed the four latest component models in Java: Enterprise JavaBeans, Spring, OSGi, and SCA. We understood that each component model has its own standards for development and assembly. The runtime environment provided

Table 3.1 Feature Comparison of Various Component Models

FEATURES	EJB	SPRING	OSGI	SCA
Standard	Yes	Yes	Yes	Yes
Component interface	Plain Old Java Interface (Business Interface)		Plain Old Java Interface	Plain Old Java Interface (Service Contract)
Component implementation	Plain Old Java Object	Plain Old Java Object	Plain Old Java Object	Plain Old Java Object
XML configuration file	`ejb-jar.xml` (optional, used in earlier versions)	`Beans.xml`	`Manifest.mf` `component.xml`	`xxx.` `composite`
Runtime environment	EJB container	Spring container	OSGi framework	SCA domain
Annotation support	Supported	Supported	Supported	Supported
Registry	Available—EJB container	Available—Spring container	OSGi service registry	SCA domain
Dependency injection	Supported	Supported	Supported	Supported
Modularity	Partial support	Partial support	Complete support	Partial support
Aspect-oriented programming	Supported	Supported	Not supported	Not supported
API	EJB API	Spring API	OSGi API	SCA API implementations
Packaging	Jar file	Jar file	Jar file with manifest metadata (bundle)	Composite
Assembly	Using Jar	Using Jar	Using bundles (runtime assembly is possible)	Using composites
Component reference	Using `@EJB` or JNDI lookup in the container	Using `Beans.xml` and bean id in the container	Using `ComponentContext`, service reference APIs and OSGi registry	Using the service address in the composite
Language	Java	Java	Java	Java, C++, BPEL, Ruby, Python, etc.

by these component frameworks helps in the execution of the components developed using the appropriate model. We also tried to understand the similarities and differences of these component models by considering a simple *age calculator component*. We briefly compared several features provided by these component models. The component models presented in this chapter are discussed in detail in the coming chapters.

Review Questions

1. What are the different types of components?
2. What is Enterprise JavaBeans?
3. What are the types of Enterprise JavaBean components?

4. What is an EJB container and its importance?

5. What is the Spring framework?

6. What are Spring beans and the Spring container?

7. What is the significance of the Spring configuration?

8. What is OSGi?

9. What is a bundle in OSGi?

10. What is the importance of the OSGi service registry?

11. What is the significance of `MANIFEST.MF` in OSGi?

12. What is `component.xml` in OSGi?

13. What is Service Component Architecture?

14. What are services in SCA, and what are the important attributes of services?

15. What are a composite and a domain in SCA?

16. How are the components registered with the component registry in EJB, Spring, OSGi, and SCA?

17. How are the components created using EJB, Spring, OSGi, and SCA invoked by an application (client)?

18. Explain the configuration mechanism available in the component models discussed in this chapter.

PART II

PRACTICE

Hands-On CODA Using Java Component Models

4

Component-Oriented Application Design and Architecture

4.1 Introduction

In this chapter, we provide ideas for the design and architecture of component-oriented applications. We present two Java SE example applications through which we elaborate the component design and architecture concepts. In the first example, the design of an existing monolithic Java application is analyzed. We then componentize this application to arrive at a component-oriented design for the application. We demonstrate that the component-oriented application is less resistive to changes. In the second example, the design of an application with multilayered architecture is presented. After analysis of the multilayered design, we demonstrate the componentization of the example application across the architecture layers.

4.2 Componentizing a Monolithic Application

Let us analyze a monolithic application that was not designed and built in a component-oriented way. The application, named *Virtual Store*, provides online front-end for a retail store. *Virtual Store* caters to the following use cases:

- *Browse Products*—The user can browse through products available in the store and view an individual product's price description.
- *Shopping Cart*—The user can add multiple quantities of a product to the shopping cart. If sufficient stock is available, *Virtual Store* adds the selected items to the shopping cart. Items in the shopping cart can be removed or modified.
- *Check-out*—After adding all the required products into a shopping cart, the user can check out of the *Virtual Store*. Stock quantities of the purchased items are reduced in the *Virtual Store* inventory.

4.2.1 Analysis of the Monolithic Implementation of the Virtual Store

Virtual Store's implementation consists of the following objects:

- *Product*—Stores the name and price of a product.
- *Inventory*—Stores multiple products available in the store.
- *Shopping Cart*—Holds products that were picked up by the user.

- *Store*—Represents the overall store. It contains an inventory and a shopping cart.
- *UI*—Serves as the user interface. It is responsible for managing user interactions with the application.

The class diagram for all of these objects is presented in Figure 4.1. This implementation of the application performs without any errors in functionality. What then is the need for componentization? The need arises because of the tight coupling between the classes and the resulting resistance for any changes to functional behavior of the application. The amount of coupling between a class and other classes can be measured by assessing the class's dependency depth. A class that has no dependency has a dependency depth of 0. Any other class that depends on a class with a dependency depth of 0 has a dependency depth of 1. Any class that depends on a class with a dependency depth of 1 would have a dependency depth of 2, and so on. Higher dependency depth implies higher tight coupling. The dependency relationships and dependency depths of the classes in the *Virtual Store* implementation are tabulated in Table 4.1.

The tight coupling results in a high resistance to change in implementation. Let us say that the online store likes to announce a promotional sale for 3 days during which a 10% discount would be applied to all items. In order to achieve this, we need to change the ShoppingCart class implementation. Based on Table 4.1, we can see that when the ShoppingCart class is changed, the Store class also needs to be recompiled. When the Store class is recompiled, the UI class also needs to be recompiled.

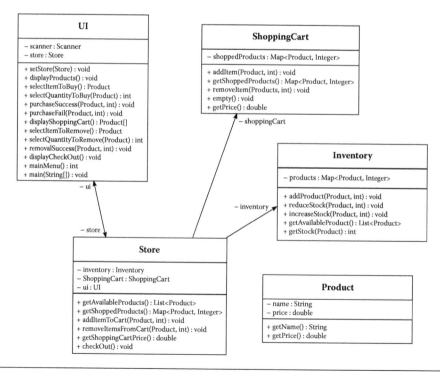

Figure 4.1   Class diagram of monolithic implementation of *Virtual Store*.

Table 4.1 Coupling Metrics of the Monolithic *Virtual Store* Implementation

NUMBER	CLASS	DEPENDS ON	DEPENDENCY DEPTH
1.	Product	—	0
2.	Inventory	Product	1
3.	Shopping Cart	Product	1
4.	Store	Inventory, ShoppingCart, Product, UI	2
5.	UI	Store, Product	2

What happens at the end of the promotional sale when the online store wants to discontinue the discounts? We need to recompile all three classes one more time. Ideally, to apply and withdraw discounts, only the implementation of the ShoppingCart class should be modified and the application should not have been affected. But due to the tight coupling, other parts of the application are also affected.

4.2.2 Componentizing the Virtual Store

We attempt to componentize the monolithic implementation of the *Virtual Store* application and then measure the amount of coupling again. In general, to componentize a monolithic application, the following rules should be followed:

1. Keep the entity classes that represent domain objects in a separate common library to be shared by all the other components. Entity classes are considered as data carrying objects, and they are not considered as components. The business entity classes can be instantiated by any other components. The instances of the business entity classes can be passed around by other components to pass data values across components.

   In the *Virtual Store* example, we have five classes in the monolithic implementation. Out of these five classes, Product class is an entity class that carries only data and does not carry any business logic. Inventory and ShoppingCart are classes with business logic. UI and Store are classes that make up the application logic.

   As per this rule, we should package the Product as part of a base library that would be shared by all the components. Product is a data carrying object and is not considered as a component. Any other component can create a new instance of Product and pass that object around to other components to pass the data.

2. Group a set of classes (one or more classes) that together provide independent business functionality into a component. Among the set of classes, they should provide a business functionality of considerable value. They can depend

on other classes for help in the process of executing the business logic of the offered functionality, but the core of the functionality should be achieved within the set of classes grouped together.

In the *Virtual Store* example, the `Inventory` class independently provides the business functionality of maintaining the inventory of the store. Hence, we create an *Inventory Component* out of the `Inventory` class. Similarly, the `ShoppingCart` class independently provides the business functionality of maintaining the shopping cart of the user. Therefore, we create a *Shopping Cart Component* out of the `ShoppingCart` class.

3. After classes are grouped into components, we need to expose the business functionality provided by the component. As per the component principle, this should be exposed as a provided interface of the component. Only the provided interface should be visible from outside the component boundary, and the internals of the component should not be exposed outside the component boundary.

In the *Virtual Store* example, from the *Inventory Component* identified in step 2, we extract an `InventoryService` interface based on the current `Inventory` class implementation, and let this component provide this interface. Similarly, from the *Shopping Cart Component* identified, we extract a `ShoppingCartService` interface based on the current `ShoppingCart` class implementation, and let this component provide this interface.

4. If two classes depend on each other mutually, they should be together in one component. Alternatively, the cyclic dependency can be broken by introducing additional classes, which can be suitably assigned to an appropriate component.

In the *Virtual Store* example, `UI` and `Store` classes mutually depend on each other, and they together handle the application logic. Hence, we group them together into an *Application Component*. This component would not provide any interface but would consume the `InventoryService` and `ShoppingCartService` interfaces provided by the above two components.

5. As a last step, we include the `InventoryService` and `ShoppingCart Service` interface definitions into the base library along with `Product` entity.

After componentizing the *Virtual Store* application along the lines outlined, we get a component architecture as depicted in Figure 4.2.

4.2.3 Analysis of the Componentized Implementation of the Virtual Store

When we perform a dependency analysis on the componentized implementation of the *Virtual Store* we get the coupling metrics tabulated in Table 4.2. When we compare this metric to that of the monolithic implementation presented in Table 4.1, we

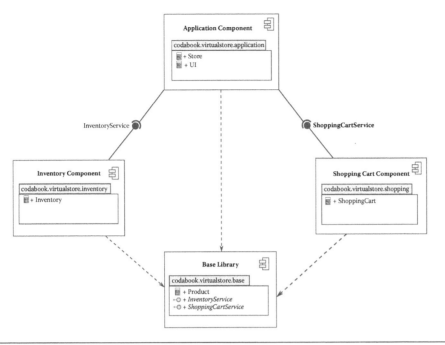

Figure 4.2 Component architecture of the componentized *Virtual Store* application.

Table 4.2 Coupling Metrics of the Componentized *Virtual Store* Implementation

NUMBER	CLASS	DEPENDS ON	DEPENDENCY DEPTH
1.	Product	—	0
2.	InventoryService	Product	0
3.	ShoppingCartService	Product	0
4.	Inventory	Product, InventoryService	1
5.	ShoppingCart	Product, ShoppingCartService	1
6.	Store	InventoryService, ShoppingCartService, Product, UI	1
7.	UI	Store, Product	1

find that the number of dependencies has increased from 8 to 12, and the highest level of dependency depth has decreased from 2 to 1 in the move from monolithic to componentized implementation of the *Virtual Store*. This implies that the coupling between the classes has been reduced in the componentized implementation. We shall demonstrate that this reduced coupling is less resistant for changes. We shall demonstrate in the next section that the changes for applying and withdrawing discounts can be accommodated in a least disruptive manner in this design.

The higher number of dependencies exhibited by the componentized implementation may sound alarming at first. But it needs some closer investigation to get the true picture. We have been following the low coupling design principle that ensures that changes made to one part in a system do not ripple across to other parts of the system. There is another design principle that qualifies coupling—coupling between two elements is especially bad if the element being depended upon is unstable in nature; if the element being depended upon is highly stable, then the coupling is acceptable. In the case of the componentized *Virtual Store* application, all the dependencies are between a class and an interface (except the dependencies on Product, UI, and Store). In the case of monolithic *Virtual Store* implementation, all the dependencies are between two classes. Interfaces are more stable compared to implementation classes. Even though the number of dependencies is more in the case of the componentized *Virtual Store*, the quality of dependencies is better and more conducive for changes compared to the monolithic implementation.

Let us extend the class-level dependency analysis to component-level dependencies. Let us perform the dependency analysis from two perspectives—build time dependencies and runtime dependencies. Table 4.3 provides the build time dependencies.

From Table 4.3, it is easy to comprehend that each component can be independently built without a dependency on other components. Table 4.4 presents the runtime dependency metrics.

We can infer that all three components require the presence of base library in the class path during the runtime. Base library is a static component and does not provide any dynamic component service. This is the reason we call it a *library* rather than a *component*. The *Application Component* requires the presence of the *Inventory Component* and the *Shopping Cart Component* at runtime. There is a little exaggeration

Table 4.3 Build Time Component Dependencies in the *Virtual Store* Implementation

NUMBER	COMPONENT/LIBRARY	DEPENDS ON	DEPENDENCY DEPTH
1.	Base library	—	0
2.	Inventory component	Base library	1
3.	Shopping cart component	Base library	1
4.	Application component	Base library	1

Table 4.4 Runtime Component Dependencies in the *Virtual Store* Implementation

NUMBER	COMPONENT/LIBRARY	DEPENDS ON	DEPENDENCY DEPTH
1.	Base library	—	0
2.	Inventory component	Base library	1
3.	Shopping cart component	Base library	1
4.	Application component	Base library, inventory component, shopping cart component	2

in the last statement. The *Application Component* requires *any* component that provides `InventoryService` and `ShoppingCartService`. It need not be the specific *Inventory Component* and *Shopping Cart Component*. This provides tremendous flexibility in making changes to an application assembly. We demonstrate this in the next section with the implementation of the change request to provide a 10% discount on the shopping cart price during the promotional offer.

4.2.4 *Accommodating Changes to the* Virtual Store

In Section 4.2.1, we proposed a change to the *Virtual Store* that requires a discount of 10% of the shopping cart price be given during some promotional period. This was a difficult proposition to handle in the monolithic implementation of the *Virtual Store*. In the componentized implementation, this can be handled easily. All it takes to change the application behavior is to replace the *Shopping Cart Component* in the application assembly with a new component, which we call the *Promotional Shopping Cart Component*. The *Promotional Shopping Cart Component* provides the same `ShoppingCartService` interface (as the original *Shopping Cart Component*), due to which the rest of the application remains unaffected. The architecture of the modified application assembly is presented in Figure 4.3.

The internal implementation of the *Promotional Shopping Cart Component* differs from the *Shopping Cart Component* internals. We present the internals of both components below so that we can understand how the 10% discount functionality is achieved.

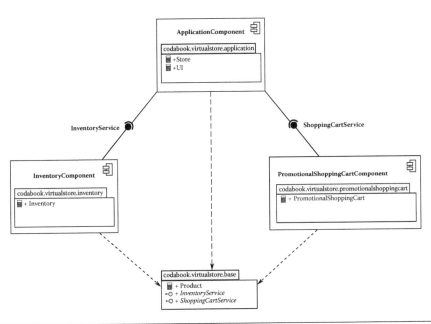

Figure 4.3   Component architecture of the *Virtual Store* application with the *Promotional Shopping Cart Component*.

The interface `ShoppingCartService` has a `getPrice()` operation defined on it as shown in the source code below:

```
public interface ShoppingCartService {
        //... some code omitted for brevity
        public double getPrice();
}
```

This method is invoked from the *Virtual Store* application component when the checkout use case is invoked. The source code below shows this invocation:

```
public class UI {
        //... some code omitted for brevity
        public void displayCheckOut() {
                double totalPrice = store.getShoppingCartPrice();
                System.out.printf("Please Pay $%1$,-8.2f\n",
                                                totalPrice);
                System.out.println("Thank you for your patronage!
                                                Please visit
                                                again!");
        }
}

public class Store {
        //... some code omitted for brevity
        public double getShoppingCartPrice() {
                return shoppingCart.getPrice();
        }
}
```

In the original application assembly, the `shoppingCart` object used by the `Store` object is the `ShoppingCartService` implementation supplied by the *Shopping Cart Component*. The internal implementation of this original component is shown below:

```
public class ShoppingCart implements ShoppingCartService,
  ComponentInterface {
        //... some code omitted for brevity
        public double getPrice() {
                double totalPrice = 0;
                for (Product product : shoppedProducts.keySet()) {
                        double unitPrice = product.getPrice();
                        int quantity = shoppedProducts.
                                                get(product);
                        double subTotal = unitPrice * quantity;
                        totalPrice + = subTotal;
                }
                return totalPrice;
        }
}
```

To accommodate the promotional 10% discount, we create a new *Promotional Shopping Cart Component*. This component also provides the same `ShoppingCartService` interface, but the implementation of the `getPrice()` method is modified to provide a 10% discount. The internal implementation of this new component is shown below:

```
public class PromotionalShoppingCart implements
   ShoppingCartService, ComponentInterface {
         //... some code omitted for brevity
         public double getPrice() {
                 double totalPrice = 0;
                 for (Product product : shoppedProducts.keySet()) {
                         double unitPrice = product.getPrice();
                         int quantity = shoppedProducts.
                                                     get(product);
                         double subTotal = unitPrice * quantity;
                         totalPrice + = subTotal;
                 }
                 return 0.9*totalPrice;
         }
}
```

When we use the *Promotional Shopping Cart Component* in the application assembly, the behavior of the application changes, and a discount of 10% is applied for each sale. At the end of the sale period, the original *Shopping Cart Component* which offers no discount can be deployed in the assembly, withdrawing the discount offer.

4.3 Componentizing Applications with Multiple Layer Architecture

In the last few sections we had analyzed a simple business application that was designed in a monolithic manner. We demonstrated how componentization can be carried out and its benefits. Many of the real-world applications follow multiple layer architecture to deal with different areas of concern such as presentation, business logic, and persistence. In the next few sections, we analyze one such example application and present mechanisms to componentize the same.

The example application we consider is a *point-of-sale* (POS) application meant for tracking orders and payments in a restaurant. The POS is used to track tables being occupied by guests and orders being made from various tables and to print bills. Apart from these operational features, the POS application can be used for restaurant administration. The total number of tables in the restaurant, foods sold in the restaurant, their prices, and the associated tax rates can be managed. The use cases to be supported by the POS application are described briefly below:

- *Guests Check-In*—This use case is invoked by the waiters when new guests arrive at the restaurant. POS displays a list of empty tables, and the waiter chooses an empty table and seats the guests at that table.

- *Place Order*—When guests from a table order food, the waiter invokes this use case. POS prompts the waiter for the table number, food item, and quantity ordered. POS consolidates and maintains orders against each table.
- *Modify Order*—The waiter can modify the quantity of any order already placed.
- *Cancel Order*—The waiter can cancel any order already placed.
- *Pay Bill*—The waiter invokes this use case to print the bill and collect payment for all items ordered from a table.
- *Guests Check-out*—When guests from a table leave, the waiter invokes this use case to mark the table as empty.
- *Collections Report*—At any point in time, the POS user can look at all the past payments collected.

In the next section, we present an existing implementation of POS, which is monolithic in nature.

4.3.1 Existing Design of the POS Layered Application

The existing implementation of POS uses a typical layered architecture pattern consisting of presentation layer, business layer, and data layer. The layered architecture is supported by the MVC (model-view-controller) design pattern. In the MVC paradigm, the model is responsible for capturing real-world business information through software objects. View is responsible for presenting the business information captured by the model visually for human consumption. The controller is responsible for handling user inputs and mediating between view and model.

In the layered architecture of POS, views and controllers belong to the presentation layer. Information exchange across the layer borders is enabled by the model objects carrying business domain data. The multiple layers of POS are shown in Figure 4.4. The arrow directions indicate the control flow, or in other words, the direction of invocation across layers. Figure 4.5 provides the list of objects present in each layer.

4.3.1.1 Objects in the Model
Model objects carry the business domain relevant information. In the restaurant business domain, we have `Food`, `Table`, `Order`, `Bill`, and `TableConfig` model objects. In addition, there is a `FoodCategory` that each `Food` belongs to; an `OrderItem`, a collection of which makes up an order; and a `BillLineItem`, a collection of which belongs to a `Bill`.

All the model objects are presented in Figure 4.6. The `Food` object is responsible for carrying information such as food name, price, tax rate, and food category. The `Table` object is responsible for storing the table number and the status on whether the table is occupied or empty. If the table is occupied, the `Table` stores an `Order` object associated to the table. The `Order` object captures items ordered from the table. Each `OrderItem` is an order for multiple quantities of a food item. The

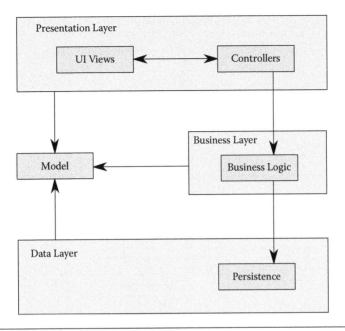

Figure 4.4 Layered architecture of the POS application.

payment toward all the items ordered from a table is captured and persists in the form of a `Bill` object. Each `OrderItem` in `Order` has a corresponding `BillLineItem` in the `Bill`.

4.3.1.2 Design of the Presentation Layer The presentation is based on a console-based UI in the current POS implementation. The presentation layer consists of views and controllers. Each UI view is responsible for showing one screen to the user and collecting inputs from the user interactively. The controller objects are responsible for processing the inputs gathered by the UI view objects. In addition, the controllers control the UI screen flow—they direct the next UI screen to be shown after each screen based on user inputs. To process the inputs given by the users, the controller objects depend on business objects in the business layer.

4.3.1.3 Design of the Business Layer The business layer contains objects that implement the business logic rules. The controllers from the presentation layer make use of the services offered by this layer. There are four business objects in the business layer, which are presented below:

- `FoodBiz`—It is responsible for the business logic associated with food creation, modification, and categorization.
- `OrderBiz`—It implements all the business logic associated with maintaining orders placed by guests at different tables, adding and modifying order items, and canceling ordered items.

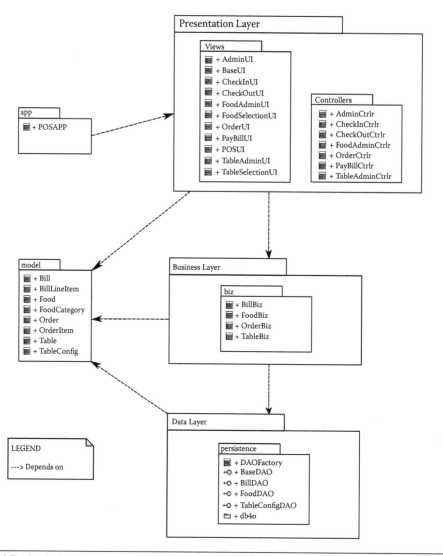

Figure 4.5   Detailed layer architecture of the POS application.

- TableBiz—It is responsible for maintaining the total number of tables based on configuration, blocking and releasing tables based on guest check-in and checkout.
- BillBiz—This object is responsible for printing the bill, and persisting bill details for future reference.

Business objects that have a need to persist the model data objects depend on the persistence layer.

4.3.1.4 Design of the Persistence Layer   The persistence layer is responsible for transferring the state information stored in the model objects to a persistent storage and for retrieving it back to in-memory objects. This layer consists of Data Access Objects (DAOs). DAO interfaces are defined for TableConfig, Food, and Bill objects.

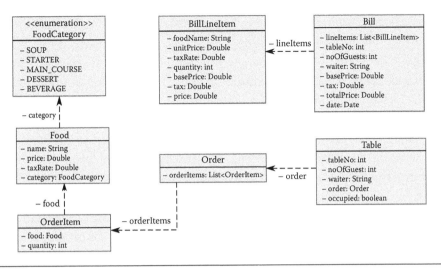

Figure 4.6 Model objects in the POS monolithic application.

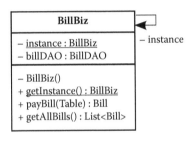

Figure 4.7 Class diagram of the `BillBiz` class.

Concrete DAOs implement these interfaces specific to the database used. Each of the generic DAOs is implemented by the Db4o specific concrete DAO object. Db4o is the object database used in the implementation.

4.3.2 Analysis of the Existing Design of the POS Application

Having analyzed the existing application in depth, which provides all the required functionalities, why should we componentize this application? Componentization in general helps in two different endeavors:

1. Improve maintainability
2. Extract reusable parts for storage and future reuse

Let us investigate the maintainability aspect. Assume that there is a new business rule to be incorporated in the POS application. The POS is supposed to charge a gratuity of 15% for any guest group consisting of 8 or more members. On analysis of the existing application architecture, the `BillBiz` is the right object to shoulder this new responsibility, because `BillBiz` implements the business logic that calculates the `Bill` amount. The `BillBiz` class diagram is presented in Figure 4.7.

The `BillBiz` object has a `payBill(Table table):Bill` method. This method implements the business logic for billing. This method can be modified to accommodate the gratuity-related business change. In addition to this change, the calculated gratuity for each bill needs to be captured in some model object and persisted. The `PayBillUI` class in the presentation layer also needs to be changed to display the gratuity amount.

If we make these changes in the existing application as is, we need to recompile and redeploy the whole application, even though the application has a layered architecture. This is due to the fact that these layers are logical and not physical. Moreover, to isolate the impact of the new business requirement, we need to isolate the Billing functionality from other functionalities such as Order Management and Food Management functionalities. Let us see how componentization can address this maintenance issue.

4.3.3 Componentizing the POS Application

Let us split the business layer of the POS into four different components as shown in Figure 4.8. By splitting the application into different components, the billing responsibility is isolated into the *Bill Component*.

In order to achieve the component structure proposed in Figure 4.8, we package the objects from the original implementation into different component packages as per Table 4.5.

As a general pattern, it can be observed that each UI component consists of a necessary view and controller objects. Each business component consists of a necessary business object and a DAO for persistence. Apart from these components, the objects from the model are packaged together as an object library, which is referred by each of these components.

Once we repackage the objects from the existing implementation into components as discussed above, we get a component architecture for the POS application as shown in Figure 4.9. In the diagram the connector with a lollipop and a receptacle represents a component assembly between two components. In a component assembly, one component exposes a service and another component consumes that service. For example,

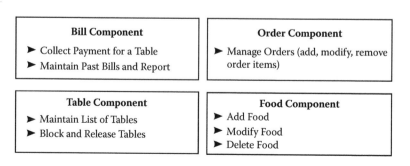

Figure 4.8 Components in the business layer of the POS application.

Table 4.5 POS Application—Mapping of Objects in Multiple Layers to Components

COMPONENT	OBJECTS	LAYER
GuestUI	CheckInUI, CheckOutUI, CheckInCtrlr, CheckOutCtrlr	Presentation
AdminUI	AdminUI, FoodAdminUI, TableAdminUI, FoodAdminCtrlr, TableAdminCtrlr	Presentation
OrderUI	OrderUI, OrderCtrlr	Presentation
BillUI	PayBillUI, PayBillCtrlr	Presentation
TableBiz	TableBiz, TableDAO	Business & Data
FoodBiz	FoodBiz, FoodDAO	Business & Data
OrderBiz	OrderBiz, OrderDAO	Business & Data
BillBiz	BillBiz, BillDAO	Business & Data

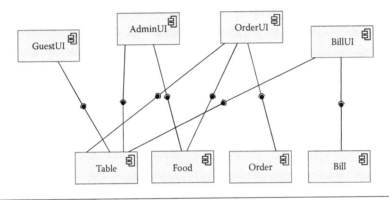

Figure 4.9 Component architecture of the POS application.

the *Table Component* exposes the TableBiz service, which is consumed by all the other components.

4.3.4 Component Replacement in the POS Application

As discussed earlier, we are processing a change request that requires an additional gratuity amount to be charged to those guest groups whose size is eight or larger. We had reasoned in the earlier analysis that the business logic change can be implemented in the BillBiz class in the *Bill Component*, in the payBill() method. Part of the code from this method is presented below:

```
public class BillBiz {
        //… some code omitted for brevity
        public Bill payBill(Table table) throws Exception {
            //… some code omitted for brevity

            Order order = table.getOrder();
            double basePrice = 0;
```

```
        double tax = 0;
        double totalPrice = 0;

        List<BillLineItem> billLineItems = new
        ArrayList<BillLineItem>();

        //Create a bill line item for each order item
        //and calculate its price components
        for (OrderItem orderItem : order.
                                getOrderedItems()) {
                Food food = orderItem.getFood();
                int quantity = orderItem.getQuantity();
        BillLineItem billLineItem = new
        BillLineItem(food.getName(),
                food.getPrice(), food.getTaxRate(),
                quantity);

        //Calculate price for individual bill line item
        double itemBasePrice =
                billLineItem.getUnitPrice()
            * billLineItem.getQuantity();
        double itemTax = itemBasePrice * billLineItem.
        getTaxRate()/100;
        double itemPrice = itemBasePrice + itemTax;

        billLineItem.setBasePrice(itemBasePrice);
        billLineItem.setTax(itemTax);
        billLineItem.setPrice(itemPrice);

        //Calculate price components for whole bill
        basePrice + = itemBasePrice;
        tax + = itemTax;
        totalPrice + = itemPrice;

        billLineItems.add(billLineItem);
    }
    Bill bill = new Bill(billLineItems, tableNo,
    noOfGuests, waiter,
            basePrice, tax, totalPrice);
    billDAO.create(bill);
    table.billPaid();

    return bill;
    }
}
```

As can be seen from the code snippet, the payBill() method obtains the Order object associated with the Table for which Bill has to be generated. For each OrderItem in the Order, a BillLineItem is generated. For each BillLineItem, the base price, tax, and total price are calculated. All

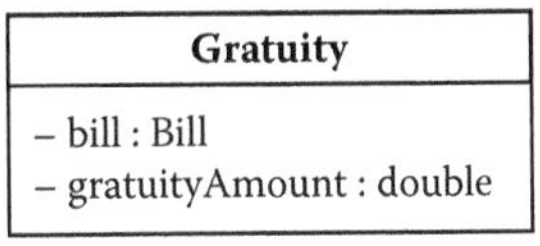

Gratuity
– bill : Bill – gratuityAmount : double

Figure 4.10 Gratuity class.

BillLineItems are kept in a collection that becomes part of the generated Bill object. The Bill object also has a total base price, total tax, and total payable amount. These values are calculated as sums of corresponding price components of the constituent bill line items. In the business logic change request, the total price of the bill should have an additional component called gratuity, if the number of guests is equal to or more than eight.

The current total price of the bill is given by

```
Total Price = Base Price + Tax
```

With the introduction of gratuity, this would have to be changed to

```
Total Price = Base Price + Tax + Gratuity
Gratuity = 0.15 * Base Price (if number of guests > = 8)
         = 0 (otherwise)
```

The payBill() method code can be modified to accommodate the above change. However, we need to capture the new gratuity element in the model objects. In order to give the least interference to other components, we introduce a new model object called Gratuity. This object is responsible for storing the gratuityAmount and the Bill object to which the gratuityAmount is applicable. The class diagram of Gratuity is presented in Figure 4.10.

We label the modified Bill component as Bill2, and the modified BillUI component as BillUI2. The modified payBill() method that implements the addition of the gratuity component to the bill is shown below:

```java
public class BillBiz {
        //… some code omitted for brevity
        public Bill payBill(Table table) throws Exception {
                //… some code omitted for brevity

                Order order = table.getOrder();
                double basePrice = 0;
                double tax = 0;
                double totalPrice = 0;

                List<BillLineItem> billLineItems = new
                    ArrayList<BillLineItem>();
```

```
//Create a bill line item for each order item and
//calculate its price components
for (OrderItem orderItem : order.getOrderedItems()) {
      Food food = orderItem.getFood();
      int quantity = orderItem.getQuantity();
      BillLineItem billLineItem = new
         BillLineItem(food.getName(),
                 food.getPrice(), food.getTaxRate(),
                    quantity);

      //Calculate price for individual bill line
      //item
      double itemBasePrice = billLineItem.
         getUnitPrice()
                 * billLineItem.getQuantity();
   double itemTax = itemBasePrice * billLineItem.
   getTaxRate()/100;
      double itemPrice = itemBasePrice + itemTax;

      billLineItem.setBasePrice(itemBasePrice);
      billLineItem.setTax(itemTax);
      billLineItem.setPrice(itemPrice);

      //Calculate price components for whole bill
      basePrice + = itemBasePrice;
      tax + = itemTax;
      totalPrice + = itemPrice;

      billLineItems.add(billLineItem);
}

//Additional logic to calculate gratuity
double gratuityAmount = 0;

if (noOfGuests > = 8) {
      gratuityAmount = basePrice * 0.15;
      totalPrice + = gratuityAmount;
}
Bill bill = new Bill(billLineItems, tableNo,
noOfGuests, waiter,
            basePrice, tax, totalPrice);
billDAO.create(bill);
table.billPaid();

if (noOfGuests > = 8) {
      Gratuity gratuityObj = new Gratuity(bill,
      gratuityAmount);
      gratuityDAO.create(gratuityObj);
}

return bill; }
}
```

As can be seen, the new code has created a Gratuity object if the number of guests is equal to or more than eight. It has also added the necessary amount to the total amount in the Bill object. The BillUI2 component would retrieve the Gratuity object associated to the bill and display the gratuity amount if it is not zero. To facilitate this retrieval, a new method called getGratuityForBill() is added to the BillBiz class in the Bill2 component. The modified BillBiz class is shown in Figure 4.11.

We reassemble the POS application by substituting Bill and BillUI components with the Bill2 and BillUI2 components. Of course, the new model object library is to be used. With these changes, the component architecture of the application is presented in Figure 4.12.

At any point in time, the Bill2 and BillUI2 components can be replaced with the old Bill and BillUI components to change the behavior of the application back to the old behavior. Thus, the evolution of the application with insertion and removal of new functionalities can be done by changing components in the application assembly without changing the application code.

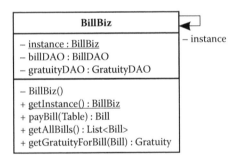

Figure 4.11 Modified BillBiz class.

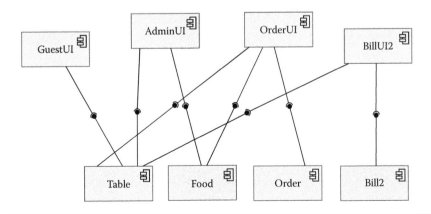

Figure 4.12 Modified POS application assembly.

4.4 Summary

In this chapter, we provided ideas on component design and architecture. We analyzed designs of existing applications, which were built in a non-component-oriented manner. We analyzed these designs and realized that these designs were resistive to changes. We presented techniques to componentize these applications and demonstrated that the componentized applications were more adaptive to changes.

Review Questions

1. What is tight coupling? Why is tight coupling not advisable?
2. How do we measure the amount of coupling present in a design?
3. What design strategies are used to lower coupling?
4. Why should the business entity objects *not* be offered as dynamic component services?
5. Why is coupling on a stable entity preferred over coupling on an unstable entity?
6. Should componentization of multiple layer applications preserve the original layering structure? Why or why not?
7. When changes are requested, is it advisable to change the provided and required interface definitions? Why or why not?

5

PRACTICING CODA WITH OSGi

5.1 Introduction

In the previous chapters, we discussed software components, component models, and component frameworks in a generic context. In this chapter, we discuss the OSGi component framework in detail. The objective of this chapter is to introduce the OSGi framework, provide sufficient information to get started with CODA practice using OSGi, and appreciate the component-oriented features of the OSGi framework. We begin with an overview of the OSGi framework architecture, the necessity of the OSGi framework, followed by an in-depth discussion of various layers of OSGi with examples.

5.2 What Is OSGi?

OSGi is a component-oriented development platform whose standards specifications are governed by the OSGi Alliance (formerly known as the Open Services Gateway Initiative). The OSGi alliance is an industry-backed nonprofit corporation. The OSGi alliance was founded in March 1999. The framework specification has gone through many releases, and the current major release version is 4.*

The OSGi standards define the OSGi framework specification. The OSGi framework provides a modularity and component layer on top of the standard Java platform. Modules in OSGi are packaged as *bundles*. A collection of bundles are deployed on the OSGi framework to form a running application. Figure 5.1 presents a graphical representation of the OSGi framework along with bundles. The OSGi framework manages the *life cycle of bundles* deployed over it. Bundles can expose their provided interfaces by registering *services*. Other bundles can consume the services registered by a bundle.

There are a number of OSGi framework implementations available from different product vendors. A few well-known framework implementations are listed below:

- Apache Felix (http://felix.apache.org)
- Eclipse Equinox (http://www.eclipse.org/equinox)
- Knopflerfish (http://www.knopflerfish.org)

The functionality of the OSGi framework is divided into multiple layers:

- Module layer
- Life cycle layer

---

* OSGi Standards Version 5 was released while the book was being written.

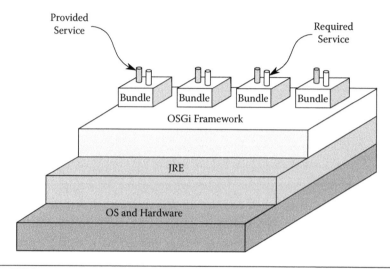

Figure 5.1   OSGi framework.

- Service layer
- Security layer
- Actual services

The module layer defines a modularity framework on top of the standard Java platform. The life cycle layer manages the life cycles of the OSGi modules (also known as bundles) deployed in the framework. The service layer provides a service registry along with a publish-lookup model for exposing services of a module. The security layer builds on top of standard Java security and provides security at the OSGi bundles level. Apart from these layers, the OSGi standard specifies a set of standard services to be provided by the OSGi runtime.

5.3 Necessity of OSGi

OSGi improvises modularization features of standard Java. Chapter 2 discussed using JAR files as physical components and Java packages as logical components. The short-coming of this approach is that the physical and logical boundaries dissolve on a flat CLASSPATH during runtime. We illustrate this with an example consisting of three JAR files: A.jar, B.jar, and C.jar files (Figure 5.2).

A.jar hosts the Java package pkg_a consisting of Class1, Class2, and Class3. B.jar hosts pkg_b consisting of Class4, Class5, and Class6. C.jar hosts pkg_c consisting of Class7. Additionally, C.jar hosts a different version of pkg_a in which a different implementation of Class2 is present. Class1 and Class3 are not present in this version of pkg_a. Similarly, C.jar hosts a different version of pkg_b which consists of a different implementation of Class5.

When these three JAR files are used in an application and deployed in a runtime environment, the versions of the classes loaded depend on the CLASSPATH

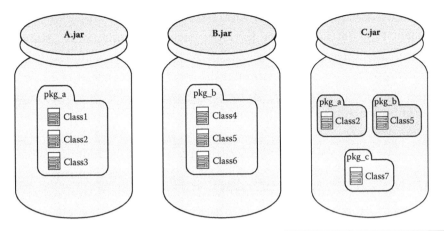

Figure 5.2 Components made up of Java package logical boundaries and JAR file physical boundaries.

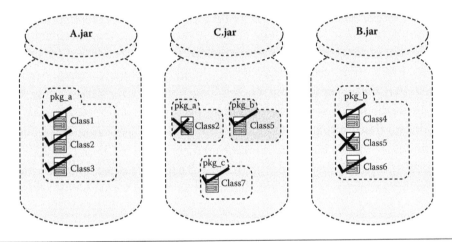

Figure 5.3 Dissolving JAR and package boundaries.

of the runtime environment. Assume that the CLASSPATH in a particular Java environment has the following precedence sequence: A.jar, C.jar, and B.jar. This CLASSPATH precedence is illustrated in Figure 5.3.

With this CLASSPATH, all three classes, Class1, Class2, and Class3 from pkg_a in A.jar are loaded, because it is the first JAR in the CLASSPATH precedence. Class5 from pkg_b and Class7 from pkg_c in C.jar are loaded because it is next in precedence. However, Class2 from pkg_a in C.jar is not loaded because it has already been loaded from A.jar. From B.jar, which is the last in precedence, Class4 and Class6 from pkg_b are loaded. Class5 from pkg_b in B.jar is not loaded because it has already been loaded from C.jar.

As a result of this class loading, Class4 and Class6 from B.jar are forced to work with Class5 in C.jar. We mentioned that Class5 implementation in C.jar is different from its implementation in B.jar. This implies that at runtime, Class4 and Class6 are working with a Class5 implementation which is different from the Class5 implementation they had worked with at development time.

Hence, the behavior of component *B* can change at runtime. The original contents of component *B*, as intended by its developer have been compromised since one of the classes of component *B* has been masked by a class from component *C* at runtime. The runtime environment determines the content and behavior of a component. Because the runtime environment can be configured with different combinations of CLASSPATH, the application can behave differently in different runtime environments. There would be no consistent component or application behavior.

The root cause for all the problems discussed above is that the component boundary that keeps all related classes of the component together at development time is dissolving and dynamically changing at runtime. The OSGi module layer solves the dissolving boundary problem of JAR and Java packages with the introduction of another layer of abstraction, called the *module layer*, around a JAR file. An OSGi module, also known as a *bundle*, is the unit of deployment in an OSGi framework. A bundle is nothing but a regular JAR file that contains class files, resource files, and metadata. The only thing special about a bundle is that it carries additional metadata relevant to OSGi in the manifest of the JAR file. Any JAR file in Java contains a manifest file called `MANIFEST.MF` placed inside a `META-INF` folder to store metadata. Apart from the regular JAR file's manifest contents, an OSGi bundle's manifest file has OSGi-specific information. When an OSGi bundle is deployed in an OSGi framework, the framework uses this information to provide stronger boundaries around the bundle.

If we convert the three JAR files from the above example to OSGi bundles, we can make bundle *A* explicitly export `pkg_a`, bundle *B* explicitly export `pkg_b`, and bundle *C* explicitly export `pkg_c`. This is illustrated in Figure 5.4. When these bundles

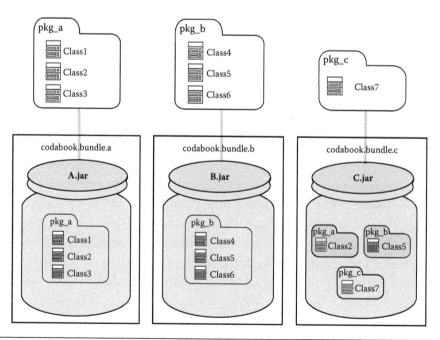

Figure 5.4   OSGi bundles provide stronger component boundaries.

are deployed into the OSGi framework, all three classes from bundle *A* and bundle *B* are loaded and are available to other bundles. However, from bundle *C*, only the `Class7` which is part of the exported `pkg_c` is loaded and made visible from outside the bundle. The other two classes, `Class2` and `Class5`, are loaded within the class loading context of bundle *C* and are not visible outside bundle *C*. This is due to the fact that the parent packages of these two classes, `pkg_a` and `pkg_b`, have not been explicitly exported. This ensures that components *A* and *B* are intact without any interference from component *C*. Moreover, the boundary is consistent irrespective of CLASSPATH definitions in the environment.

We have gained a finer control around physical and logical boundaries of a component using OSGi bundles. Bundles are more powerful than JAR files in enforcing module boundaries, because a bundle needs to explicitly define what portion of its internal code is externally visible. Similarly, a bundle must explicitly declare any external dependencies that it has with the code exposed by other bundles. The OSGi framework matches the exports and imports of deployed bundles to dynamically wire (compose) the entire application. This process of bundle resolution ensures consistency among the different bundles in terms of versions and other constraints. An application in OSGi is nothing but a collection of bundles with explicitly defined dependencies. Having obtained a feel for how the OSGi helps to improve the bare component constructs of standard Java, let us understand the OSGi framework in more detail. In the next section we provide more details on the module layer and OSGi bundles.

5.4 The OSGi Module Layer

The OSGi module layer defines the *OSGi module*, also known as a *bundle*. A bundle is deployed as a JAR file. All JAR files carry a manifest file in the location META-INF/ MANIFEST.MF. The OSGi framework defines manifest headers specific to the OSGi platform. A bundle can use these headers to provide descriptive information about itself to the OSGi environment.

Most of the metadata in an OSGi bundle is meant for the OSGi framework to read and interpret. The OSGi framework uses this information to provide runtime support for the deployed bundle. But some pieces of information in the metadata are meant for human consumption so that they can understand what the bundle does and where the bundle came from. These attributes are completely optional and are ignored by the OSGi framework. An example manifest file, presented below, shows some attributes meant for human consumption:

```
Bundle-Name: POS Model
Bundle-Description: Model package for Point of Sale Application
Bundle-DocURL: http://www.codabook.com/pos/model/doc
Bundle-Vendor: CODA Book
```

Some of the manifest attributes define the identity of a bundle. `Bundle-SymbolicName` is one such attribute that assigns a unique name to a bundle. In an OSGi environment, two deployed bundles cannot have the same `Bundle-SymbolicName`. However, it is allowed to have different versions of the same bundle (with the same symbolic name). The `Bundle-Version` attribute defines the version of the bundle. The value of the `Bundle-Version` attribute follows a common OSGi version number format of the form *x.y.z*. The first number, *x*, is called a *major number*. The second number, *y*, is called a *minor number*. The third number, *z*, is called a *micro number*. The common version format also specifies a fourth component called a *qualifier*. The qualifier can contain alphanumeric characters. For example, 2.0.0.beta is a valid version number. The symbolic name and version together uniquely identify a bundle:

```
Bundle-SymbolicName: codabook.osgi.pos.model
Bundle-Version: 1.0.0.qualifier
```

Bundles are deployed into the OSGi runtime environment. An application is made of interacting bundles, which are deployed in an OSGi runtime framework. Bundles can hide Java packages within them so that these packages and the classes they contain are not shared outside the host bundle. Bundles need to explicitly specify the list of Java packages they want to share with other bundles.

In a standard Java platform, when a JAR file is in the CLASSPATH, the JVM has an implicit policy of searching all folders inside the JAR file relative to the root folder in the JAR file, as if they were package names corresponding to the requested class. For example, to locate `foo.bar.clazz` inside a JAR, the JVM will look for the `foo/bar/clazz.class` file. OSGi class path searching is different from the above JVM class search inside JAR files. The OSGi framework's class searching algorithm is influenced by the code visibility–related metadata specified in the bundle manifest file. Code visibility–related manifest information consists of the following:

- Internal bundle class path
- Exported internal code
- Imported external code

5.4.1 *Internal Bundle Class Path*

We discussed that during class loading, the JVM searches all the folders in a standard JAR file. However, OSGi framework class loading does not search all the folders in a bundle JAR file. Instead it searches only in the folders that are explicitly specified in a manifest attribute. This manifest attribute is called a `Bundle-Classpath`. This parameter influences the class path search within the scope of a bundle. An example of this attribute from a manifest file is as follows:

```
Bundle-ClassPath:.,other-classes/,embedded.jar
```

In this bundle, all the classes relative to the root folder of the JAR file are searched due to the first entry "." in the `Bundle-ClassPath`. The next entry `other-classes/` forces the OSGi runtime framework to search for classes inside the folder `other-classes` relative to the root of the JAR file. The next entry `embedded.jar` points to another JAR file embedded within this bundle JAR file. All class files within that embedded JAR file are also searched. If no `Bundle-ClassPath` is specified in the manifest file, the OSGi framework provides a default value of "." which makes the search similar to that done in regular JAR files, a relative search from the root folder. However, if a `Bundle-ClassPath` is mentioned in the manifest file and it does not include ".", then the class files relative to the root folder are not searched; only the locations specified by the `Bundle-ClassPath` attribute are searched.

5.4.2 Exported Internal Code

A bundle can access its internal code using the `Bundle-ClassPath` as we saw in the last subsection. But how can a bundle make use of code that is part of another bundle? Or how can a bundle expose its internal code to be consumed by other bundles? In order to expose some part of its internal code as public API accessible from another bundle, the bundle must use the `Export-Package` manifest attribute. By default, the bundle exports nothing, and none of its code is visible from other bundles. The bundle exposes its internal code by specifying the list of Java packages exported by it. But please note that exposing a package does not automatically expose its descendant packages. For example, if you export `foo.bar.pkg`, then `foo.bar.pkg.sub` is not exported; if you would also like to export `foo.bar.pkg.sub`, you must explicitly export it. Following is an example from a manifest file:

```
Export-Package: codabook.osgi.pos.model
```

5.4.3 Imported External Code

Internal code exposed by a bundle can be consumed from another bundle through the `Import-Package` attribute. We should not confuse the *import* Java keyword with the `Import-Package` OSGi manifest attribute. The purpose of the Java *import* keyword is to manage the namespaces. The *import* keyword provides a convenience to you so that you need not use fully qualified class names inside your code. The *import* keyword does not provide any code visibility. The `Import-Package` operation from the manifest file, on the other hand, is meant for visibility control. An example from a manifest file is as follows:

```
Import-Package: codabook.osgi.pos.model
```

To understand the OSGi modules concept through an example, consider some of the components we introduced in the point-of-sale (POS) application in Chapter 4.

The `Table` component contained the business logic associated with seating guests and checking out guests from a table. The `GuestUI` component contained the presentation logic associated with the check-in and check-out of guests. All the components depended on the `POSModel` object library.

We consider the two components (`GuestUI` and `Table`) and the `POSModel` object library shown in Figure 5.5 for conversion to the OSGi component model. All three of them are JAR files that house certain Java packages within them. We convert them into three OSGi modules with code sharing across them as defined by Table 5.1.

The internals of the three JAR files remain as is, except for the manifest information. The manifest file of the `POSModel` bundle is presented below. Pay special attention to exported package information.

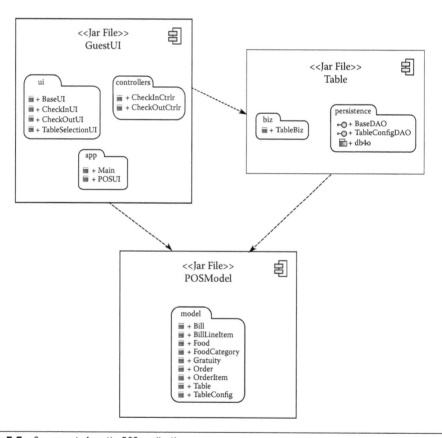

Figure 5.5   Components from the POS application.

Table 5.1   Code Visibility across OSGi Modules of the POS Application

BUNDLE NAME	EXPORTED PACKAGES	IMPORTED PACKAGES
POSModel	model	—
Table	biz	model
GuestUI	—	biz, model

```
Manifest-Version: 1.0
Bundle-ManifestVersion: 2
Bundle-Name: POSModel
Bundle-SymbolicName: codabook.osgi.pos.model
Bundle-Version: 1.0.0.qualifier
Export-Package: codabook.osgi.pos.model
```

The manifest file for the Table bundle is shown below. Pay special attention to exported and imported package information.

```
Manifest-Version: 1.0
Bundle-ManifestVersion: 2
Bundle-SymbolicName: codabook.osgi.pos.table
Bundle-Version: 1.0.0.qualifier
Export-Package: codabook.osgi.pos.table.biz
Import-Package: codabook.osgi.pos.model
```

The manifest file for the GuestUI bundle is shown below. Pay special attention to imported package information.

```
Manifest-Version: 1.0
Bundle-ManifestVersion: 2
Bundle-SymbolicName: codabook.osgi.pos.guestui
Bundle-Version: 1.0.0.qualifier
Import-Package: codabook.osgi.pos.model,
                codabook.osgi.pos.table.biz
Main-Class: codabook.osgi.pos.guestui.app.Main
```

These three bundles satisfy the export and import requirements of one another as shown in Figure 5.6. We demonstrate how these three bundles can be deployed in an OSGi runtime framework in the next section.

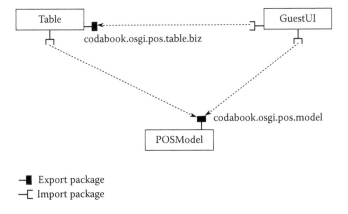

Figure 5.6 The POS application assembly using OSGi bundles.

5.5 OSGi Runtime Framework

OSGi bundles are deployed onto OSGi runtime framework. There are many different ways of deploying the bundles onto OSGi runtime framework. In an IDE like Eclipse, one can choose the run configuration to target an OSGi platform. The OSGi framework implementation (Equinox in the case of Eclipse) would then be started, and the bundles selected in the run configuration would be deployed on this runtime.

Alternatively, the framework can be started programmatically. The OSGi specification defines a `FrameworkFactory` API that should be implemented by the OSGi framework implementation. The `FrameworkFactory` defines a single method `newFramework()`. This method returns an object of type `Framework`. `Framework` is another standard API defined in the OSGi specifications, through which we can deploy bundles. The following launcher code snippet demonstrates how this can be achieved:

```
FrameworkFactory fwFactory =
        ServiceLoader.load(FrameworkFactory.class)
        .iterator().next();
Framework framework = fwFactory.newFramework(null);
framework.init();

BundleContext bndlCtxt = framework.getBundleContext();
File folder = new File(".");
for (File file : folder.listFiles()) {
        if (file.getName().endsWith(".jar")) {
                Bundle bundle = bndlCtxt.installBundle(file.
                toURI().toString());
        }
}

framework.start();
```

Using `java.util.ServiceLoader`, we load the `FrameworkFactory` object.[*] Once we have the `FrameworkFactory`, we request for a new `Framework` object instance from it. Before we install any bundle onto the framework, we need to initialize the framework. We do that by calling the `init()` method on the `framework` object. In the example code above, we look for all JAR files in the current folder and install them as bundles in the OSGi framework. Once we install all the bundles, we can start the framework by calling the `start()` method on the `framework` object. This would start the framework along with all the bundles deployed in it. To deploy the three OSGi bundles (`Table`, `GuestUI`, and `POSModel`) we created for the POS

---

[*] We need to have an OSGi framework implementation JAR file in our class path; for example, in the case of Eclipse Equinox, the file is named `org.eclipse.osgi_3.8.0.v20120529-1548.jar`; the portion of the file name that follows the `*.osgi_` may differ depending on the version of Eclipse and Equinox in your environment.

application in the last section, we just need to copy JAR files of these bundles in the folder from which we are running the above launcher. Because the launcher loads all the JAR files in the current folder onto the OSGi framework, all three bundles would get deployed onto the framework.

5.6 OSGi Life Cycle Layer

The module layer defines an OSGi bundle. The life cycle layer defines how a bundle is installed, activated, updated, and uninstalled. Once deployed onto an OSGi runtime framework, a bundle can be in one of the following states:

- *Installed*—A bundle can be installed by another bundle. Once a bundle is installed, an object of type *Bundle* is returned by the framework runtime. All life cycle operations such as starting, stopping, or uninstalling of the bundle can be performed only through this object.

- *Resolved*—Once a bundle is installed, the framework analyzes its manifest to determine the dependencies of the bundle. The framework resolves the import-package dependencies of the bundle by looking for other bundles that export the required packages. If the bundle dependencies are successfully resolved, the bundle's state is changed to *Resolved* from *Installed*. For example, the Table bundle discussed in the last section declares that it imports the `codabook.osgi.pos.model` package. To resolve this dependency, the framework looks for a bundle that exports this package. Since the `POSModel` bundle exports this package, the status of the Table bundle is changed to *Resolved*.

- *Starting*—A bundle in `Resolved` state can be started by calling the `start()` method on the `Bundle` object. The bundle is in an intermediate `Starting` state from the moment it receives the `start()` command until it transitions to `Active` state.

- *Active*—After a bundle has received a `start()` command, it gets activated after a transition state of `Starting`. Just before the bundle is activated, the framework checks if there is a `BundleActivator` defined in the manifest. If there is one, then the framework calls the `start()` method on the defined bundle activator. The `BundleActivator` provides a means for the bundle developer to interfere with the bundle life cycle events.

- *Stopping*—An active bundle can be stopped by calling the `stop()` method on the `Bundle` object. The bundle transitions through the `Stopping` state to reach the `Resolved` state. If a bundle activator is defined in the manifest, the framework calls the `stop()` method on the bundle activator. This intervention provides an opportunity for the bundle developer to clean up any resources being used by the bundle before it stops.

- *Uninstalled*—A bundle can be uninstalled by calling the `uninstall()` method on the `Bundle` object. When a bundle is uninstalled, the framework

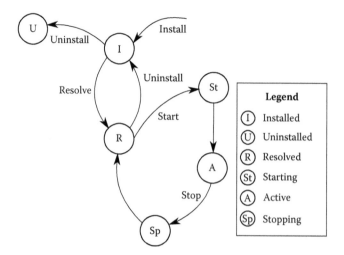

Figure 5.7   The OSGi bundle life cycle state transition.

notifies all the other bundles. If the bundle had exported any package and it is currently in use by other bundles, then the exported packages would continue to be available until the framework is stopped in spite of the uninstallation of the bundle.

The life cycle states of a bundle and the state transitions are illustrated in Figure 5.7.

The life cycle layer defines a `BundleContext` API that the bundle developer can use to gain access to runtime framework services. When the life cycle layer calls the `start()` and `stop()` methods of the `BundleActivator`, the `BundleContext` object is passed as an argument. Alternatively, `BundleContext` can be obtained from the `Bundle` object. Part of the `BundleContext` API is presented below:

```
public interface BundleContext {
...
String getProperty(String key);
Bundle getBundle();
Bundle installBundle(String location, InputStream input)
                        throws BundleException;
Bundle installBundle(String location) throws BundleException;
Bundle getBundle(long id);
Bundle[] getBundles();
void addBundleListener(BundleListener listener);
void removeBundleListener(BundleListener listener);
void addFrameworkListener(FrameworkListener listener);
void removeFrameworkListener(FrameworkListener listener);
...
}
```

All the installed bundles in the framework can be obtained from the `BundleContext` using the `getBundles()` method call. `BundleContext` was used to install the bundles in the launcher example code we presented in Section 5.5. We extended the launcher below so that it would invoke the main() method after starting the bundles:

```
framework.init();
BundleContext bndlCtxt = framework.getBundleContext();
Bundle mainBundle = null;

File folder = new File(".");
for (File file : folder.listFiles()) {
            if (file.getName().endsWith(".jar")) {
                    Bundle bundle = bndlCtxt.
                        installBundle(file.toURI().toString());

                    if (bundle.getHeaders().
                            get("Main-Class") ! = null)
                    {
                            mainBundle = bundle;
                    }
            }
    }
        framework.start();
```

In the above launcher code, we obtain the BundleContext from the Framework instance. Using BundleContext, we install all the JAR file bundles found in the current folder. After installing each bundle, we also check if the bundle is the main bundle for the application. This is verified by checking if the bundle has a Main-Class attribute.* If so, we store the reference of this bundle. After installing all the bundles, they are in an Installed state. When we call the framework.start() method, all these bundles are Resolved by the framework, and finally made Active. However, if any of the bundle dependencies are not fulfilled, those bundles do not change the state from Installed. After the bundles have been started, we invoke the main method of the identified main bundle using the remaining launcher code shown below:

```
if (mainBundle ! = null) {
        String mainClassName = mainBundle.getHeaders().get("Main-
                            Class");
        Class mainClass = mainBundle.loadClass(mainClassName);
        Method mainMethod = mainClass.getMethod("main", String[].
                            class);
        String[] params = null;
        mainMethod.invoke(null, (Object) params);

}
```

Using this launcher code, when we deploy the three bundles of the POS application described earlier, we can see that the assembled application can run two of the use

---

* Note that this is a JAR file manifest header and not an OSGi manifest header.

cases: Guests Check-In and Guests Check-Out. However, there is one snag in this implementation: the GuestUI bundle is tightly coupled to the Table bundle as it invokes the TableBiz implementation through a *new* operation as shown below:

```
TableBiz tableBiz = new TableBiz();
```

In the next section, we discuss the OSGi service layer and show how it can solve this problem of bundle level coupling.

5.7 OSGi Service Layer

While the module layer defines concrete component boundaries, the OSGi service layer defines a model for dynamic collaboration among bundles across the boundaries. The service layer provides a publish, find, and bind model of collaboration. An OSGi bundle can *publish* a set of services through the OSGi service registry. Other bundles query the OSGi service registry to *locate* and *bind* with the services that they require. The service registry checks the list of registered services and returns a service reference that matches the query. The requiring bundle binds with the service reference and consumes its services. Instead of querying the registry, the bundles can opt to be notified by the OSGi service registry whenever a registration or unregistration event happens. Once the notification arrives, the bundles can bind or unbind with an appropriate service.

A service consists of a *service interface* and a *service object*. The service interface is akin to a provided interface of a component, and the service object is akin to an internal component implementation of the provided interface. The service interface defines a set of API operators. A service interface represents a conceptual contract between the provider and consumer. A service object provides implementation of the service. When a bundle registers a service with the service registry, it registers a service object against a service interface. The bundle that registered a service owns the service object. When the bundle is stopped, the service and service object are unregistered.

Let us consider the example of the Table bundle from the last section. We can let this bundle expose its functionality by registering a service, and let the GuestUI bundle consume it by querying the OSGi registry. This would solve the problem of direct coupling between these two bundles. In order to publish its functionality as a service, the Table bundle needs to define a service interface. We extract an ITableBiz Java interface from the TableBiz class implementation. The interface code is as follows:

```
public interface ITableBiz {
        public int getNoOfTables();
        public List<Table> getOccupiedTables();
        public List<Table> getEmptyTables();
        public void occupyTable(Table table, int noOfGuests,
            String waiter) throws Exception;
```

```
    public void unOccupyTable(Table table) throws Exception;
    public void canPayBill(Table table) throws Exception;
    public void reconfigureTables(int newNoOfTables) throws
        Exception;
    public void canTableTakeOrders(Table table) throws
        Exception;

}
```

Once the service interface is defined, the service can be registered from the *Activator* of the bundle using the BundleContext API. The TableBundleActivator code that registers the service is shown below. A new instance of TableBiz class, which implements the ITableBiz interface, is created and registered as the service object:

```
public class TableBundleActivator implements BundleActivator {

    @Override
    public void start(BundleContext context) throws Exception {
        context.registerService(ITableBiz.class, new
            TableBiz(), null);
    }

    @Override
    public void stop(BundleContext context) throws Exception {
    }

}
```

Once a bundle registers a service, the service functionality is made available to other bundles under the runtime framework's control. A potential consumer can use the service registry to search for providers of a particular service. Once it finds a service provider, it can bind and use the service. A dependency exists between the bundle owning a service and any other bundle that consumes the service. This dependency is managed by the OSGi framework. The framework is aware of which bundles are using a particular service being offered by a bundle. When a bundle is stopped, the framework automatically removes the entries of all the services registered by the bundle.

Registered services are referenced through a ServiceReference API object. The ServiceReference provides an indirection level that decouples direct dependency on the service object. The ServiceReference object carries the properties and other metadata information of the service that it represents. A bundle that wants to just examine the properties of the service provided by another bundle can do so with the help of a ServiceReference object. Once the bundle chooses to make use of the service, it can pass the ServiceReference to the BundleContext to get the service object. The ServiceReference object is valid only as long as the service object is registered.

In the POS example, let us consider the consumption of the `ITableBiz` service registered by the `Table` component. The `GuestUI` component is in need of this service. Inside the `GuestUI` component, we have a `TableBizHolder` class, which serves as the helper class to locate the `ITableBiz` service. The code of the helper method `getTableBiz()` inside the `TableBizHolder` class is presented:

```
public ITableBiz getTableBiz() {
        ServiceReference<ITableBiz>
        tableBizServiceRef = bundleContext
                    .getServiceReference(ITableBiz.class);
        return bundleContext.getService(tableBizServiceRef);
}
```

The service layer provides a procedural service model where the publishing bundle takes the responsibility of publishing the service, and the consuming bundle takes the responsibility of finding and binding to the service. Instead of this procedural service registration and lookup, services can be defined declaratively using OSGi declarative services. In the next section, we discuss the OSGi declarative services specification.

5.8 OSGi Declarative Services Specification

On top of the service layer, OSGi specifications define a set of core services that may be provided as part of the OSGi framework. Logging service, configuration service, and HTTP service are some of the example services. All of these services are defined as part of the OSGi compendium service specifications. One of the compendium services is OSGi declarative services. Declarative services let the bundle developers publish and consume services declaratively through the OSGi service layer.

In the declarative services model, a service provided by a bundle is described by a *service component*. The service component description is interpreted at runtime to create and destroy service objects as necessary. The service component is sometimes referred to as simply the *component*. The service component is declared in a *component description* file, which is an XML file inside the bundle. The component description files are read and acted upon by Service Component Runtime (SCR). A component declares the services that it provides and also the dependencies it has on the other components through the *references*.

To declare a component in a bundle, the following three things are required:

- An XML file that contains the component description
- A pointer to the component description file location using the bundle manifest header `Service-Component`
- An implementation class as defined by the component description

Let us explain these steps through the POS example's `Table` bundle and `ITableBiz` service interface that it offers. Inside the `Table` bundle's `META-INF` folder, we create a new `component.xml` file whose contents are shown below:

```
<?xml version = "1.0" encoding = "UTF-8"?>
<scr:component xmlns:scr = "http://www.osgi.org/xmlns/scr/v1.1.0"
name = "codabook.osgi.pos.table">
  <implementation class = "codabook.osgi.pos.table.biz.TableBiz"/>
  <service>
   <provide interface = "codabook.osgi.pos.table.ifce.ITableBiz"/>
  </service>
</scr:component>
```

We dissect this file line by line to understand it. The first line is a standard XML file header:

```
<?xml version = "1.0" encoding = "UTF-8"?>
```

The second line defines a root XML element of type `component`, within the namespace `scr`. The component element has been given the name `codabook.osgi.pos.table`:

```
<scr:component xmlns:scr = "http://www.osgi.org/xmlns/scr/v1.1.0"
name = "codabook.osgi.pos.table">
```

The third line defines the implementation class for the component. This is the *service object* that we discussed in the service layer:

```
<implementation class = "codabook.osgi.pos.table.biz.TableBiz"/>
```

The fourth to sixth lines define the service provided by the component. The service is the same as the *service interface* that we discussed in the service layer:

```
<service>
  <provide interface = "codabook.osgi.pos.table.ifce.ITableBiz"/>
</service>
```

Finally, the seventh line closes the XML element component that was declared in the second line:

```
</scr:component>
```

In the component description XML file, we declared a component, gave it a name, defined the implementation class for the component, and defined its provided interface (through the service XML element). A component description file can declare more than one component. A component can provide more than one interface. Once the component description file has been created, a pointer to the component description file is required from the manifest. The MANIFEST.MF file for the Table component is shown below:

```
Manifest-Version: 1.0
Bundle-ManifestVersion: 2
Bundle-SymbolicName: codabook.osgi.pos.table.service
Bundle-Version: 1.0.0.qualifier
Export-Package: codabook.osgi.pos.table.ifce
Import-Package: codabook.osgi.pos.model
Service-Component: META-INF/component.xml
```

The Service-Component manifest header points to the component description file. One important point to note with respect to declarative services is that, unlike in the service layer implementation, we do not require a Bundle Activator class to register the service. The declaration of the service inside the component description file and its inclusion in the manifest file through the Service-Component header are read by the SCR of the declarative service, and it performs an autoregistration of the ITableBiz service interface along with the TableBiz service object.

Now that the service is published, it has to be consumed. The consumption of one component by another component is aided through a reference in the component description file. Once a reference is defined in a component description, the SCR reads this information at runtime, locates the provided service that matches this reference, and binds. This autowiring and resolving is similar to the resolving of export and import packages at the bundle layer. This means less work to the component developer, as there is no need for manual lookup and binding in the bundle activator class. Let us see how the GuestUI component can consume the ITableBiz service published by the Table component.

We create a component.xml file inside the GuestUI component:

```
<?xml version = "1.0" encoding = "UTF-8"?>
<scr:component xmlns:scr = "http://www.osgi.org/xmlns/scr/v1.1.0"
    name = "codabook.osgi.pos.guestui.service">
        <implementation class =
            "codabook.osgi.pos.guestui.controllers.CheckInCtrlr"/>

        <reference bind = "setTableBiz" cardinality = "1..1"
            interface = "codabook.osgi.pos.table.ifce.ITableBiz"
            name = "ITableBiz" policy = "static"/>
</scr:component>
```

The structure of the component description file is similar to the structure of the component description file we presented for the Table component. We dissect this file line by line to understand it.

The first line is a standard XML file header:

```
<?xml version = "1.0" encoding = "UTF-8"?>
```

The second line defines a root XML element of type component, within the namespace scr. The component element has been given the name "codabook.osgi.pos.guestui.service".

```
<scr:component xmlns:scr = "http://www.osgi.org/xmlns/scr/v1.1.0"
     name = "codabook.osgi.pos.guestui.service">
```

The third line defines the implementation class for the component. This is the *service object* that either provides or requires the service:

```
<implementation class =
     "codabook.osgi.pos.guestui.controllers.CheckInCtrlr"/>
```

The fourth line specifies the *required interface* of this component through a *reference* element. The reference element has many attributes through which details of the required interface are specified. The *bind* attribute specifies a method from the component implementation class, which should bind the required interface. The *cardinality* attribute defines how many instances of the references can be passed to this component. The policy attribute can specify if the assignment of the references should be *static* or *dynamic*. In the case of a *static* binding policy, the referred service is searched for only once during this component's activation and wired to this component. The framework does not intervene and revoke this binding even if the referred service is unregistered. In the case of the dynamic binding policy, the framework tracks the *reference* service even after it has been bound and revokes the *reference* or supplies it with another available *reference* should this *reference* service disappear:

```
<reference bind = "setTableBiz" cardinality = "1..1"
     interface = "codabook.osgi.pos.table.ifce.ITableBiz"
     name = "ITableBiz" policy = "static"/>
```

Finally, the fifth line closes the XML element component that was declared in the second line:

```
</scr:component>
```

Using the declarative services, we have let the TableBiz component expose a service that was consumed by the GuestUI component. This is illustrated in Figure 5.8. The same component composition was achieved using only the service layer, without using declarative services in the last section. Using declarative services has reduced our job as component developers since the registration and lookup of services has been automated.

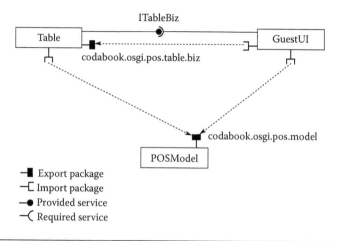

Figure 5.8   The POS application assembly using OSGi declarative services.

5.9 Summary

This chapter discussed component-oriented features provided by the OSGi service framework. The chapter introduced the OSGi framework. We used an example application assembly to demonstrate the necessity of the OSGi component model on top of simple packages and the JAR file–based Java component model. We discussed how the OSGi module layer enforces the component boundaries. We discussed the use of the life cycle layer to deploy and assemble multiple OSGi bundles into one application. This was followed by a discussion of the OSGi service layer, with an example application assembly that used the OSGi service registry to publish, find, and bind with services. Finally, we discussed how the OSGi declarative services specification can ease component development in a declarative way.

Review Questions

1. What is wrong with the JAR file–based component model?
2. How does OSGi overcome the problems of flat CLASSPATH?
3. Are all OSGi bundles JAR files? Are all JAR files OSGi bundles? Explain with examples.
4. How is the unique identity of an OSGi bundle defined?
5. Do all OSGi bundles need to export one or more packages?
6. Can an OSGi bundle transition its state from installed to active? Why or why not?
7. How does the OSGi framework carry out bundle resolution? Is the same resolution mechanism applicable to the OSGi service layer?
8. What are the elements of an OSGi service?
9. How do you register an OSGi service?
10. How do you find an OSGi service?

11. How do you bind to an OSGi service?
12. Why do we need declarative services?
13. Can an OSGi component provide more than one interface? How?
14. Can an OSGi component require more than one interface? How?
15. Do declarative services provide autowiring of required and provided interfaces? How?
16. In what way does declarative services specification enhance upon the service layer specification?

6
PRACTICING CODA WITH SCA

6.1 Introduction

In the last chapter, we discussed practicing CODA using the OSGi component framework. The objective of this chapter is to introduce practicing CODA using the Service Component Architecture (SCA) component model and framework. The SCA component model was introduced in Chapter 3 along with other component models. This chapter provides additional details pertaining to the SCA framework. The chapter provides sufficient information to get started with CODA practice using SCA, and lets the readers appreciate the component-oriented features of the SCA framework. The chapter starts with background information on SCA standards, followed by technical concepts associated with SCA, and this is followed by an explanation of the SCA application programming interface through example code snippets.

6.2 What Is Service Component Architecture?

Service Component Architecture (SCA) is a component model based on Service Oriented Architecture (SOA). The fundamental premise of SCA is that business functionalities are available as software services, which can be composed together to form an application. SCA supports the creation of new services that are tailor-made for an application, as well as reuse of existing software assets by exposing them as services. The SCA component model supports a wide range of programming languages and a variety of distribution technologies such as Web Services, Java RMI, and IIOP.

SCA standards were originally specified by an industry body called *Open SOA*. The standards are currently maintained by another industry standards body—*OASIS* (Organization for the Advancement of Structured Information Standards). Many vendors such as IBM, Oracle, Fabric3, and Apache provide implementation of the SCA framework. We use the *Apache Tuscany* implementation for the examples in this chapter.

6.3 SCA Concepts

6.3.1 Component

Central to the SCA technology is the component, which is the atomic unit of construction. An *SCA Component* is a *configured instance of an implementation* (Figure 6.1). An *implementation* is a piece of a software program which provides

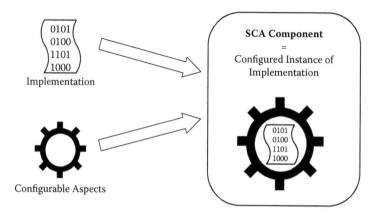

Figure 6.1   An SCA component is a configured instance of an implementation.

business functionality. SCA allows the implementation to be sourced from a variety of programming platforms including many programming languages, scripting languages, and declarative languages. As long as the implementation contains some business functionality, it can be turned into an SCA component. SCA calls these variations in implementations the *implementation types*. A component's implementation type can be any one of Java, BPEL, or PHP, and so on.

SCA defines the configurable aspects of the component as a *component type*. There are five configurable aspects for a component:

- Service
- Reference
- Producer
- Consumer
- Property

A *service* is the SCA equivalent of a *provided interface* of a component. SCA components expose the business functionality implemented by them through *services*. A component can depend on services provided by other components. These dependencies are known as *references*. A *reference* is the SCA equivalent of the *required interface* of a component. A component can have *properties* that can be set to specific values at the time of deployment. Data values assigned to properties would be able to manifest the business functions of the component in a predetermined way.

Apart from sharing the business functions through exposure of services and consumption through references, components can share business functions through the publisher-subscriber mechanism as well. A *producer* component publishes the list of events that it would generate. A *consumer* component subscribes for the kind of events it is interested in consuming. The producer-consumer mechanism is not currently supported for the Java implementation type. Hence, we will not discuss it further. The SCA standard defines a diagrammatic symbol to represent the component. Figure 6.2 provides the symbol notations.

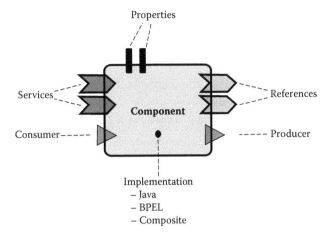

Figure 6.2   SCA symbol for a component.

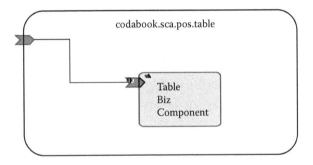

Figure 6.3   `PosTable` composite.

6.3.2 Composite

An SCA application is constructed through the assembly of components. The assembly of SCA components is known as a *composite*. A composite is primarily a collection of components. The constituent components can be implemented using different technologies. Each component would have services and references. In addition to the list of components, the composite consists of wiring elements that connect references of a component to the services provided by other components. Services, references, and properties of constituent components can be promoted to the level of composite. Using the promoted elements, the composite can offer services, have references to services that are provided elsewhere outside of this composite, and have properties that can be configured. Composites can also play the role of a component in another composite assembly. Thus, an application can be made up of a hierarchy of composites and components. SCA composites are defined through an XML file with a `.composite` extension. A composite can be diagrammatically represented using the component symbol introduced earlier. An example composite diagram is presented in Figure 6.3. In this diagram, note that the service provided by the `TableBizComponent` has been promoted to the level of composite.

6.3.3 Wiring

When SCA components are assembled together into a composite, the references of individual components have to be fulfilled through the services provided by other components. An SCA *wire* specifies this runtime association between the requiring reference and the providing service. Some of the services offered by the constituent components of a composite can be *promoted* to the level of composite so that these services can be consumed from outside the composite. Similarly, some of the references of the internal components can be promoted to the level of composites so that these references can be fulfilled from outside the composite.

6.3.4 SCA Runtime and Domain

SCA composites are deployed to SCA runtime for execution. SCA runtime is the component framework that implements the SCA component model. For example, *Apache Tuscany* is an SCA runtime. Many SCA runtime instances can be combined to form an SCA *domain*. A domain hosts components and composites associated with one administrative boundary. A domain can consist of multiple SCA runtime instances hosted across multiple physical nodes. During deployment, components in a composite can get deployed onto different nodes in the SCA domain.

In the next few sections, we demonstrate the steps involved in the creation, composition, and consumption of SCA components and composites.

6.4 Creating an SCA Component from Java Implementation

As mentioned earlier, an SCA component is nothing but a configured instance of an implementation. Once we have a business logic implementation in Java, we need to declare the configurable aspects of the implementation (i.e., services, references, and properties). The mechanism of declaring configurable aspects of an implementation vary from one implementation platform to the other. For Java, SCA annotations are used in the source code to declare the configurable aspects of the implementation. During deployment of the component, the configurable aspects are configured. Configuration involves providing values to the properties and wiring the references to appropriate services.

Consider the *point-of-sale* (POS) application for restaurants that was introduced in Chapter 4. We shall convert the existing business implementation in this application to SCA components. We consider the two components (`GuestUI` and `Table`) and the `POSModel` object library shown in Figure 6.4 for conversion to the SCA component platform.

The `Table` component shown in Figure 6.4 implements business functions related to the management of tables in the restaurant such as configuring the

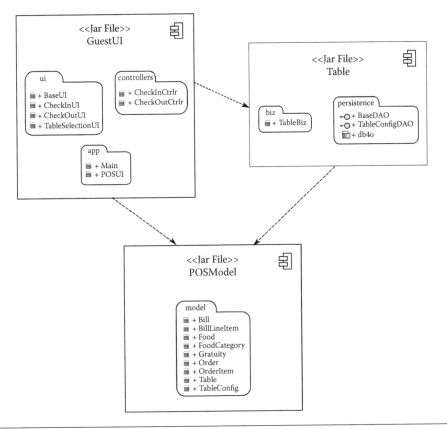

Figure 6.4   Components from the POS application.

number of tables, occupying a table, and vacating a table. All of these business functions are implemented in the `TableBiz` class inside this component. This component can be converted to an SCA component exposing a service. The SCA component is named `TableComponent`. The service can be exposed as a Java interface `ITableBiz`.

The `GuestUI` component in Figure 6.4 implements business functions related to guest check-in and guest check-out. Check-in related implementation is in the `CheckInCtrlr` class, and check-out related implementation is in the `CheckOutCtrlr` class. We create two SCA components from these implementations, one `CheckInCtrlrComponent` providing `ICheckIn` service and another `CheckOutCtrlrComponent` providing `ICheckOut` service. We also see from the existing component structure in Figure 6.4 that `CheckInCtrlrComponent` and `CheckOutCtrlrComponent` would depend on the `ITableBiz` service provided by the `TableBizComponent`. This dependency is shown in Figure 6.5.

Let us see how to declare the SCA configurable aspects on the existing Java implementation code. The existing `Table` component implements business functionality in the class `TableBiz`. This business functionality will be exposed as a service with Java interface `ITableBiz`. The definition of `ITableBiz` is refactored from the `TableBiz` implementation:

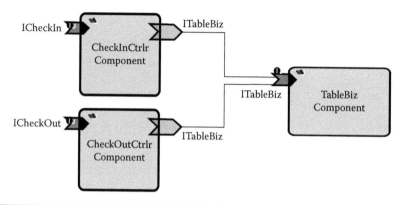

Figure 6.5   Component dependencies within the POSGuest composite.

```
public interface ITableBiz {
        public int getNoOfTables();
        public List<Table> getOccupiedTables();
        public List<Table> getEmptyTables();
        public void occupyTable(Table table, int noOfGuests,
        String waiter)
                        throws Exception;
        public void unOccupyTable(Table table) throws Exception;
        public void canPayBill(Table table) throws Exception;
        public void reconfigureTables(int newNoOfTables) throws
        Exception;
        public void canTableTakeOrders(Table table) throws
        Exception;
}
```

Now we need to declare the ITableBiz as the service being offered by
the TableBiz implementation class. In order to make this declaration we use
@Service SCA annotation on the implementation class. The service interface
is also specified along with the annotation. The @Service annotation informs
the SCA runtime that this implementation provides an SCA service with interface
ITableBiz. An SCA component can configure this implementation and expose
a service with interface ITableBiz. The SCA annotations on the implementation
code are shown below:

```
@Service(ITableBiz.class)
@Scope("COMPOSITE")
public class TableBiz implements ITableBiz {
        //… some code omitted for brevity
}
```

In addition to the @Service annotation, we see another @Scope annotation in
the above implementation. We can define the life cycle scope of the implementation
through @Scope annotation. If we assign a value of *"COMPOSITE"* to @Scope

annotation, then SCA runtime will ensure that it would appear as if a single instance of the implementation is being used across all the clients of the component. The state of the component would be shared across all the client components. If we assign a value of *"STATELESS"* to @Scope annotation, the state of the component is not preserved, and each time the client component acquires an instance of the implementation, it would have no correlation to the implementation instance acquired earlier. Since the TableBiz implementation needs to remember the set of tables occupied across different calls from clients, we would like the implementation to remember the state. Hence, we use *"COMPOSITE"* scope as shown in the code above.

From the GuestUI component in Figure 6.4, we identified two business functionality implementation classes CheckInCtrlr and CheckOutCtrlr. We refactor these implementation classes to retrieve two Java interfaces ICheckIn and ICheckOut, the source code of which are given below:

```
public interface ICheckIn {
        public void invokeCheckIn();
}

public interface ICheckOut {
        public void invokeCheckOut();
}
```

Both the CheckInCtrlr and the CheckOutCtrlr implementations have a dependency on the ITableBiz interface. Since this dependency is an SCA reference, which is a configurable aspect, we declare this configurable aspect on the implementation using the annotation @Reference as shown below for the CheckInCtrlr class:

```
@Service(ICheckIn.class)
public class CheckInCtrlr implements ICheckIn {

        private CheckInUI checkInUI;
        private ITableBiz tableBiz;

        @Reference
        public void setTableBiz(ITableBiz tableBiz) {
                this.tableBiz = tableBiz;
        }

        //... some code omitted for brevity
}
```

The CheckInCtrlr implementation requires an object of type ITableBiz. It declares this as an SCA *reference*, a configurable aspect of the SCA component. This is done by using the @Reference SCA annotation on the setter method of the member variable tableBiz. By declaring this as a configurable aspect, the implementation does not bother with obtaining a reference to the member variable `tableBiz`. The component configuration that uses this implementation will provide a reference object. It can do this by wiring the SCA component's reference to the `ITableBiz` service provided by another component. When the component is deployed into the SCA runtime, the runtime will use the setter method annotated with `@Reference` to pass the wired reference into the `CheckInCtrlr` implementation. The `CheckOutCtrlr` implementation has a similar source code that is presented below:

```
@Service(ICheckOut.class)
public class CheckOutCtrlr implements ICheckOut {

        private CheckOutUI checkOutUI;
        private ITableBiz tableBiz;

        @Reference
        public void setTableBiz(ITableBiz tableBiz) {
                this.tableBiz = tableBiz;
        }

        //... some code omitted for brevity
}
```

Now that we modified the implementations of all the POS components to define the configurable aspects, it is time to actually configure these configurable aspects and create SCA components out of the implementations.

6.5 Creating SCA Components and Composites

As discussed earlier, an SCA component is a configured instance of an implementation. So far we discussed how to declare the configurable aspects of the existing implementation through SCA annotations. In this section we discuss how to configure the implementations to turn them into components, and how to assemble components into composites. Both these actions are done through a composite definition XML file. The resultant composite is presented in Figure 6.6.

In the definition file, the *composite* XML element represents the composite. It is usually the root element of the XML definition file. A portion of an example composite file is shown below. The boldfaced portion defines the root XML element, which is of type *composite*:

```
<?xml version = "1.0" encoding = "UTF-8"?>
<sca:composite xmlns:sca = "http://www.osoa.org/xmlns/sca/1.0"
autowire = "false" name = "posguest" targetNamespace = "http://
          eclipse.org/POSGuestApp/src/posguest">
          ...
</sca:composite>
```

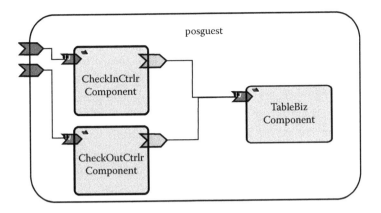

Figure 6.6   SCA composite diagram for the `POSGuest` application.

The *composite* XML element can have a few attributes such as *name* and *autowire*. The value of the *name* attribute defines the name of the composite. In the example shown above, the name of the composite has been defined as `posguest`. The value of the *autowire* attribute decides whether the components within the composite would be wired automatically by the SCA runtime or not. If *autowire* is assigned a value of *true*, then the SCA runtime would match the "reference" of the individual component to the "service" of other components within the composite. The runtime then automatically wires the service providing the component to the requiring component. If the *autowire* is assigned a value of false, then the composer of the composite must supply the wiring information manually. In the example composite file shown above, the *autowire* attribute is assigned a value of *false*. The composite element can have many types of children elements. We list below some of the children types of interest to us:

- *component*—The component element defines a constituent component of the composite. The composite may consist of 0 or more components. Each component holds a configured implementation that implements part of the business logic contained in the composite. The XML declaration of the component ties a specific implementation class to the internals of the defined component. For example, the `TableBizComponent` from the POS example will be mapped to the implementation class `TableBiz`.
- *service*—The service element defines the public services provided by the composite, which can be accessed from outside the composite. The composite's services involve promotion of any of the services offered by the constituent components. By promoting a service offered by an internal component, the composite makes the service accessible from outside the composite. For example, `ICheckIn` and `ICheckOut` services offered by `CheckInCtrlrComponent` and `CheckOutCtrlrComponent` are promoted to be available from outside the composite.
- *reference*—The reference element defines the dependencies the composite may have on services provided elsewhere, outside of this composite. The

composite's references involve the promotion of any of the references required by the constituent components. In the POS example, we do not have any unfulfilled references within the composite that need to be promoted.

- *wire*—The wire element defines a connection between one of the constituent component's reference and another constituent component's service. When the *autowire* attribute of the composite and individual components is turned off, the composite definition must contain wire elements to fulfill the required interfaces of all the constituent components (fulfill references of all the components). For example, the `CheckInCtrlrComponent`'s reference of `ITableBiz` is wired to the `ITableBiz` service provided by `TableBizComponent` in the `posguest` composite.

6.5.1 Component Element of a Composite

The composite is primarily a collection of components wired together. The list of components that constitute a composite are declared as children elements of the composite in the XML composite definition file. An example of three components under the `posguest` composite is shown below:

```xml
<?xml version = "1.0" encoding = "UTF-8"?>
<sca:composite xmlns:sca = "http://www.osoa.org/xmlns/sca/1.0"
autowire = "false" name = "posguest" targetNamespace = "http://
eclipse.org/POSGuestApp/src/posguest">

    <sca:component name = "TableBizComponent"> …
                                    </sca:component>
    <sca:component name = "CheckInCtrlrComponent"> …
                                    </sca:component>
    <sca:component name = "CheckOutCtrlrComponent"> …
                                    </sca:component>
    …
</sca:composite>
```

The three components within the composite each have a name—`TableBiz Component`, `CheckInCtrlrComponent`, and `CheckOutCtrlrComponent` —as defined by the *name* attribute of the `sca:component` XML element. Each component definition includes some children elements. The children elements of a component can be any of the following types:

- Implementation
- Service
- Reference
- Property

The *implementation* child element defines the implementation type of the component and the corresponding implementation artifact. For Java, the `implementation`.

java is the XML element, and it has an attribute called *class* through which the implementing Java class can be specified. As an example, the implementation for the CheckInCtrlrComponent is defined as below:

```
<?xml version = "1.0" encoding = "UTF-8"?>
<sca:composite xmlns:sca = "http://www.osoa.org/xmlns/sca/1.0"
autowire = "false" name = "posguest" targetNamespace = "http://
eclipse.org/POSGuestApp/src/posguest">

        <sca:component name = "CheckInCtrlrComponent">
          <sca:implementation.java
            class = "codabook.sca.pos.guestui.CheckInCtrlr"/>
          ...
        </sca:component>

...
</sca:composite>
```

The *service* child element of a component configures the service configurable aspect declared in the implementation. Recollect that we declared the CheckIn Ctrlr class to be providing service with interface ICheckIn through the annotation @Service(ICheckIn.class) in the implementation source code. A component can have zero or more *service* child elements. The *service* element can have a *name* attribute and zero or one *interface* child element. For Java, the interface. java XML element is used to define the interface of the component. As an example, the ICheckIn service offered by the CheckInCtrlrComponent is shown below:

```
<?xml version = "1.0" encoding = "UTF-8"?>
<sca:composite xmlns:sca = "http://www.osoa.org/xmlns/sca/1.0"
autowire = "false" name = "posguest" targetNamespace = "http://
eclipse.org/POSGuestApp/src/posguest">

        <sca:component name = "CheckInCtrlrComponent">
            <sca:service name = "ICheckIn">
                <sca:interface.java
                    interface = "codabook.sca.pos.guestui.
                    ICheckIn"/>
            </sca:service>
              ...
        </sca:component>
...
</sca:composite>
```

A *reference* defines the dependency that an implementation has on a service provided by another component. The *reference* child element of a *component* element configures a reference of the component. A component may have zero or more references. Recollect that we declared the @Reference annotation on the setter method of the tableBiz member variable of the CheckInCtrlr class. To configure this reference, we create a *reference* element under the CheckInCtrlrComponent with the *name* attribute tableBiz. Notice that the name of the configured reference should match the name of the declared reference in the source code. The reference element can be wired to a target service element within the composite using the *target* attribute. As an example, the tableBiz reference of the CheckInCtrlrComponent is shown below:

```
<?xml version = "1.0" encoding = "UTF-8"?>
<sca:composite xmlns:sca = "http://www.osoa.org/xmlns/sca/1.0"
autowire = "false" name = "posguest" targetNamespace = "http://
eclipse.org/POSGuestApp/src/posguest">

        <sca:component name = "CheckInCtrlrComponent">
            <sca:reference name = "tableBiz"
                    target = "TableBizComponent/ITableBiz"/>
            ...
        </sca:component>
...
</sca:composite>
```

Property elements in a component let us configure the value of property-configurable aspects declared in the implementation.

6.5.2 Service Element of a Composite

The service element of a composite lets the composite expose services to components outside the composite. The services to be exposed by the composite have to be provided by constituent components within the composite. Those services that need to be exposed outside get promoted from the component level to the composite level using the *service* XML element under the composite. As an example, consider the promotion of the ICheckIn service of the CheckInCtrlrComponent to outside the composite as shown below:

```
<?xml version = "1.0" encoding = "UTF-8"?>
<sca:composite xmlns:sca = "http://www.osoa.org/xmlns/sca/1.0"
autowire = "false" name = "posguest" targetNamespace = "http://
eclipse.org/POSGuestApp/src/posguest">

        <sca:service name = "ICheckIn"
            promote = "CheckInCtrlrComponent/ICheckIn"/>
...
</sca:composite>
```

Notice that the *service* XML element can be present inside the *component* element as well as the *composite* element. When inside the *component* it is used to configure a service being offered by that component. When inside a *composite* it is used to promote a *component*-level service to the *composite* level.

6.5.3 Reference Element of a Composite

The reference element of a composite lets the composite declare its dependency on services external to the composite. The references of the composite have to be consumed by constituent components within the composite. These references are defined under the constituent components of the composite, and they get promoted so that they get exposed outside. The promotion to the composite level happens with the use of the *reference* XML element under the composite, similar to the service element promotion explained above.

Notice that the *reference* XML element can be present inside the *component* element as well as the *composite* element. When inside the *component* it is used to configure a reference required by that component. When inside a *composite* it is used to promote a *component*-level reference to the *composite* level. This enables the supply of the reference from *components* outside of the *composite*.

6.5.4 Property Element of a Composite

The property element of a composite lets the internals of the composite be configured from the outside. A property of the constituent component of the composite gets promoted to the level of composite similar to the manner in which the service and reference of the components were promoted. This property, when configured from outside the composite, directly affects the internal component that exported the property. For example, if the `TableBizComponent` had a property called `noOfTables`, this property can be promoted to the level of `posguest` composite. If the `posguest` composite is configured with the property value of 100, the `noOfTables` property in the `TableBizComponent` is assigned a value of 100.

6.6 PosGuest Composite

In the last section, we discussed various aspects of how to create a `posguest` composite from `TableBiz`, `CheckInCtrlr`, and `CheckOutCtrlr` implementations. The complete composite file is presented below:

```
<?xml version = "1.0" encoding = "UTF-8"?>
<sca:composite xmlns:sca = "http://www.osoa.org/xmlns/sca/1.0"
autowire = "false" name = "posguest" targetNamespace = "http://
eclipse.org/POSGuestApp/src/posguest">

<sca:component name = "TableBizComponent">
  <sca:implementation.java
     class = "codabook.sca.pos.table.TableBiz"/>

  <sca:service name = "ITableBiz">
    <sca:interface.java
    interface = "codabook.sca.pos.model.ITableBiz"/>
  </sca:service>
</sca:component>
```

```
<sca:component name = "CheckInCtrlrComponent">
 <sca:implementation.java
  class = "codabook.sca.pos.guestui.CheckInCtrlr"/>

 <sca:service name = "ICheckIn">
  <sca:interface.java
  interface = "codabook.sca.pos.guestui.ICheckIn"/>
 </sca:service>

 <sca:reference name = "tableBiz"
  target = "TableBizComponent/ITableBiz"/>
</sca:component>

<sca:service name = "ICheckIn"
        promote = "CheckInCtrlrComponent/ICheckIn"/>

<sca:component name = "CheckOutCtrlrComponent">
    <sca:implementation.java
     class = "codabook.sca.pos.guestui.CheckOutCtrlr"/>

    <sca:service name = "ICheckOut">
      <sca:interface.java
        interface = "codabook.sca.pos.guestui.ICheckOut"/>
    </sca:service>

    <sca:reference name = "tableBiz"
     target = "TableBizComponent/ITableBiz"/>
  </sca:component>

<sca:service name = "ICheckOut"
        promote = "CheckOutCtrlrComponent/ICheckOut"/>

</sca:composite>
```

As can be seen from the XML file, the composite is made of three components—
`TableBizComponent`, `CheckInCtrlrComponent`, and `CheckOutCtrlr`
`Component`—wired together. Two of the services, `ICheckIn` and `ICheckOut`,
from the internal components `CheckInCtrlrComponent` and `CheckOut`
`CtrlrComponent` have been promoted and exposed outside the composite.
The references for `tableBiz` in both the `CheckInCtrlrComponent` and
`CheckOutCtrlrComponent` have been wired to the `TableBiz` component's
`ITableBiz` service.

6.7 Deploying and Consuming SCA Composites

SCA components are deployed onto an SCA runtime. Multiple SCA runtime
instances can be clubbed under one SCA domain. The SCA domain offers many infrastructure services defined by SCA specifications. The SCA domain also facilitates the

distributed deployment of components on multiple SCA runtimes hosted in different nodes in different physical locations. It is also possible to deploy the composites programmatically as shown in the code below:

```
import org.apache.tuscany.sca.host.embedded.SCADomain;

public class GuestApp {

        public static void main(String[] args) {
                SCADomain scaDomain = SCADomain
                        newInstance("posguest.composite");
                ICheckIn checkIn = scaDomain.getService
                        (ICheckIn.class,
                        "CheckInCtrlrComponent/ICheckIn");

                ICheckOut checkOut = scaDomain.getService
                        (ICheckOut.class,
                        "CheckOutCtrlrComponent/ICheckOut");

                POSUI posUI = new POSUI();
                posUI.setCheckIn(checkIn);
                posUI.setCheckOut(checkOut);
                posUI.displayUI();
        }
}
```

The above code uses the Apache Tuscany implementation of SCA runtime. The `posguest` composite is deployed into the SCA domain through the statement `SCADomain.newInstance("posguest.composite")`. Once the composite is deployed, we consume the services provided by the composite through the `getService()` method of `SCADomain` object. For example, to get the `ICheckIn` service, we use the `scaDomain.getService(ICheckIn.class,` `"CheckInCtrlrComponent/ICheckIn")` statement. The first argument is the interface class, and the second argument is the service URI, which takes the form of `"component _ name/service _ name"`. Once the services are obtained, the client can use them as normal Java objects.

6.8 Summary

In this chapter we introduced the SCA framework. A component is the atomic unit of construction in SCA. A component is a configured instance of an implementation. The implementation could be constructed using any one of the many programming platform choices. Implementations are configured using composite files. Using composite files, multiple components can be assembled together into a composite. Composites can be deployed onto SCA domains, and the services exposed by the composites can be consumed by client programs. SCA is a programming platform which is distribution protocol neutral; it provides multiple choices with respect to implementation languages and distribution deployment technologies, from which a suitable technology can be chosen. We demonstrated assembling SCA components into an application using the POS example. In the process, we learned how to declare configurable aspects of existing Java implementation, how to configure the implementations into components, and how to assemble the components into a composite application.

Review Questions

1. What is SCA? Who defines SCA standards?
2. Give some examples of SCA runtime implementations.
3. What is a component in SCA?
4. What are the configurable aspects of an implementation?
5. What is a composite?
6. What is a service?
7. What is a reference?
8. What is a property?
9. How are composites made from components?
10. Can a composite play the role of a component? Why or why not?

7

ENTERPRISE COMPONENT-ORIENTED DEVELOPMENT AND ASSEMBLY USING JAVA PLATFORM, ENTERPRISE EDITION

7.1 Introduction

Efficiency gained through CODA practice is at its best when we use component models like OSGi and SCA. In previous chapters, we understood how the components can be developed, assembled, and deployed using OSGi and SCA. Java Platform, Enterprise Edition, is a standardized popular platform for developing enterprise applications using Java. In this chapter, we discuss the various component models and frameworks supported by Java Platform, Enterprise Edition (referred to as Java EE) for developing enterprise applications. Java EE provides a standard platform for developing, assembling, and deploying enterprise components that are spread across multiple tiers in an N-tier architecture.

As discussed in Chapter 3, components can be classified into different types depending on where and how they can be used. Java EE provides the following components based on the N-tier architecture:

- Presentation tier components
- Business tier components
- Persistence tier components

Presentation tier components are also referred to as Web tier components of an enterprise application. Business tier components contain the business logic of the enterprise application. These components are POJO-based Java classes. Persistence tier components are reusable components used for representing the data in the persistence tier of an enterprise application.

7.2 Presentation Tier Components

Presentation tier components are the components in the Web tier (presentation tier) of an enterprise application. Presentation tier components contain the presentation logic (also referred to as user interface logic) for the application. Because these components are used in the Web tier, they are popularly known as Web components.

The Java EE Platform provides several Web component models like Java Servlet, Java Server Pages (JSP), and Java Server Faces (JSF) for developing Web applications using Web components. Components are developed, assembled, and deployed in a container that provides the runtime for the components. Containers are the component runtime frameworks that provide services for the components deployed in them. Web components are deployed in Web containers that provide the runtime support for the components as per the Java EE platform specifications.

7.2.1 Web Component Model—Java Servlet

In this section, we discuss the Java Servlet component model in brief from the perspective of component creation, assembly, and deployment. We discuss the Java Server Pages and Java Server Faces component models in the subsequent sections.

Java Servlet is a standardized powerful, reliable, and efficient component model for creating dynamic Web components in Java that can serve HTTP request and response. Java Servlet is a specification of the Java EE platform. Java Servlet is written as a Java class implementing the *Servlet* API defined by the Java Servlet specification. The *Servlet* API defines the behavior of the Web component that can handle the HTTP request. The *Servlet* API is an interface that defines the method signatures for a Web component. The *Servlet* API is inherited by the *HttpServlet* API, which defines HTTP-specific behavior for the implementing component. Any servlet component has to implement either the *Servlet* API or *HttpServlet* API to handle any dynamic Web request. The servlet component typically contains the user interface logic for representing a dynamic UI. The servlet component model is one of the important Java EE Web component models. A servlet is created using the *Servlet* API provided by the Java EE platform and deployed in the Web container for execution as shown in Figure 7.1.

A sample `AgeCalculatorServlet` that calculates the age of a person based on the date of birth entered by the user is shown below. In this example, it is assumed that

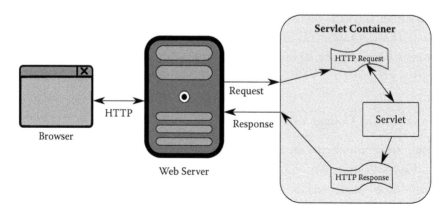

Figure 7.1   Servlet and Servlet container.

the user sends the year of birth, month, and date to the servlet that takes these values for calculating the current age:

```
package codabook.agecalculator.web;

import java.io.IOException;
import java.io.PrintWriter;
import java.util.Calendar;
import java.util.GregorianCalendar;
import javax.servlet.ServletException;
import javax.servlet.http.HttpServlet;
import javax.servlet.http.HttpServletRequest;
import javax.servlet.http.HttpServletResponse;

public class AgeCalculatorServlet extends HttpServlet {

  protected void processRequest(HttpServletRequest request,
     HttpServletResponse response)
       throws ServletException, IOException {
     response.setContentType("text/html;charset = UTF-8");
     PrintWriter out = response.getWriter();

     String year = request.getParameter("year");
     String month = request.getParameter("month");
     String date = request.getParameter("date");

     try {
         Calendar dateOfBirth = new GregorianCalendar();
         dateOfBirth.clear();
         dateOfBirth.set(Integer.parseInt(year), Integer.
         parseInt(month) - 1, Integer.parseInt(date));
         Calendar rightNow = new GregorianCalendar();

         int currentYear = rightNow.get(Calendar.YEAR);
         int currentMonth = rightNow.get(Calendar.MONTH);
         int currentDate = rightNow.get(Calendar.DATE);

         int birthYear = dateOfBirth.get(Calendar.YEAR);
         int birthMonth = dateOfBirth.get(Calendar.MONTH);
         int birthDate = dateOfBirth.get(Calendar.DATE);

         int age = 0;

         boolean isCurrentYearBdayPassed =
                 (currentMonth > birthMonth)
             || ((currentMonth = = birthMonth)
             && (currentDate > = birthDate));

         if (isCurrentYearBdayPassed) {
            age = currentYear - birthYear;
         } else {
```

```
            age = currentYear - 1 - birthYear;
        }
        PrintWriter out = response.getWriter();
         out.println("Your age is <b> " + age);
        } finally {
            out.close();
    }
}


/**
 * Handles the HTTP <code>GET</code> method.
 * @param request servlet request
 * @param response servlet response
 * @throws ServletException if a servlet-specific error occurs
 * @throws IOException if an I/O error occurs
 */
@Override
protected void doGet(HttpServletRequest request,
    HttpServletResponse response)
        throws ServletException, IOException {
    processRequest(request, response);
}


/**
 * Handles the HTTP <code>POST</code> method.
 * @param request servlet request
 * @param response servlet response
 * @throws ServletException if a servlet-specific error occurs
 * @throws IOException if an I/O error occurs
 */
@Override
protected void doPost(HttpServletRequest request,
    HttpServletResponse response)
        throws ServletException, IOException {
    processRequest(request, response);
}
}
```

The servlet component is mostly used as a controller in the MVC model. The servlet component contains the logic for processing the request, invoking the model and presenting the response to the client who has sent the request. Servlets also play a key role in controlling application flow. A servlet is typically accessed by a JSP or other view components. Servlets can be composed with other components as well.

7.2.2 Web Component Model—Java Server Pages

Java Server Pages is an extension to the servlet component technology. Java Server Pages (JSP) was introduced to make writing presentation logic simpler and easier.

JSP is also a standard specification part of the Java EE Platform. The component architecture of JSP is similar to the servlet except that the JSP is not a Java class. It is a text-based document with a `.jsp` extension which is deployed in the Web container. The Web container generates a servlet from the JSP text document and executes the JSP page as a servlet using the JSP API. JSP is more like HTML with Java code embedded in it using scriptlets. JSP provides a clean separation between content presentation logic and content generation logic. In addition to JSP, there are several new technologies like Facelets available for creating the presentation logic.

7.2.3 Web Component Model—Java Server Faces

Java Server Faces is a standardized component model for creating component-based server-side UI in Java. Java Server Faces (JSF) is a standard part of the Java EE platform. The JSF component model provides built-in API for creating UI components and managing their state, a library for using UI components, and a framework for handling the navigation and flow for the Web application. JSF is referred to as a component-based design model because it internally uses other Web component models like servlet and JSP. JSF uses an inbuilt servlet called *FacesServlet* for handling the navigation and flow (typically as a controller) and JSP and facelets as the view templating system. Facelets is preferred over JSP for representing the Web pages (view) in JSF. The JSF component model helps to

- Create UI using reusable and extensible UI components
- Place the UI component in the page with the help of simple tags
- Bind the UI component in the view page to the property of the server-side managed bean
- Wire component-generated events to server-side application code

The JSF component model provides some reusable and extensible UI components for UI input and output like text field, text area, button, label, table, and so forth. These UI components are represented by Java classes and placed in the Web pages with the help of the tag library provided by JSF. The tag libraries provided by JSF are:

- JSF HTML Tag Library (used with prefix *h* with namespace `"http://java.sun.com/jsf/html"`)
- JSF Core Tag Library (used with prefix *f* with namespace `"http://java.sun.com/jsf/core"`)
- Facelets Tag Library (used with prefix *ui* with namespace `"http://java.sun.com/jsf/facelets"`)

The properties and functions of the UI components in the Web pages are mapped to a Plain Old Java Object (POJO) class called managed bean on the server side. Managed beans in JSF represent the model in the MVC architecture. The JSF component model binds the properties of the UI components in the view page to the appropriate property of the model which is the managed bean. JSF has an event and listener model that allows UI component-generated events to be captured. This event model is similar to the event model in Java. There is also a validation model for validating the data from the UI components and a conversion model for getting and setting the component data from a UI component to a server-side component like a managed bean.

The JSF component model completely manages the interaction between UI components and the server-side managed bean. The managed beans are identified using @ManagedBean annotation. The scope of the bean, like request, session, or application, should also be mentioned while creating a managed bean using @RequestScoped, @SessionScoped, or @ApplicationScoped annotations. These annotations help the container to manage the state of the managed bean appropriately. The managed bean is referred to in the facelets using JSF expressions represented by #{...}. Similarly, validators and convertors are POJOs implementing the respective APIs. Any dynamic content from any of the managed bean, validator, or converter is accessed by the view with the help of this expression.

Let us try to understand the JSF component model with an example. A sample facelets file named checkOut.xhtml is presented below:

```xml
<?xml version = '1.0' encoding = 'UTF-8' ?>
<!DOCTYPE html PUBLIC "-//W3C//DTD XHTML 1.0 Transitional//EN"
    "http://www.w3.org/TR/xhtml1/DTD/xhtml1-transitional.dtd">
<html xmlns = "http://www.w3.org/1999/xhtml"
  xmlns:h = "http://java.sun.com/jsf/html"
  xmlns:ui = "http://java.sun.com/jsf/facelets">
  <h:head>
    <title>Guest CheckOut</title>
  </h:head>

  <h:body>
    <h3> Guest CheckOut </h3>
    <h:form id = "checkOutForm">
      <h:outputText
        value = "SORRY - None of the tables is occupied!"
        rendered = "#{checkOutBean.occupiedTables.size() eq 0}"/>
      <br/>
      <h:outputText value = "Please choose a table to checkout
          guests from"/> <br/>
      <h4> Occupied Tables- - - - </h4>

      <h:panelGrid columns = "1" border = "1">
        <ui:repeat var = "tables" value = "#{checkOutBean.
          occupiedTables}">

          <h:commandButton value = "#{tables.getTableNo()}"
                     action = "#{checkOutBean.
                            checkOut(tables.getTableNo())}"/>
```

```
            </ui:repeat>
        </h:panelGrid>

        <h:outputText style = "color:red" value = "#{checkOutBean.
            displayMessage}"/>
        <br/> <br/>
        <h:commandLink id = "home" action = "index">Home
            </h:commandLink>
    </h:form>

  </h:body>
</html>
```

Facelets has a .xhtml extension, and it uses JSF tag libraries. It is evident from the boldfaced namespaces in the sample code that this example is using the JSF HTML tag library (with prefix *h*) and the facelets tag library (prefix *ui*). This page uses a managed bean object called checkOutBean, which refers to the managed bean component CheckOutBean. The JSF component model provides the binding between the UI components (like the command button and the text fields) with the server-side component managed bean. Optionally, an XML file named faces-config.xml can be used to represent the binding information like the name of the managed bean, the scope, and the fully qualified name. The CheckOutBean component accessed by the page is shown below:

```
package pos.managedbean;

import java.util.List;
import javax.ejb.EJB;
import javax.faces.bean.ManagedBean;
import javax.faces.bean.RequestScoped;
import pos.ejb.TableBeanRemote;
import pos.ejb.helper.Table;

@ManagedBean
@RequestScoped
public class CheckOutBean {

  private List<Table> occupiedTables;
  private String displayMessage;

  @EJB
  private TableBeanRemote tableBean;
  public CheckOutBean() {
  }

  public List<Table> getOccupiedTables() {
    this.occupiedTables = tableBean.getOccupiedTables();
    return occupiedTables;
  }
```

```java
  public void setOccupiedTables(List<Table> occupiedTables) {
    this.occupiedTables = occupiedTables;
  }

  public String getDisplayMessage() {
    return displayMessage;
  }

  public void setDisplayMessage(String displayMessage) {
    this.displayMessage = displayMessage;
  }

  public void checkOut(Integer tableNo) {
    displayMessage = tableBean.unOccupyTable(tableNo);
  }

}
```

The managed bean is a POJO identified with @ManagedBean annotation. The bean component contains simple properties and methods. The properties displayMessage and occupiedTables are bound with the UI components. The properties must have setter and getter methods for the container to read and write value for the UI components. This component need not maintain the state and hence is declared to be a request scoped object. The CheckOutBean component is accessed by facelets for the presentation logic. As mentioned earlier, the managed bean acts as a model and helps in binding the properties with the UI component. This in turn invokes business tier components for the business logic. The managed bean components compose with the business components for executing the business logic functionality.

7.2.4 Web Container

Web container is the component runtime for the Web components. The Web components created using models like Java Servlet, JSP, and JSF are deployed in the Web container. The Web container provides runtime services like life cycle service and system services to the components deployed in it. The Web containers are provided by the application servers adhering to the standard Java EE platform specification.

7.2.5 Packaging Web Components

Web components are packaged and assembled in a *Web ARchive (WAR)* file. A WAR file has a .war extension and contains Web components, static resources like HTML, CSS, helper classes, and other libraries that are referred by the Web components. There is also an XML file called web.xml, referred to as the *Deployment Descriptor*, which contains the metadata information about the various Web components that need to be handled by the Web container. The web.xml is crucial for the

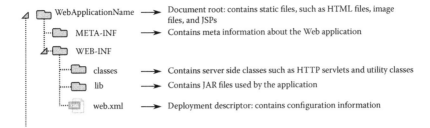

Figure 7.2   Structure of a WAR file.

Web container. The Web container will execute the components developed using the Web component models discussed in the previous sections based on the information provided in the web.xml. The servlet component will be executed by the container only if it is specified in the web.xml. This gives the component runtime the flexibility to handle the life cycle of the components managed by it. The WAR file structure is represented in Figure 7.2.

A sample web.xml having entries for servlets, JSP and JSF is shown below:

```xml
<?xml version = "1.0" encoding = "UTF-8"?>
<web-app version = "2.5" xmlns = "http://java.sun.com/xml/ns/
    javaee" xmlns:xsi = "http://www.w3.org/2001/XMLSchema-instance"
    xsi:schemaLocation = "http://java.sun.com/xml/ns/javaee http://
    java.sun.com/xml/ns/javaee/web-app_2_5.xsd">
  <context-param>
    <param-name>javax.faces.STATE_SAVING_METHOD</param-name>
    <param-value>client</param-value>
  </context-param>
  <servlet>
    <servlet-name>Faces Servlet</servlet-name>
    <servlet-class>javax.faces.webapp.FacesServlet</servlet-class>
    <load-on-startup>1</load-on-startup>
  </servlet>
  <servlet-mapping>
    <servlet-name>Faces Servlet</servlet-name>
    <url-pattern>/faces/*</url-pattern>
  </servlet-mapping>
  <session-config>
    <session-timeout>
      30
    </session-timeout>
  </session-config>
  <welcome-file-list>
    <welcome-file>faces/welcomeJSF.jsp</welcome-file>
  </welcome-file-list>
</web-app>
```

In this sample, the FacesServlet provided by the JSF component model is used. It is evident from the sample that the FacesServlet component is identifed by a name and is executed by the component runtime only for a specific `url-pattern` as mentioned in the `web.xml`. The `FacesServlet` will handle the requests coming with the `/faces/*` url pattern. The recent Servlet 3.0 specification introduced the annotations for Web components, which has made the `web.xml` deployment descriptor optional. Servlet components can be identified with the `@WebServlet` annotation in the source code. The Web container will execute these components based on the information in the source code of the components. It is also evident that the Java Server Pages components are executed by the container based on the request, and there is no need for an entry in the `web.xml`. Similarly, the JSF managed beans and other UI components like validators and convertors need not be specified in the `web.xml` because they are managed using source code annotations.

7.3 Business Tier Components

Business components in the Java EE platform are typically represented as POJOs using the Enterprise JavaBeans (EJB) component model. The EJB component model is a standard specification that helps to create, assemble, and deploy Java components. Enterprise JavaBeans are the distributed business components that contain the business logic for the enterprise application. Typically, EJBs are deployed in the EJB containers that are the component runtime provided by the application servers. EJBs are distributed and transaction oriented in nature. The Enterprise JavaBean is considered to be one of the most important component models as well as a significant part of the Java EE platform. EJBs are normally accessed through the presentation tier components like managed beans and servlets. The EJB standard has come a long way from its initial version EJB 1.0 to the current version EJB 3.2, and this chapter discusses the features provided by EJB 3.2.

An Enterprise JavaBean component is represented as a combination of an interface called *Business Interface* and an implementation class, which is the *EJB Component*. The business interface is a Plain Old Java Interface (POJI), and the business component is represented as a POJO (Plain Old Java Object). The enterprise bean component can be accessed by either a remote or a local client. A remote client accesses the enterprise bean component using a remote protocol like RMI or IIOP. A local client can access the bean component from the same JVM where the bean component is deployed.

7.3.1 Business Interface

The business interface for the enterprise bean contains the signatures of the business methods. The business interface is the *provided interface* of an EJB component. Only this interface is exposed to the clients. The business interface can be a remote interface or a local interface. Remote interfaces are used by clients for remote invocation, and local interfaces are used by clients for local invocation. Business interfaces are identified as remote using the `@Remote` annotation, and local interfaces are identified using the `@Local` annotation on the source code of the business interface. The local business interface is optional (i.e., when the client is accessing the EJB component using local invocation, it can directly invoke the EJB component without using an interface). Enterprise clients like servlets and managed beans are not required to have a business interface when they try to access the enterprise bean component using local invocation. They can access the bean component using dependency injection, which refers the bean component directly rather than through an interface.

7.3.2 EJB Container

EJBs are deployed in *EJB containers*, which is the component runtime that provides services for the EJB components. EJB containers manage the life cycle of the EJB components—they create, manage, and destroy the objects based on the different types of EJB components and their usage. These containers are rich in features, provide a variety of services for the business components deployed in them. They enable scalability and portability of the enterprise application, besides helping to bring in reusability and ease of use. Some of the crucial services provided by the EJB container are

- Life cycle service
- Security service
- Transaction service

7.3.3 Enterprise JavaBean Component Types

Enterprise bean components are broadly classified into the following types:

- Stateless Session Beans
- Stateful Session Beans
- Singleton Session Beans
- Message-Driven Beans

7.3.3.1 Stateless Session Beans   A stateless session bean is a type of EJB component that contains no conversational state between methods. Stateless session bean instances are not shared between clients. They are used for single method request/response communication between the client and the component. However, stateless session bean instance variables can contain state but are valid only for the method invocation. Because all instances are stateless, any instance of a stateless session bean can be used for servicing any client. Because of this nature, a stateless session bean is highly scalable and can support a large number of concurrent clients.

The stateless session bean component implements the business operations defined in the business interface. The stateless session bean component is identified through `@Stateless` metadata annotation or using the XML deployment descriptor.

A sample business interface and the stateless session bean component are shown below. The business interface is a remote interface and declares the business methods.

```java
package pos.ejb;

import java.util.List;
import javax.ejb.Remote;
import pos.ejb.helper.FoodCategory;
import pos.entity.Food;


@Remote
public interface FoodBeanRemote {
  public String createNewFood(String name, Double price,
            Double taxRate, FoodCategory category);
  public String modifyFood(String oldName, Food modifiedFood);
  public String deleteFood(Food food);

  public List<Food> findAllFoods();
  public List<Food> findFoodsByCategory(FoodCategory foodCategory);
  public FoodCategory[] getFoodCategories();
}
```

The business component `FoodBean` implements the `FoodBeanRemote` as shown below. Since the bean component need not maintain a conversational state between business methods, it is declared as a stateless session bean. Every business method has its data for performing the business logic; hence, it is stateless.

```java
package pos.ejb;

//import….


@Stateless
public class FoodBean implements FoodBeanRemote {
  private EntityManagerFactory emf;
  private EntityManager em;
  private EntityTransaction transaction;

  @PostConstruct
  public void initialize() {
    emf = Persistence.createEntityManagerFactory
                    ("CODAPOSJavaEEEJBPU");
```

```
  em = emf.createEntityManager();
  transaction = em.getTransaction();
}


public String createNewFood(String name, Double price,
                      Double taxRate, FoodCategory
category) {
      //business logic

}

public String modifyFood(String oldName, Food modifiedFood) {


      //business logic
}

public String deleteFood(Food food) {
      //business logic
}

public List<Food> findAllFoods() {
      //business logic
}

public List<Food> findFoodsByCategory(FoodCategory foodCategory) {
      //business logic
}

public FoodCategory[] getFoodCategories() {
      //business logic
}
}
```

7.3.3.2 Stateful Session Beans   A stateful session bean is a type of EJB component that maintains a conversational state for a single client. Unlike a stateless session bean component, the stateful session bean instance contains a conversational state that will be retained for a single client across method invocations and transactions. The conversational state is the session object of the client.

The stateful session bean component implements the business operations defined in the business interface. The stateful session bean component is identified through @Stateful metadata annotation or by using an XML deployment descriptor.

Ideally, the stateful session bean continues to be associated with the client until the client chooses to log out of the application. However, it is possible that in cases where these beans are engaged with a client in a long drawn-out session, delay could arise from the client side. To efficiently manage the stateful session bean instances, a container may temporarily transfer the state of such an idle stateful session bean instance to some secondary storage. This is called *passivation*. The transfer back from secondary storage is called *activation*.

7.3.3.3 Singleton Session Beans   A singleton session bean is a type of EJB component that is introduced in the EJB 3.1 specification. A singleton session bean component is shared between clients and allows for concurrent access. This bean component is used for sharing application-wide data.

A singleton session bean is instantiated once per application. That means there can be only one singleton session bean instance per application for each JVM. This is similar to the concept of the `ServletContext` in Java Servlet API, which helps to manage an *application* scope object. Singleton session bean components can be effectively used for caching. Singleton session bean components are created during application startup and destroyed during application shutdown.

The singleton session bean component implements the business operations defined in the business interface. The singleton session bean component is identified through `@Singleton` metadata annotation or using an XML deployment descriptor.

7.3.3.4 Message-Driven Beans   The Message-Driven Beans (MDB) is a type of EJB component that is a stateless, lightweight, and asynchronous message consumer. They are associated with messaging systems and have no direct client interaction. Message-driven beans contain the business logic of the enterprise application. The architecture and functionality of MDBs are quite different from session beans. A client cannot access a message-driven bean directly, it accesses it only by sending a message to a message destination where the message-driven bean is registered as a listener. Hence, MDBs do not have any business interface. MDBs typically listen to a message destination like JMS (Java Message Service) Queue or Topic and consume messages asynchronously.

When a message arrives at the destination, the container activates the message-driven bean component by calling its `onMessage` method that contains the business logic for processing the message. The message-driven bean, like any other JMS message consumer, receives the message and handles its processing.

The message-driven bean component is identified through `@MessageDriven` metadata annotation or by using the XML deployment descriptor. The details of the message destination to which the message-driven bean component is associated are also given through source code annotations or by using a deployment descriptor. Typically, the message-driven bean is associated with a Queue or Topic using the `activationConfig` element of the `@MessageDriven` annotation or `activation-config` property element in the deployment descriptor.

A message-driven bean can use dependency injection mechanisms to refer to other resources in the environment. If a message-driven bean uses a dependency injection, the container injects the required references when the bean instance is created.

Let us try to understand how different a message-driven bean is from a session bean through an example. A sample message-driven bean associated with a message destination called `simpleQueue` is shown below:

```
package codabook.mdb.ejb;

import java.util.logging.Level;
import java.util.logging.Logger;
import javax.ejb.ActivationConfigProperty;
import javax.ejb.MessageDriven;
import javax.jms.JMSException;
import javax.jms.Message;
import javax.jms.MessageListener;
import javax.jms.TextMessage;


@MessageDriven(mappedName = "jms/simpleQueue", activationConfig = {
   @ActivationConfigProperty(propertyName = "acknowledgeMode",
       propertyValue = "Auto-acknowledge"),
   @ActivationConfigProperty(propertyName = "destinationType",
       propertyValue = "javax.jms.Queue")
 })
public class DemoMDB implements MessageListener {

 public DemoMDB() {
 }


 public void onMessage(Message message) {
   if(message! = null) {
     try {
         TextMessage msg = (TextMessage) message;
         String text = msg.getText();
         //business logic
     } catch (JMSException ex) {
       Logger.getLogger(DemoMDB.class.getName()).log(Level.
         SEVERE, null, ex);
     }
   }
 }
}
```

It is evident that the message-driven bean does not have a business interface and hence has no direct client interaction. The message-driven bean component is associated with a messaging interface named `javax.jms.MessageListener`, which is part of the messaging system. The `DemoMDB` is a listener and implements the `MessageListener` interface which represents the business interface. The `onMessage` method in the `MessageListener` interface acts as a business method. All message-driven bean components implement the `onMessage` method, and whenever

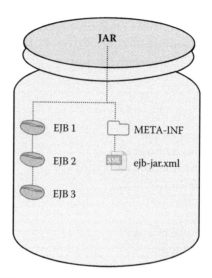

Figure 7.3   Structure of a JAR file.

there is a new message on the `SimpleQueue` this method is invoked by the container with the `Message`.

7.3.4 Packaging Enterprise JavaBean Components

Enterprise bean components are typically packaged in a *Java ARchive (JAR)* file. Optionally, the JAR file can have a metadata XML file named `ejb-jar.xml`, which is used to override all the default annotations present in the source code. The structure of the JAR file is shown in Figure 7.3.

Enterprise bean components are packaged as JAR files and are composed with the presentation tier components and the persistence tier components for the presentation and the persistence logic. All these components are composed as a package in an *Enterprise ARchive (EAR)* file that will have a `.ear` extension. In an EAR file, the JAR file having enterprise bean components is packaged along with the Web components in a WAR file. The structure of the EAR file with the Web components and the enterprise components is shown in Figure 7.4.

From the EJB 3.1 specification, the enterprise bean components need not be packaged separately in a JAR file, they can be placed under the classes folder of the WAR file along with the servlets directly as shown in Figure 7.5.

7.3.5 Accessing Enterprise JavaBean Components

A client can locate an enterprise bean component's business interface using lookup in the JNDI namespace or through dependency injection as discussed in Chapter 3. Clients accessing enterprise beans (except message-driven beans) can be either remote or local clients. Enterprise bean components are accessed by the presentation tier

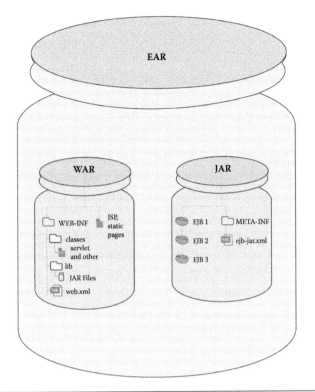

Figure 7.4 Structure of an EAR file.

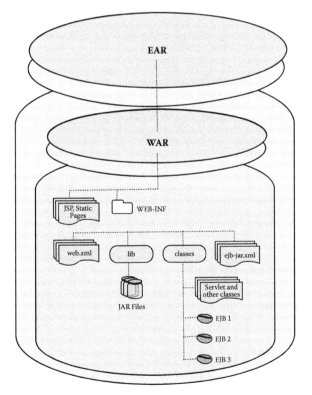

Figure 7.5 Structure of an EAR file from EJB 3.1.

components or in some cases by client applications directly. Typically, servlet components and managed bean components will invoke the enterprise bean components for the business logic.

The EJB components are not instantiated directly using the *new* operator. For accessing EJB components, dependency injection is used for getting a reference to the component deployed in the container. The idea is to avoid direct creation of objects using the *new* operator. Dependency injection for EJB components is provided through a metadata annotation @EJB. The annotation @EJB specifies a reference to the business interface. When this annotation is used, the container will provide a reference of the component to the clients. A local client for EJB simply uses the @EJB to get a reference to the component.

In the JSF section, we used the CheckOutBean example to understand the managed bean. A closer look at the CheckOutBean reveals that the managed bean tries to access an enterprise bean component. Facelets invoke the managed bean, which in turn invokes the session bean named TableBean through the business interface TableBeanRemote using the @EJB annotation as shown below. The container will inject a reference of the bean to the @EJB annotation, and the client will be able to invoke the business methods.

```
package pos.managedbean;

import java.util.List;
import javax.ejb.EJB;
import javax.faces.bean.ManagedBean;
import javax.faces.bean.RequestScoped;
import pos.ejb.TableBeanRemote;
import pos.ejb.helper.Table;

@ManagedBean
@RequestScoped
public class CheckOutBean {

   private List<Table> occupiedTables;
   private String displayMessage;

   @EJB
   private TableBeanRemote tableBean;

   public CheckOutBean() {
   }

   public List<Table> getOccupiedTables() {
     this.occupiedTables = tableBean.getOccupiedTables();
     return occupiedTables;
   }
```

```
  public void setOccupiedTables(List<Table> occupiedTables) {
    this.occupiedTables = occupiedTables;
  }

  public String getDisplayMessage() {
    return displayMessage;
  }

  public void setDisplayMessage(String displayMessage) {
    this.displayMessage = displayMessage;
  }

  public void checkOut(Integer tableNo) {
    displayMessage = tableBean.unOccupyTable(tableNo);
  }

}
```

Enterprise bean components may also use dependency injection to acquire references to other resources like data source and messaging systems as discussed in Section 7.3.3.4. Session bean clients can access the session beans both synchronously and asynchronously.

A remote client for EJB, where injection is not possible, has an alternative way of accessing EJB components. It can use JNDI API for locating the components in the container with a string name called a JNDI name. For a JNDI lookup, the container responds with the reference of the component which will be used by the clients.

A message-driven bean cannot be accessed by clients directly because they are asynchronous message listeners. This is a type of EJB component that is activated by the arrival of a message in a message destination, so clients cannot directly invoke any of the methods in the message-driven bean. From a client's view, a message-driven bean is a simple JMS message consumer. The client sends the message to a JMS destination—Queue or Topic—for which the message driven bean is a registered listener. For the client, the message-driven bean is not visible.

7.4 Persistence Tier Components

Persistence components contain the persistence logic in an enterprise application. The Java EE platform provides an API (*Java Persistence API*) for developing and deploying persistence components using Java. Java Persistence API (JPA) is a lightweight, POJO-based component model for object relational mapping. Components in JPA are POJO, and there is no business interface (no direct interface association). The JPA components are identified with the help of metadata annotations in the source code or in the optional deployment descriptors provided by the JPA. The JPA API is packaged in javax.persistence and its subpackages. The component runtime for the persistence components is provided by the persistence providers who provide an implementation of the JPA specification standard.

7.4.1 Entity

The component in JPA is called an *entity*. An entity is a lightweight persistent domain object. An entity is identified using the @Entity annotation or through the XML deployment descriptor file. The persistence state of an entity is represented by instance variables of the entity component. An entity class typically represents a table in a relational data store, and the instance variables map to the respective columns in the table. The persistent state of an entity is accessed using property access or field access. By default all the properties of the entity class are persistent in nature (persisted into data store) except the ones that are marked with the @Transient annotation.

Every entity must be associated with a *primary key*. The primary key represents the primary key column in the data store, which can be simple or composite. Instance variable representing primary key is identified using the @Id annotation. For the composite primary key, a separate class is defined with the @IdClass or @ Embeddable annotation.

For example, a table Food can be represented as a Food entity as shown below. The component Food is a POJO with the @Entity annotation and accessor methods. In this example, the primary key column in the table is the food name that is declared using the @Id annotation.

```
package pos.entity;

//imports....

@Entity
@NamedQueries({
  @NamedQuery(name = "Food.findAll",
           query = "SELECT f FROM Food f"),
  @NamedQuery(name = "Food.findByCategory",
     query = "SELECT f FROM Food f
     WHERE f.category = :category")})

public class Food implements Serializable {

  @Id
  private String name;
  private Double price;
  private Double taxRate;

  @Enumerated(EnumType.STRING)
  private FoodCategory category;

  public Food() {
  }
```

```
  public Food(String name, double price, double taxRate,
        FoodCategory category) {
    this.name = name;
    this.price = price;
    this.taxRate = taxRate;
    this.category = category;
  }

  public FoodCategory getCategory() {
    return category;
  }

  public void setCategory(FoodCategory category) {
    this.category = category;
  }

  public String getName() {
    return name;
  }

  public void setName(String name) {
    this.name = name;
  }

  public Double getPrice() {
    return price;
  }

  public void setPrice(Double price) {
    this.price = price;
  }

  public double getTaxRate() {
    return taxRate;
  }

  public void setTaxRate(Double taxRate) {
    this.taxRate = taxRate;
  }
}
```

The relationships between entities are depicted with the help of source code annotations. Both multiplicity and directions in relationships can be specified using the annotations. The annotations @OneToOne, @OneToMany, @ManyToOne, and @ManyToMany are used on entities to represent the multiplicity association between entities. The directions in the relationships (unidirectional or bidirectional) are depicted using the attribute mappedBy element of the annotation. The mappedBy element is used in bidirectional relationships. The annotation @JoinColumn is used to represent the foreign key relationships in the data store.

7.4.2 Entity Manager

Entity classes are typically managed by an API called `EntityManager` provided by the JPA. The entity manager acts like a container and manages the life cycle of entities. The entity manager is used for persisting entities, to retrieve entities, to query entities using query APIs, and to manage the persistence state of the entities. The entity manager manages the entity and its life cycle in a *persistence context*. A persistence context represents a set of entity instances that are active with a unique identity. Typically, an instance of `EntityManager` represents the persistence context. The set of entities that can be managed by the entity manager is defined in a single group called a *persistence unit*. A persistence unit defines the set of all entity classes that are related and grouped by the application and are collocated in a single database.

In Java EE environments, the persistence context can be managed either by the application or by the container. An entity manager for which the container manages the persistence context is called a *container-managed entity manager*. A container-managed entity manager's life cycle is managed by the Java EE container.

In rare cases where the application is used outside the Java EE container, applications access stand-alone persistence contexts. An entity manager that is used by the application to create and destroy a persistence context (application managing the persistence context) is termed an *application-managed entity manager*. An application-managed entity manager's life cycle is managed by the application. All Java EE Web and EJB containers support both container-managed entity managers and application-managed entity managers.

The persistence context (an instance of `EntityManager`) can be created manually or by using a dependency injection. The container-managed entity manager is obtained using the dependency injection on the persistence context. The annotation `@PersistenceContext` is used for creating an instance of entity manager:

```
@PersistenceContext
EntityManager em;
```

The application-managed entity manager is obtained using an `EntityManager Factory`. For a container-managed environment (Java EE), the `EntityManager Factory` is injected by the container with the help of the persistence unit:

```
@PersistenceUnit(unitName = "OrderPU")
EntityManagerFactory emf;
EntityManager em = emf.createEntityManager();
```

For a non-container-based environment, the `EntityManagerFactory` is created manually with the help of a persistence provider. In the code snippet below, `Persistence` is the class provided by EclipseLink for managing the persistence:

```
EntityManagerFactory emf =
        Persistence.createEntityManagerFactory("OrderPU");
EntityManager em = emf.createEntityManager();
```

7.4.3 Persistence Provider

JPA is a specification that defines standards for creating and assembling persistence components. A Java EE platform supporting JPA must provide a *persistence provider* that will actually manage the persistence with the data store. The persistence provider acts as the component framework for the persistence components. The persistence provider provides a component runtime for the persistence entities. There are several providers of JPA, and some of the popular providers are

- Oracle EclipseLink
- JBoss Hibernate
- Apache OpenJPA

Persistence providers provide persistence service to the components deployed in a Java EE container. Persistence providers are easily configurable in a JPA environment. A persistence provider helps in creating the persistence unit and the persistence context. It plays an important role in the creation of an instance of `EntityManagerFactory`.

7.4.4 Packaging Entities

Entities are packaged in a JAR file. The JAR file representing a persistence component will have the following:

- Entity components
- Persistence mapping XML file
- Driver for the data source
- Additional libraries

The persistence mapping XML file is a configuration file that contains important metadata information used by the Java EE container for creating `EntityManagerFactory`. The persistence mapping XML file is called `persistence.xml`. The `persistence.xml` contains a unique persistence unit, persistence provider details, the entity classes, and the information related to data store connectivity. A sample `persistence.xml` using *EclipseLink* as the persistence provider and having a persistence unit as `DemoJPA` and some entity components is shown below:

```
<?xml version = "1.0" encoding = "UTF-8"?>
<persistence version = "1.0"
        xmlns = "http://java.sun.com/xml/ns/persistence" xmlns:xsi
           = "http://www.w3.org/2001/XMLSchema-instance"
```

```
xsi:schemaLocation = "http://java.sun.com/xml/ns/
    persistence http://java.sun.com/xml/ns/persistence/
    persistence_1_0.xsd">
    <persistence-unit name = "DemoJPA">
            <provider>org.eclipse.persistence.jpa.
                PersistenceProvider</provider>
            <class>codabook.demo.jpa.Employee</class>
            <class>
                codabook.demo.jpa.PermanentEmployee</class>
            <class>codabook.demo.jpa.ContractEmployee</class>
            <properties>
                <property name = "javax.persistence.jdbc.
                    driver" value = "fully qualified
                    driver class"/>
                <property name = "javax.persistence.jdbc.
                    url" value = "jdbc url"/>
                <property name = "javax.persistence.jdbc.
                    user" value = "username"/>
                <property name = "javax.persistence.jdbc.
                    password" value = "password"/>
            </properties>
    </persistence-unit>
</persistence>
```

7.4.5 Accessing Entities

Entities are created directly using a *new* operator because they are POJO classes. An entity instance created is a new record created in the data store. Entities are managed by the `EntityManager` which actually represents the component runtime. An entity manager instance is associated with a persistence context. The entity manager is used to create persistent entity instances, remove persistent entity instances, find persistent entity instances using a primary key, and select specific persistent entity instances using a query API within a persistence context.

Entities are accessed by the business components like enterprise bean components or Web components like servlets and managed beans. These components typically get an instance of entity with the help of the `EntityManager` API. Based on the type, the entity manager is created and entities are managed.

For example, the `FoodBean` enterprise bean component used in the stateless session bean (refer to Section 7.3.3.1) accesses the `Food` entity for the persistence management and executes its business logic as shown below. The entity manager is created with the help of the persistence provider:

```
@Stateless
public class FoodBean implements FoodBeanRemote {
  private EntityManagerFactory emf;
```

```java
private EntityManager em;
private EntityTransaction transaction;

@PostConstruct
public void initialize() {
  emf = Persistence.createEntityManagerFactory
                      ("CODAPOSJavaEEEJBPU");
  em = emf.createEntityManager();
  transaction = em.getTransaction();
}

public String createNewFood(String name, Double price,
                 Double taxRate, FoodCategory category) {

  transaction.begin();

  Food food = new Food(name, price, taxRate, category);
  em.persist(food);

  transaction.commit();

  return "SUCCESS - New food item created successfully";
}

public String modifyFood(String oldName, Food modifiedFood) {

  transaction.begin();

  em.merge(modifiedFood);

  transaction.commit();
  return "SUCCESS - Food successfully modified";
}

public List<Food> findAllFoods() {
  return em.createNamedQuery("Food.findAll").getResultList();
}

public List<Food> findFoodsByCategory(FoodCategory foodCategory) {
  return em.createNamedQuery("Food.findByCategory").
     setParameter("category", foodCategory).getResultList();
}

public FoodCategory[] getFoodCategories() {
  return FoodCategory.values();
}
}
```

7.5 Enterprise CODA Using Java EE—An Example

In this section, we discuss the componentization of the POS example application explained in Chapter 4 using the Java EE platform. Let us take the Guest Check-In use case to see how it can be realized using various Java EE components. As discussed in Chapter 4, this use case is invoked by the waiters when new guests arrive at the restaurant. When this use case is invoked, the POS application displays a list of empty tables, and the waiter chooses an empty table and seats the guests at the table. Table 7.1 provides the list of components for the Check-In use case in Java EE and the corresponding components in the component model discussed in Chapter 4.

The view component is a facelets application named `checkIn.xhtml`. This view page displays the UI components to take the number of guests and the waiter name. When the waiter chooses a particular table, the table number, guests' details, and waiter name are sent to the managed bean named `CheckInBean`. The source code of the view component is shown below:

```
<?xml version = '1.0' encoding = 'UTF-8' ?>
<!DOCTYPE html PUBLIC "-//W3C//DTD XHTML 1.0 Transitional//EN"
      "http://www.w3.org/TR/xhtml1/DTD/xhtml1-transitional.dtd">
<html xmlns = "http://www.w3.org/1999/xhtml"
  xmlns:h = "http://java.sun.com/jsf/html"
  xmlns:ui = "http://java.sun.com/jsf/facelets">
  <h:head>
    <title>Guest CheckIn</title>
  </h:head>
  <h:body>
    <h3> Guest CheckIn </h3>
    <h:form id = "checkInForm">
      <h:panelGrid columns = "2">
        <h:outputText value = "Enter the number of guests"/>
        <h:inputText value = "#{checkInBean.noOfGuests}"/>

        <h:outputText value = "Enter the waiter name"/>
        <h:inputText value = "#{checkInBean.waiterName}"/>

      </h:panelGrid>
      <h:outputText value = "Please choose a table to seat the
      guests"/> <br/>
```

Table 7.1 POS Application Components for Check-In Use Case

TIER	JAVA EE COMPONENT	PLAIN JAVA COMPONENT (REFER TO CHAPTER 4)
Presentation	`checkIn.xhtml` (facelets)	`CheckInUI.java`
	`CheckInBean.java` (managed bean)	`CheckInCtrlr.java`
Business	`TableBean.java` (EJB component)	`TableBiz.java`
	`TableBeanRemote.java` (business interface)	`Table.java`
	`Table.java` (helper class)	
Persistence	`TableConfig.java` (entity class)	`TableConfigDAO.java`

```
    <h:panelGrid columns = "1" border = "1">
      <ui:repeat var = "tables"
              value = "#{checkInBean.emptyTables}">
        <h:commandButton value = "#{tables.getTableNo()}"
              action = "#{checkInBean.checkIn(tables.get TableNo
    ())}"/>
      </ui:repeat>
    </h:panelGrid>

    <h:outputText style = "color:red"
        value = "#{checkInBean.displayMessage}"/>
    <br/> <br/>
    <h:commandLink id = "home" action = "index">Home
        </h:commandLink>
  </h:form>

  </h:body>
</html>
```

The CheckInBean is a request scoped managed bean because the bean does not maintain any state with the view. The view components are mapped to the properties of the managed bean. The CheckInBean contains the properties like emptyTables, noOfGuests, waiterName, and displayMessage, which are used by the view page. The managed bean uses a helper class named Table, and it invokes the EJB component named TableBean that contains the business logic for managing the tables. The TableBean is invoked by the managed bean using the remote interface TableBeanRemote as shown below:

```
package pos.managedbean;

//imports

@ManagedBean
@RequestScoped
public class CheckInBean {

  private List<Table> emptyTables;
  private Integer noOfGuests;
  private String waiterName;
  private String displayMessage;

  @EJB
  private TableBeanRemote tableBean;

  public CheckInBean() {

  }
```

```
//setter and getter methods

public void checkIn(Integer tableNo) {
  displayMessage = tableBean.occupyTable(tableNo, noOfGuests,
    waiterName);
}

}
```

The EJB component is modeled as a singleton object because it is used to manage application-wide data. The `TableBean` in turn uses the `TableConfig` entity for getting the total available tables. The `TableConfig` provides the persistent information in the data store. The remote interface of the bean, bean implementation class, and entity class are represented below:

Business Interface: TableBeanRemote

```
package pos.ejb;

//imports…
@Remote
public interface TableBeanRemote {

  public String occupyTable(Integer selectedTableNo, int
    noOfGuests, String waiter);

  //Other business methods
}
```

Bean Component: TableBean

```
package pos.ejb;

//imports…..

@Singleton
public class TableBean implements TableBeanRemote {

  private List<Table> tables;
  private EntityManagerFactory emf;
  private EntityManager em;
  private EntityTransaction transaction;
  private TableConfig tableConfig;

  @PostConstruct
  public void initialize() {
    tables = new ArrayList<Table>();
    emf = Persistence.createEntityManagerFactory
              ("CODAPOSJavaEEEJBPU");
```

```
    em = emf.createEntityManager();
    transaction = em.getTransaction();
}

public String occupyTable(Integer selectedTableNo, int
noOfGuests, String waiter) {

  Table table = tables.get(selectedTableNo-1);

  Order order = new Order();

  table.occupy(noOfGuests, waiter, order);

  return "SUCCESS - Check in completed successfully";
}

//Other business methods…..

}
```

Entity: TableConfig

```
package pos.entity;

import java.io.Serializable;
import javax.persistence.Entity;
import javax.persistence.Id;

@Entity
public class TableConfig implements Serializable {

  @Id
  private Integer noOfTables;

  public Integer getNoOfTables() {
    return noOfTables;
  }

  public void setNoOfTables(Integer noOfTables) {
    this.noOfTables = noOfTables;
  }
}
```

The various components used for building the use case are represented in Figure 7.6.

The presentation tier components are packaged in a WAR file and deployed in the Web container hosted by the application server. The business tier components and the persistence tier components are packaged together in a JAR file and deployed in the EJB container provided by the application server. The open source persistence provider *EclipseLink* is used for this example.

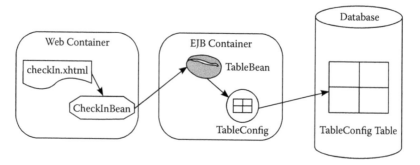

Figure 7.6   Java EE components and container for Guests Check-In use case.

7.6 Summary

In this chapter, we discussed the various component models supported by the Java EE platform. The component models are spread across multiple tiers in an N-tier architecture. Java Servlet, Java Server Pages, and Java Server Faces are the presentation tier component models. The JSF component model helps to create the UI component and binds the properties of the UI components with the managed bean on the server side. The Web components are created and deployed in the Web container, which is the component framework. Enterprise JavaBean is the component model used in the business tier. EJB components are deployed in the EJB container which provides the component framework. Java Persistence API is the component model for the persistence tier. We discussed each of the component models to understand how they aid in component development and deployment. We also discussed how to build the Guests Check-In use case of the POS application using the Java EE component models.

Review Questions

1. What is a Java EE platform?
2. What are the different types of components provided by Java EE?
3. What are the component models provided by Java EE in the presentation tier?
4. What is a managed bean and its role?
5. What is the role of a servlet in the MVC architecture?
6. What are the different types of enterprise bean components?
7. How are message-driven beans different from session beans?
8. Explain stateless session bean, stateful session bean, and singleton session bean.
9. What are the different types of clients for an enterprise bean?
10. What is an entity?
11. What are persistence providers?
12. What are Web containers and EJB containers?
13. What is persistence context?
14. What is persistence unit?

15. What is an entity manager and its significance?
16. How is an entity component accessed?
17. What are the various configuration files used in presentation tier components, business tier components, and persistence tier components?
18. How are the different types of components packaged and deployed in the Java EE platform?

8

ENTERPRISE COMPONENT-ORIENTED DEVELOPMENT AND ASSEMBLY USING THE SPRING COMPONENT MODEL

8.1 Introduction

Spring is an open source component model based on the Java platform for building an end-to-end enterprise application. Spring was written initially by Rod Johnson and was first released in June 2003. Spring components are POJO based and have an advantage that they do not need heavyweight containers; lightweight Web containers are sufficient.

We had a brief introduction to the Spring component model in Chapter 3. In this chapter, we will understand how the Spring component model can be used to build an enterprise application. Spring has a module for MVC architecture, which facilitates the building of Web applications and a module for data access facilitating data store access. We discuss how the Spring MVC module and data access components help in building enterprise applications.

8.2 Spring Component Model

The core Spring component model includes *Spring beans* (the component), which are essentially POJOs deployed in a *Spring container*. The Spring container instantiates the bean components based on a configuration that is specified through either an *XML file* or *annotations*.

Dependency injection is at the heart of the Spring framework. Dependency injection plays an important role in the binding and wiring of components in Spring. Dependency injection helps to bind independent components together without using the *new* operator. The components that are dependent on other components define their dependencies through annotations on constructor arguments or properties. The container will inject the dependencies while creating and instantiating these components. Dependency injection provides a high level of decoupling. Usually, components that have dependencies look up for other components which will provide the required services. In the case of dependency injection, the requiring component does not perform the lookup but just specifies the list of dependencies, and the framework provides the requiring component with instances of other components that fulfill the dependencies. Because the dependency lookup and wiring are performed by the framework rather than the components, this is referred to as the principle of Inversion of Control (IoC). Dependency injection exists in two forms:

- Constructor-based dependency injection
- Setter-based dependency injection

Constructor-based injection occurs when a component's constructor is invoked with parameters representing dependent components. Setter-based injection occurs when the setter method of the component is invoked with the dependent component.

Spring has many positive features such as being lightweight and modular. Spring provides a number of modules for component development and is organized in a modular fashion. Some of the important modules referred to in this chapter are:

- Core module
- Bean module
- Context module
- Expression language (EL) module
- Web module
- Web servlet module
- Data layer module

The high-level architecture of a Spring framework with some important modules is shown in Figure 8.1.

Each module has a number of classes and packages but not all are loaded. Only the required modules and classes are loaded, and the rest are ignored. The modules are organized into multiple containers like core, Web, and data layer.

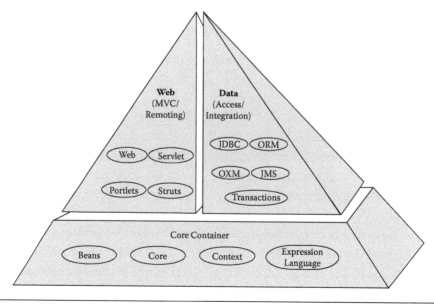

Figure 8.1   High-level architecture of the Spring framework.

The core container consists of core, beans, context, and expression language modules that are fundamental to any Spring application. The core module is the core of the component model; it provides fundamental features like dependency injection. The bean module is useful for the instantiation of the beans and is used extensively by the Spring component framework. The context module is used on top of the core and bean modules for initializing the context for the beans. The context module plays an important role in loading the components defined and configured for the application. The EL module is used for dynamic querying of components.

The Web container is built on top of the core container. The Web and Web servlet modules that are part of the Web container are useful for building the Web components for the enterprise applications using the Spring framework. The Web module provides the basic features of a Web application, and the Web servlet module provides an implementation of the Spring MVC architecture for Web applications.

Modules in the data layer help to provide data access from the Web and business components. The data layer contains various modules as listed below:

- *JDBC module*—This module provides the JDBC abstraction layer and helps to avoid tedious JDBC coding.
- *ORM module*—This module provides integration for object relational mapping APIs such as JPA, Hibernate, JDO, etc.
- *JMS module*—This module provides access for producing and consuming messages.
- *OXM module*—This module provides Object/XML binding.

We use some of the modules in the example application discussed in Section 8.7 of this chapter.

8.3 Spring Container

The Spring container is the component runtime of the Spring component model. The container takes the responsibility of instantiating components, configuring properties of components, and wiring them together as per dependency injection information specified. The container completely manages the life cycle of components from their creation through to their destruction. The configuration specifies the list of components to be instantiated and how they should be glued together. The Spring container is built on the principle of IoC. The container uses dependency injection to manage the relationships across multiple components deployed in the container. Dependency information is specified by the component developer in the configuration metadata. The configuration metadata are specified using either an XML file or Java annotations.

The Spring container is of two types:

- Spring `BeanFactory` container
- Spring `ApplicationContext` container

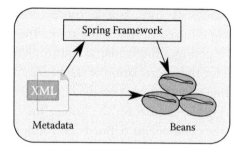

Figure 8.2 Spring container working model.

The Spring BeanFactory container is the simplest container that is an implementation of the Factory design pattern. The Spring ApplicationContext container is an enhanced container that includes all the functionality provided by the BeanFactory container and additionally provides features required for enterprise functionality. The ApplicationContext container provides several ways to load the bean definitions from the configuration file. It allows loading the configuration XML file from a file system through a class named FileSystemXmlApplicationContext, from the CLASSPATH using a class called ClassPathXmlApplicationContext, and from a Web application through the class WebXmlApplicationContext. The working model of a Spring container is represented in Figure 8.2.

8.4 Spring Beans

Spring beans play the role of business components in the Spring component model. They are developed and deployed in the Spring container which manages their life cycles. The instantiation of beans is managed by the container with the help of the configuration file. Spring beans are POJOs and are categorized into two types:

- Singleton
- Prototype

If a Spring bean is singleton, only a single instance of the bean is created per each Spring container. The single instance is cached and used for subsequent requests. If a Spring bean is prototype, any number of instances can be created based on the requests. By default, the Spring bean is singleton in nature. The type of bean is specified in the bean definition configuration file.

8.5 Spring Configuration

Spring provides three configurations as mentioned below:

- XML-based configuration file
- Annotation-based configuration
- Java-based configuration

The most popular configuration mechanism is through the XML file. This configuration file can have any name, but it is usually named `Beans.xml`. This file plays a critical role in managing bean instances. A Spring container loads the XML file and manages the beans defined in the file. The XML file contains the configuration metadata, which are used by the container for creating bean instances, managing beans' life cycle methods, and managing beans' dependencies. The configuration file allows the creation of objects with different initialization values without impacting the source code.

8.6 Spring MVC Model

The Spring MVC model helps in creating Web components for the enterprise application. A typical application that uses the MVC model has the following components:

- `DispatcherServlet`
- Web configuration file
- Controllers
- Views

8.6.1 DispatcherServlet

The MVC model provides the servlet component named `DispatcherServlet`, which acts as a front controller for all incoming requests. The `DispatcherServlet` in turn dispatches the request to handlers, controllers, view resolvers, and finally the views. The handlers help in mapping the request to appropriate controllers. The controllers must be defined for handling the request. The view resolvers help in choosing a view, and the controller passes the model data to the view that is presented.

`DispatcherServlet` is provided by the Spring component model. As discussed in Chapter 7, any servlet component in a Web application must have an entry in the `web.xml`, which is the deployment descriptor. The `web.xml` will have the entry as shown below:

```
<?xml version = "1.0" encoding = "UTF-8"?>
<web-app xmlns:xsi = "http://www.w3.org/2001/XMLSchema-instance"
    xmlns = "http://java.sun.com/xml/ns/javaee" xmlns:web =
    "http://java.sun.com/xml/ns/javaee/web-app_2_5.xsd"
    xsi:schemaLocation = "http://java.sun.com/xml/ns/javaee http://
    java.sun.com/xml/ns/javaee/web-app_2_5.xsd" id = "WebApp_ID"
    version = "2.5">
  <display-name>SpringPOS</display-name>
  <servlet>
  <servlet-name>appServlet</servlet-name>
  <servlet-class>org.springframework.web.servlet.
  DispatcherServlet</servlet-class>
  </servlet>
```

```
    <servlet-mapping>
    <servlet-name>appServlet</servlet-name>
    <url-pattern>/</url-pattern>
    </servlet-mapping>
</web-app>
```

8.6.2 Web Configuration File

In addition to the web.xml, the Spring MVC component model requires an additional configuration file that is also an XML file for handling the Web request. This configuration file will have the name:

```
[name of dispatcher servlet]-servlet.xml
```

For example, with reference to the web.xml defined above, the name of the configuration file will be appServlet-servlet.xml. Alternatively, the name of the configuration file can have a different name, and it can be specified using the contextConfigLocation parameter in the init-param element in the web.xml as shown below:

```
<?xml version = "1.0" encoding = "UTF-8"?>
<web-app xmlns:xsi = "http://www.w3.org/2001/XMLSchema-instance"
    xmlns = "http://java.sun.com/xml/ns/javaee" xmlns:web =
    "http://java.sun.com/xml/ns/javaee/web-app_2_5.xsd"
    xsi:schemaLocation = "http://java.sun.com/xml/ns/javaee http://
    java.sun.com/xml/ns/javaee/web-app_2_5.xsd" id = "WebApp_ID"
    version = "2.5">
    <display-name>SpringPOS</display-name>
    <servlet>
    <servlet-name>appServlet</servlet-name>
    <servlet-class>org.springframework.web.servlet.
        DispatcherServlet</servlet-class>
    <init-param>
    <param-name>contextConfigLocation</param-name>
    <param-value>/WEB-INF/spring/appServlet/servlet-context.xml
        </param-value>
    </init-param>
    </servlet>
    <servlet-mapping>
    <servlet-name>appServlet</servlet-name>
    <url-pattern>/</url-pattern>
    </servlet-mapping>
</web-app>
```

The name of the file in this case is servlet-context.xml, and it is placed under the WEB-INF/spring folder. When a web.xml file is loaded by the Spring container, the component runtime will look for a xxx-servlet.xml file depending on the entry in `web.xml`. The configuration file is used to define all the Spring beans that will be used by the `DispatcherServlet`. The Web configuration file also has information about the controllers and the details of the views used in the application. The content of a sample Web configuration file is shown below:

```xml
<?xml version = "1.0" encoding = "UTF-8"?>
<beans xmlns = "http://www.springframework.org/schema/beans"
           xmlns:context = "http://www.springframework.org/
           schema/context"
           xmlns:xsi = "http://www.w3.org/2001/XMLSchema-
           instance"
           xsi:schemaLocation = "http://www.springframework.
           org/schema/beans http://www.springframework.org/
           schema/beans/spring-beans-3.1.xsd http://www.
           springframework.org/schema/context http://www.
           springframework.org/schema/context/spring-context-
           3.1.xsd">

           <context:component-scan
                 base-package = " codabook.demoweb.controller "/>

           <bean class = "org.springframework.web.servlet.view.
              InternalResourceViewResolver">
                    <property name = "prefix"
                                value = "/WEB-INF/jsp/"/>
                    <property name = "suffix" value = ".jsp"/>
           </bean>
</beans>
```

8.6.3 Controller

Controllers handle the user interactions invoked on view objects. They invoke the appropriate business logic to handle the request and create response views that show modified models in the application. Unlike other component models that typically have a single controller, Spring allows the creation of multiple controllers. The controller details are specified in the Web configuration file. Either the controller name is specified or the folder where the controller is available is mentioned in the Web configuration file. Controllers are POJOs annotated with the `@Controller` annotation. The controller uses the `@RequestMapping` annotation to map a user request to either a specific method or to the whole controller class. The mapped method either handles the request by itself or interacts with Spring beans that implement business logic. Business logic invocation results are passed back to the view using model objects. A sample controller is represented below:

```java
package codabook.demoweb.controller;

//imports
```

```
@Controller
public class DemoSpringWebController {

    @RequestMapping(value = "/demo", method = RequestMethod.GET)
    public String sayHello(Model model) {
        model.addAttribute("greetingmsg",
            "Hello, This is Spring MVC!!!");
        return "sayhello";
    }


    @RequestMapping(value = "/test", method = RequestMethod.GET)
    public String displayHello(Model model) {
        model.addAttribute("greetingmsg",
            "Hello, This is from displayHello Method......");
        return "sayhello";
    }

}
```

The controller has two methods, sayHello and displayHello, mapped to two different URL requests, /demo and /test, respectively, using the @Request Mapping annotation. The value attribute in the annotation specifies the URL to which the method is mapped, and the method attribute specifies the HTTP method for handling the request, which is HTTP GET request in this case. Both the methods have Model as an attribute. The Model is an API provided by the Spring MVC, which is used to transfer the data from the controller to the view. The values to be returned to the view will be set in this model as attributes, and these attributes are accessible to the views to present the response of the request. The return value of the methods is usually a string, which is the name of the view to be presented as the response.

In this example, the class is identified as a controller using the @Controller annotation, and this class will be loaded by the container during initialization of the Web configuration file by looking for an entry for the Spring MVC annotation scanning. The Web configuration file should have an element <context:component-scan...> to load and activate all the required components having the @Controller and the @RequestMapping annotations in the application context. The entry for the controller in the Web configuration file is shown below in the boldfaced text:

```
<?xml version = "1.0" encoding = "UTF-8"?>
<beans xmlns = "http://www.springframework.org/schema/beans"
        xmlns:context = "http://www.springframework.org/
        schema/context"
        xmlns:xsi = "http://www.w3.org/2001/XMLSchema-
        instance"
        xsi:schemaLocation = " http://www.springframework.
        org/schema/beans http://www.springframework.org/
```

```
schema/beans/spring-beans-3.1.xsd http://www.
springframework.org/schema/context http://www.
springframework.org/schema/context/spring-context-
3.1.xsd">

    <context:component-scan
        base-package = " codabook.demoweb.controller "/>

    <bean class = "org.springframework.web.servlet.view.
    InternalResourceViewResolver">
            <property name = "prefix"
                    value = "/WEB-INF/jsp/"/>
            <property name = "suffix" value = ".jsp"/>
    </bean>
</beans>
```

8.6.4 *Views*

Spring view components can be constructed using any Web presentation technology like JSP, JSON, XML, XSLT, and so forth. We use JSP in our examples. The views are specified in the Web configuration file using a bean component provided by Spring MVC. This bean is called `InternalResourceViewResolver`, which helps to resolve the view names. The return value from the controller is the name of the view to be presented, and this bean plays a critical role in identifying and invoking the view from the appropriate location. A sample configuration is shown below:

```
<?xml version = "1.0" encoding = "UTF-8"?>
<beans xmlns = "http://www.springframework.org/schema/beans"
        xmlns:context = "http://www.springframework.org/
            schema/context"
        xmlns:xsi = "http://www.w3.org/2001/XMLSchema-
        instance"
        xsi:schemaLocation = " http://www.springframework.
        org/schema/beans http://www.springframework.org/
        schema/beans/spring-beans-3.1.xsd http://www.
        springframework.org/schema/context http://www.
        springframework.org/schema/context/spring-context-
            3.1.xsd">

    <context:component-scan
        base-package = "codabook.demoweb.controller "/>

    <bean class = "org.springframework.web.servlet.view.
        InternalResourceViewResolver">
            <property name = "prefix"
                    value = "/WEB-INF/jsp/"/>
            <property name = "suffix" value = ".jsp"/>
    </bean>
</beans>
```

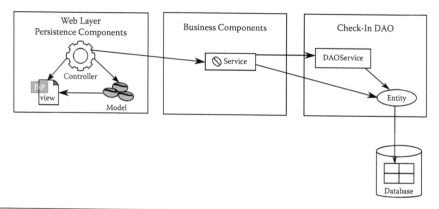

Figure 8.3   Spring components across layers.

In this example, the views will have a .jsp extension, and the views are located under a folder /WEB-INF/jsp. If the return value from the controller is sayHello, the sayHello.jsp from the folder /WEB-INF/jsp is returned as a view. Figure 8.3 shows how the Spring MVC components can be used across various layers.

8.7 Enterprise CODA Using the Spring MVC Model—An Example

In this section, we discuss the componentization of the POS example using the Spring MVC model. Let us take the example of the Guest Check-In use case, which was discussed in the previous chapter, to understand Java EE component models. Let us see how this use case can be realized using the Spring MVC model. We use Spring DAO with Hibernate for connecting to the data store. As we know, this use case is invoked by the waiters whenever there is a new guest in the restaurant. In this use case, the application displays a list of empty tables; the waiter chooses an empty table and allocates this to a guest.

Table 8.1 discusses the various components that will be used as part of this use case.

We will use the Spring MVC components for realizing the model. The web.xml for this example is shown below:

```
<?xml version = "1.0" encoding = "UTF-8"?>
<web-app …..>
        <display-name>SpringPOS</display-name>
        <servlet>
        <servlet-name>appServlet</servlet-name>
        <servlet-class>org.springframework.web.servlet.
        DispatcherServlet</servlet-class>
        <init-param>
                <param-name>contextConfigLocation</param-name>
                <param-value>
                        /WEB-INF/spring/appServlet/servletcontext.xml
                </param-value>
        </init-param>
        <load-on-startup>1</load-on-startup>
```

Table 8.1   Spring Components for Guests Check-In Use Case

COMPONENT	COMPONENTS IN SPRING MVC MODEL	COMPONENTS FROM POS APPLICATION	COMPONENTS IN JAVA EE PLATFORM
Presentation tier	`checkIn.jsp,` `checkInSuccess.jsp` (JSP views) `CheckInController.` `java` (controller) `Table.java` (model)	`CheckInUI.java,` `CheckInCtrlr.java` `Table.java`	`checkIn.xhtml` (Facelets) `CheckInBean.java` (managed bean)
Business tier	`TableService.java`	`TableBiz.java`	`TableBean.java` (EJB component) `TableBeanRemote.` `java` (business interface) `Table.java` (helper class)
Persistence tier	`TableConfig.java` `TableConfigDAO.java` `TableConfigDAOImpl.` `java`	`TableConfigDAO.` `java`	`TableConfig.java` (entity class)

```
        </servlet>
        <servlet-mapping>
        <servlet-name>appServlet</servlet-name>
        <url-pattern>/</url-pattern>
        </servlet-mapping>
</web-app>
```

The request for this application will be handled by the `DispatcherServlet`. The Web configuration file for this application is `servlet-context.xml`, and it has been mentioned using the `contextConfigLocation` element. The `servlet-context.xml` is shown below:

```
<?xml version = "1.0" encoding = "UTF-8"?>
<beans xmlns = "http://www.springframework.org/schema/beans"
    ....>

    <!- Scans within the base package of the application for
    @Components to
            configure as beans- >
    <!- @Controller, @Service, @Configuration, etc.- >
    <context:component-scan
            base-package = "codabook.pos.spring"/>

    <!- Enables the Spring MVC @Controller programming model- >
    <mvc:annotation-driven/>

    <bean
            class = "org.springframework.web.servlet.view.
            InternalResourceViewResolver">
```

```
                    <property name = "prefix"
                            value = "/WEB-INF/views/"/>
                    <property name = "suffix" value = ".jsp"/>
        </bean>

        <import resource = "dao-context.xml"/>

</beans>
```

The Web configuration file servlet-context.xml contains the elements that are helpful in loading the bean definitions with the @Component annotations and view resolvers, which help in choosing the views and references to any other configuration file to be loaded. The container will look for controllers, models, and service components under the package codabook.pos.spring as mentioned by the <context:component-scan.... > element. The views are JSP pages and are invoked by the InternalResourceViewResolver from the folder WEB-INF/views. Another configuration file for data access named dao-context.xml is also imported by the Web configuration file.

8.7.1 View Components

The presentation tier components used in this model are JavaServer Pages (JSP), a POJO as a controller and as a model. The view component is a JSP page that displays the list of available tables by taking the information from the model. The waiter assigns a particular table to guests by entering the guest details and the waiter name. The JSP page uses the UI components like label, text field, list, button, and so forth, provided by the Spring MVC model in the user interface. The JSP page code is shown below:

```
<%@ taglib uri = "http://www.springframework.org/tags/form" prefix
    = "form"%>
<html>
<body>
<div align = "center">
        <form:form method = "post" action = "checkin"
            modelAttribute = "table">
                <table style = "text-align: left">
                <tr>
                <td>TableNo</td>
                <td><form:select path = "tableNo">
                <form:option value = "0">
                  Select a Table
                </form:option>
                <form:options items = "${emptyTablesList}"
                            itemValue = "tableNo"
                            itemLabel = "tableNo"/>
                </form:select></td>
                </tr>
```

```
                        <tr>
                                <td>Number of Guests</td>
                                <td>
                                  <form:input path = "noOfGuests"/>
                                </td>
                        </tr>
                        <tr>
                                <td>Waiter Name</td>
                                <td><form:input path = "waiter"/>
                                <br/></td>
                        </tr>
                        <tr>
                        <th colspan = "2"><input type = submit value
                        = "Check IN"/></th>
                        </tr>
                </table>
        </form:form>
</div>
</body>
</html>
```

It is evident from the code above that the JSP page takes the list of available tables from the model through ${emptyTablesList}. The Spring container provides the linkage between the JSP page and the model. The values from the model are fetched by the container and displayed in the JSP page.

A POJO is used as a controller that handles the request for the specific URL request named /checkin. When there is a request for this URL, the DispatcherServlet delegates the request to the controller, which addresses this particular request mapped to the @RequestMapping annotation. The controller handles the request based on @RequestMapping annotation. The controller takes the responsibility of handling business logic and the navigation of the Web pages. For executing the business logic, the controller in turn invokes a business component named TableService for getting the list of available empty tables and to check in a particular table with the guest details and the waiter details. The controller also allows setting the return values as model attributes, and these attributes are accessed by the view to display the result. In this case, the model uses a POJO named Table for carrying data between requests. As discussed earlier, each of the methods in the controller returns the name of the view to be presented next. The source code of the controller is shown below:

```
package codabook.pos.spring.controller;

//imports

@Controller
@RequestMapping(value = "/checkin")
public class CheckInController {
```

```
@Resource
private TableService tableService;

@RequestMapping(method = RequestMethod.GET)
public String invokeCheckIn(Model model) {
        model.addAttribute("emptyTablesList",
        tableService.getEmptyTables());
        model.addAttribute("table", new Table());
        return "checkIn";

}

@RequestMapping(method = RequestMethod.POST)
public String checkIn(
        @ModelAttribute("table") Table table,
        BindingResult result,
        Model map,
        HttpServletResponse response) {

        try {
                tableService.occupyTable(
                    tableService.getTables().get
(table.getTableNo() - 1),
                table.getNoOfGuests(),
                table.getWaiter()
            );
        } catch (Exception e) {
                return "redirect:/checkin";
        }

        map.addAttribute("occupiedTables",
                tableService.getOccupiedTables());
        return "checkInSuccess";

}

}
```

In this example, the class is identified as a controller using the @Controller annotation, and this class will be loaded by the container during initialization of the Web configuration file by the entry <context:component-scan...>. The controller has two methods, invokeCheckIn and checkIn, mapped to the same URL request /checkin using the @RequestMapping annotation, but they are invoked for two different HTTP requests, GET and POST, which are specified in the *method* attribute. Both methods have Model as an attribute. First, the list of empty tables is fetched from the TableService, which is the business component that contains the business logic for the application. The return value from the business component and the Table POJO are set as attributes to the model. These attributes are accessible to the views checkIn.jsp to present the response of the request.

When a waiter chooses a table and allocates for a guest, the second method `checkIn` is invoked using the `HTTP POST` request. This method gets the details of the `Table` from the request, and again the business component methods are invoked for occupying a table. The return values are added to the model, and the response is sent to the `checkInSuccess.jsp` view, which displays the result.

From the source code, it is evident that the controller handles the request, invokes the appropriate service method, and invokes the business component for executing the business logic and setting the value of the attributes to the model. It is clear that the object of the business component `TableService` is not created by the controller. The reference of the business component `TableService` is obtained by the controller from the container using dependency injection, which is the core feature of the Spring component model. Because interfaces are not used in the Spring model, dependency injection helps in obtaining the required references of the components. The annotation `@Resource` is used to specify the required component references. This annotation is part of the Java API, and its use on the `TableService` indicates to the container that an object of `TableService` is the resource that needs to be injected at the reference that happens during runtime.

8.7.2 Business Components

`TableService` is the business component that contains the business logic for the check-in use case. `TableService` contains the logic to get the list of available tables, to occupy an available table, and to get the list of occupied tables. The `TableService` component is a POJO annotated with the `@Service` annotation of the Spring component model. The `@Service` annotation is an extension of the `@Component` annotation in Spring, which is used for identifying service components (business components are popularly known as service components in Spring). This annotation allows the component runtime to detect the business components through CLASSPATH scanning. Alternatively, the details of the Spring beans can be entered in the Web configuration file. It is also possible to have a separate XML file for all business components, which can be imported in the Web configuration file using the *import* element. The business component in turn accesses the data store using a DAO pattern. A separate DAO named `TableConfigDAO` is defined. The source code of the `TableService` business component is shown below:

```
package codabook.pos.spring.service;

//imports....

@Service
public class TableService {

        private TableConfigDAO tableConfigDAO;
        private TableConfig tableConfig;
```

```
List<Table> tables;

public List<Table> getTables() {
        return tables;
}


@Autowired
public TableService(TableConfigDAO tableConfigDAO) {
        this.tableConfigDAO = tableConfigDAO;
        this.tables = new ArrayList<Table>();
        tableConfig = this.tableConfigDAO.
        findTableConfig();

        if (tableConfig = = null) {
                tableConfig = new TableConfig();
                tableConfig.setNoOfTables(10);
                this.tableConfigDAO.create(tableConfig);
        }

        for (int tableNo = 1; tableNo < = tableConfig.
        getNoOfTables(); tableNo++) {
                Table table = new Table(tableNo);
                tables.add(table);
        }
}

public int getNoOfTables() {
        return tableConfig.getNoOfTables();
}

public List<Table> getOccupiedTables() {
        //business logic
}

public List<Table> getEmptyTables() {
        //business logic
}

public void occupyTable(Table table, int noOfGuests,
String waiter)
                throws Exception {

        //business logic
}

}
```

From the source code it is clear that the business component is a POJO annotated with the @Service annotation. The Spring container will locate the component using this annotation and inject a reference of this bean to the controller component. Another interesting aspect to notice in the `TableService` is that the constructor is not a default one and has a parameter of type `TableConfigDAO`. As mentioned earlier, the `TableService` in turn makes use of other POJOs for the data store access using the DAO pattern.

The `TableConfigDAO` is one such component that is accessed by the `TableService` business component. The `TableConfigDAO` is instantiated by the component runtime and injects a reference of the implementation of this DAO interface in the constructor of `TableService` (constructor-based dependency injection). The annotation `@Autowired` plays a major role in binding references between two bean components. The Spring container uses dependency injection between collaborating beans through this annotation. The `@Autowired` annotation helps the container to literally wire two bean components. The `@Autowired` annotation can be used to wire beans in the constructor, setting methods and properties of the bean component. In this example, when the `TableService` object is created, the `TableConfigDAO` object is injected to the constructor by the container.

8.7.3 Persistence Components

The Spring component model provides a variety of options for data store access. Let us discuss the DAO pattern in this example. DAO stands for Data Access Object, which is used for database access. This is a design pattern that defines a mechanism for accessing an underlying data store through some common mechanisms like JDBC, JPA, and JDO. Usually this pattern defines the read-write operations to be performed on the data store through an interface. These operations are implemented and supported by the underlying runtime that supports the DAO. Spring offers support for JDBC, Hibernate, JPA, and JDO as the underlying technologies. We discuss how Hibernate is used as the runtime for data access using DAO.

There is an entity* component named `TableConfig`, which is a persistence component that stores the number of tables in the restaurant. This is the same `Tableconfig` entity component, a POJO that was discussed in Chapter 7. The `TableConfig` entity source code from Chapter 7 is shown below:

```
@Entity
public class TableConfig {
        @Id
        @GeneratedValue(strategy = GenerationType.IDENTITY)
        private int id;
        private int noOfTables;
```

---

* To understand *entity*, refer to the persistence tier components in Chapter 7.

```
public int getId() {
        return id;
}

public int getNoOfTables() {
        return noOfTables;
}

public void setNoOfTables(int noOfTables) {
        this.noOfTables = noOfTables;
}

public void setId(int id) {
        this.id = id;
}

public TableConfig() {

}
}
```

This entity is retrieved, modified, and stored into persistence storage by the TableConfigDAO. The TableConfigDAO inherits from BaseDAO, which defines the basic read and write operations to be performed on the entity, and it is implemented in BaseDAOImpl. The source code of the DAO interfaces and implementations are as shown below:

```
package codabook.pos.spring.dao;

public interface BaseDAO {
        public void create(Object obj);
        public void update(Object obj);
        public void delete(Object obj);
}

package codabook.pos.spring.dao;

//imports…..

@Repository
public class BaseDAOImpl implements BaseDAO {

        private SessionFactory sessionFactory;
        private Session session;

        @Autowired
        public BaseDAOImpl(SessionFactory sessionFactory) {
                this.sessionFactory = sessionFactory;
                session = this.sessionFactory.openSession();
        }
```

```
public void create(Object obj) {
        try {
                Transaction transaction = session.
                beginTransaction();
                session.save(obj);
                transaction.commit();
        } catch (Exception e) {
                System.out.println(e.getMessage());
        }
}

public void update(Object obj) {
        try {
                Transaction transaction = session.
                beginTransaction();
                session.update(obj);
                transaction.commit();
        } catch (Exception e) {
                System.out.println(e.getMessage());
        }
}

public void delete(Object obj) {
        try {
                Transaction transaction = session.
                beginTransaction();
                session.delete(obj);
                transaction.commit();
        } catch (Exception e) {

                System.out.println(e.getMessage());
        }
}

}

package codabook.pos.spring.dao;

import codabook.pos.spring.model.TableConfig;

public interface TableConfigDAO extends BaseDAO {
        public abstract TableConfig findTableConfig();
}

package codabook.pos.spring.dao;

//imports….

@Repository
```

```
public class TableConfigDAOImpl extends BaseDAOImpl implements
TableConfigDAO {
        private SessionFactory sessionFactory;
        private Session session ;
        @Autowired
        public TableConfigDAOImpl(SessionFactory sessionFactory){
                super(sessionFactory);
                this.sessionFactory = sessionFactory;
                session = this.sessionFactory.openSession();
        }

        public TableConfig findTableConfig() {
                return (TableConfig) session.get(TableConfig.
                class,1);

        }

}
```

The DAO implementation class implements the DAO interface and is annotated with the @Repository annotation so that the Spring container can identify this class quickly using CLASSPATH scanning. This annotation is similar to the @Service annotation, which is an extension of the @Component discussed in Section 8.7.2. This also uses the @Autowired annotation to get wired with the SessionFactory, which is responsible for managing the session with the data store. The DAO pattern implementation is provided by *Hibernate*, an open source framework for accessing a data store. Spring DAO in this example internally uses Hibernate through configuration. Hibernate provides the component runtime for persisting and accessing entity components through the DAO objects. The configuration file is an XML file that contains the details of the entities and the DAO classes along with the data store details. The configuration file is dao-context.xml, and this is imported in the servlet-context.xml. At the time of loading of the Web application, both servlet-context.xml and dao-context.xml files and all the components specified in them are loaded and instantiated by the container. The import of dao-context.xml in the Web configuration file servlet-context.xml is shown below:

```
<?xml version = "1.0" encoding = "UTF-8"?>
<beans ..........>
      <context:component-scan
          base-package = "codabook.pos.spring"/>

      <!— Enables the Spring MVC @Controller programming model— >
      <mvc:annotation-driven/>

      <bean
            class = "org.springframework.web.servlet.view.
            InternalResourceViewResolver">
```

```
            <property name = "prefix"
                        value = "/WEB-INF/views/"/>
            <property name = "suffix" value = ".jsp"/>
    </bean>

    <import resource = "dao-context.xml"/>
</beans>
```

The dao-context.xml lists the entity components, the configuration properties of Hibernate, and the database details like the name of the driver, location of the data store, user name, password, and so forth. The database details are provided through a separate file named jdbc.properties. The content of the dao-context.xml is shown below:

```
<beans ................>

    <context:property-placeholder location = "classpath:jdbc.
        properties"/>

    <tx:annotation-driven transaction-manager =
        "hibernateTransactionManager"/>

    <bean id = "sessionFactory"

class = "org.springframework.orm.hibernate3.annotation.
    AnnotationSessionFactoryBean">
            <property name = "dataSource"
                        ref = "dataSource"/>
            <property name = "annotatedClasses">
            <list>
                    <value>
                        codabook.pos.spring.entity.TableConfig
                    </value>
            </list>
            </property>
    </bean>

    <bean id = "hibernateTransactionManager"
            class = "org.springframework.orm.hibernate3.
                HibernateTransactionManager">
            <property name = "sessionFactory"
                        ref = "sessionFactory"/>
    </bean>

    <bean id = "dataSource"
            class = "org.springframework.jdbc.datasource.
                DriverManagerDataSource">
            <property name = "driverClassName"
                        value = "${database.driver}"/>
            <property name = "url" value = "${database.url}"/>
```

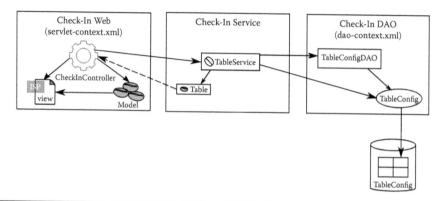

Figure 8.4   Spring components of the POS Guest Check-In.

```
<property name = "username"
          value = "${database.user}"/>
<property name = "password"
          value = "${database.password}"/>
</bean>

</beans>
```

Figure 8.4 depicts the details of the presentation components, business (service) components, and persistence components and the configuration files used in realizing the Guests Check-In use case using the Spring MVC components.

8.8 Summary

This chapter discussed the Spring core and Spring MVC model. The components in Spring are called Spring beans, and the component runtime is the Spring container. We understood that dependency injection is the core of the Spring model. Dependency injection is a principle of Inversion of Control (IoC). The Spring container supports constructor-based injection and setter-based injection. We discussed the various modules provided by the Spring model and the different components provided by the Spring MVC model.

In Spring MVC, the `DispatcherServlet` acts as a front controller receiving all the requests and passing them to the appropriate controllers. Multiple controllers can be defined in the Spring model, which is loaded by the Web configuration file. We discussed the model, view, and controller components and Web configuration files. The Web configuration file defines beans and other resources required by the container for executing the application.

We discussed the persistence components and how Spring provides integration to the data store using various techniques like JDBC, JDO, and ORM. We discussed each of the components to understand how they aid in enterprise component development and deployment. We also discussed how to build the Guests Check-In use case of the POS application using the Spring MVC components for the presentation, Spring service components for the business, and Spring DAO components for the data access layer.

Review Questions

1. What is a Spring container?
2. What are Spring beans?
3. What is Spring configuration, and what are the various configurations?
4. What are the two types of Spring beans?
5. What is a dispatcher servlet?
6. How is the Spring MVC model configured in a Web application?
7. What is the Web configuration file in the Spring MVC model and its significance?
8. How are controllers represented in the Spring MVC model?
9. How are two Spring beans wired automatically by the container?
10. How are the business components in Spring represented and identified?
11. What are the various options for persistence access in Spring?
12. Explain how Spring DAO can be implemented.

9

ENTERPRISE COMPONENT-ORIENTED DEVELOPMENT AND ASSEMBLY USING ENTERPRISE OSGI

9.1 Introduction

In the last few chapters, we discussed Component-Oriented Development and Assembly using various component models like OSGi, SCA, Java EE, and Spring. In this chapter, we discuss enterprise component development and assembly using the Enterprise OSGi specification. In Chapter 5, we learned about the OSGi component model in detail. In this chapter, we discuss how enterprise OSGi helps to build enterprise applications on top of OSGi runtime. The objective of this chapter is to give a brief overview of Enterprise OSGi services and give details of how to build enterprise components using Enterprise OSGi services.

9.2 Enterprise OSGi—An Introduction

Enterprise OSGi is a specification that extends the OSGi core framework for building enterprise applications. The Enterprise OSGi specification latest release version is v5.0. The Enterprise OSGi specification is based on core OSGi. There is an expert group within the OSGi Alliance called the OSGi Enterprise Expert Group (EEG), which is responsible for defining the technical requirements and specifications for enterprise application scenarios. The services for the Enterprise specification have been designed to integrate with OSGi and cooperate with each other.

Although the OSGi framework is simple to use, there is some amount of infrastructure code visible from the application code of a bundle. The Enterprise OSGi specification helps to solve this issue through Enterprise OSGi services. The Enterprise OSGi specification supports multiple component models that are highly interoperable and based on dependency injection. The dependency injection feature in the component models helps in decoupling the code from the OSGi APIs. These models provide an OSGi bundle programming model with minimal implementation dependencies and virtually less complex Java code. The component models supported by the Enterprise OSGi specification based on dependency injection are *declarative services specification* and *Blueprint container specification*.

The *declarative services specification* provides dependency injection for services. It handles life cycle dynamics by notifying the component or managing the component's life cycle. The OSGi declarative services specification was briefly discussed in Chapter 5. Please refer to Section 5.8 for details on the OSGi declarative services specification.

The *Blueprint container specification* is based on the Spring dynamic module project. It provides a general dependency injection framework. The services are supported by proxying them and damping their life cycles. This specification defines a dependency injection framework specifically for OSGi bundles, which understands the unique dynamic nature of services. Bundles in this programming model contain a number of XML definition resources that are used by the Blueprint container to wire the application together and start when the bundle is active.

Apart from the declarative services and Blueprint container specifications, the Enterprise OSGi defines various other specifications for OSGi-based services like:

- *Remote Services*—This specification allows the bundles to communicate through services hosted on remote systems.
- *Log Service*—This specification defines a general purpose message logger for the OSGi framework.
- *Web Application Service*—This specification is defined for Web components like servlet and JSP. This specification details how Web components packaged in WAR or Web application bundles (WABs) can be deployed in an OSGi framework and use OSGi services.
- *Http Service*—This specification defines how bundle developers can use common communication and interface technologies like HTTP, HTML, XML, and servlet.
- *Management and Configuration Services*—This specification defines the support for managing the servers and the applications in an enterprise system within the OSGi framework. This specification in turn makes use of JMX Management Extensions for managing the servers.
- *Naming and Directory Services*—This specification defines the naming and directory services that provide vendor-neutral APIs that allow the client to interact using naming services.
- *JDBC Service*—This specification defines the JDBC service for interacting with the database.
- *JPA Service*—This specification defines how bundles can access and use Java Persistence API (JPA) units in an application within an OSGi framework.
- *JTA Transaction Service*—This specification defines transaction services and synchronization registry services that are based on Java EE transaction services.

9.3 Enterprise OSGi—Application Structure

Enterprise applications typically spread across various tiers of the N-tier architecture. Applications built for N-tier architecture contain presentation components in the presentation tier, business components containing business logic in the business tier, and persistence components for connecting to the data store in the persistence tier. Components for an enterprise application are built using Enterprise OSGi services like a Web application service, JPA service, OSGi declarative services, and Blueprint container services as mentioned in the previous section. The components are packaged and deployed in the form of bundles. An enterprise application built using Enterprise OSGi specification services is typically composed of Web application bundles, Blueprint context bundles, and persistence bundles that together provide complete business functionality.

Web application bundles contain presentation/Web components like Servlet, Java Server Pages. Web components are packaged as bundles with manifest information and deployed in the OSGi framework. The Web container based on the Java EE platform runs the Web application in the OSGi runtime.

Business components are typically POJOs containing business logic packaged as bundles and deployed in the OSGi framework. Declarative services specification or Blueprint container specification is used for registering the services provided by the business component with the OSGi service registry. In Chapter 5, we already discussed creating business components using the declarative services specification, so in this chapter we focus on the Blueprint container specification and see how an enterprise application can be built using OSGi Blueprint bundles with the underlying Java EE platform.

Persistence components are JPA entities created using Java Persistence API. Persistence components are also packaged as bundles called persistence bundles. The persistence bundle defines the entities and persistence units through a JPA persistence configuration file along with manifest information. The OSGi JPA service provider registers JPA `EntityManager` and `EntityManagerFactory` in the OSGi service registry. Components in need of persistence service can look up `EntityManager` and `EntityManagerFactory` in the service registry and use them without knowing the details of the underlying persistence provider. In the next few sections we discuss how a Web applications bundle is created and deployed using a Web application service, how business component bundles are created using a Blueprint container, and how persistence bundles are created and deployed in the OSGi environment using JPA Service of Enterprise OSGi specifications.

An enterprise application having the Web components in the Web application bundle, business components in the Blueprint context bundle, and persistence components in the persistence bundle is shown in Figure 9.1.

9.4 Web Application Service

In Chapter 7, we learned how Servlet and Java Server Pages serve as the Web components for the Java EE platform. Web applications in OSGi continue to use Servlet and Java Server Pages as Web components, but they have the additional benefit of running in an OSGi framework. The Web application services specification of the Enterprise OSGi specification defines how Web components can be packaged and deployed in an

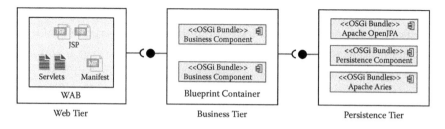

Figure 9.1   Enterprise OSGi application structure.

OSGi framework. Web applications in OSGi are packaged as bundles and are called *Web application bundles (WABs)*.

In simple terms, a WAB is the OSGi version of WAR. The WAB typically contains the structure of a regular bundle with the regular OSGi headers in the MANIFEST.MF. Apart from the usual headers, WABs will have an additional header Web-ContextPath that specifies the application context path. The Enterprise OSGi specification gives the flexibility of bundling a Web application as a WAR or JAR file with manifest headers. The MANIFEST.MF file should be included in the Web application. A sample MANIFEST.MF with the manifest header for a WAB is shown below:

```
Manifest-Version: 1.0
Bundle-ManifestVersion: 2
Bundle-Name: codabook.pos.eosgi.web
Bundle-SymbolicName: codabook.pos.eosgi.web
Bundle-Version: 1.0.0.qualifier
Web-ContextPath:/codabook_pos
Import-Package: javax.servlet;version = "2.5.0",
javax.servlet.http;version = "2.5.0",
javax.servlet.jsp,
javax.servlet.jsp.el,
javax.servlet.jsp.tagext
Bundle-ActivationPolicy: lazy
```

From the manifest information shown above, it is clear that this is a regular manifest file with one additional header Web-ContextPath specific to WAB as boldfaced above. This header is crucial in identifying a bundle as a WAB. The application will have /codabook_pos as the context path. The difference between the WAR file and WAB is shown in Figure 9.2.

9.5 Blueprint Container Specification

Business components are implemented as POJOs and are deployed as bundles using the OSGi declarative services specification or Blueprint container specification. The Blueprint is a standardized dependency injection framework that can handle

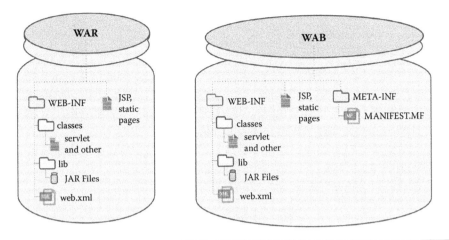

Figure 9.2   Differences between WAR and WAB.

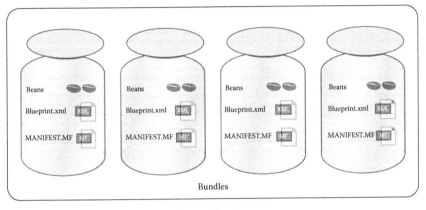

Figure 9.3   Blueprint container.

the dynamic nature of OSGi services—services can be made available and unavailable anytime. This specification consists of the following:

- Blueprint container
- Blueprint bundles
- Blueprint XML file
- Beans (components)

The Blueprint container having bundles, a manifest file, and Blueprint XML file is shown in Figure 9.3.

The Blueprint container is the runtime for the business components using the Blueprint specification. The container is responsible for instantiation of components by looking up the information in the Blueprint XML file. The container first parses the XML file for the information. The container also ensures that all the services and their references are satisfied before instantiation of components. The container registers all the declared services in the Blueprint XML file with the service registry and binds the components together.

Like any OSGi application, a Blueprint-based application will also have a bundle as its deployable entity. A Blueprint bundle will have one or more associated Blueprint XML files, and the MANIFEST.MF file will have an additional manifest header Bundle-Blueprint identifying the bundle as a Blueprint bundle. A Blueprint bundle is shown below with the manifest headers:

```
Manifest-Version: 1.0
Bundle-ManifestVersion: 2
Bundle-Name: TableBizService
Bundle-SymbolicName: codabook.pos.eosgi.table
Bundle-Version: 1.0.0.qualifier
Export-Package: codabook.pos.eosgi.postable.biz.api
Import-Package: codabook.pos.eosgi.model.entities,
codabook.pos.eosgi.model,
javax.persistence;version = "2.0.0"
Bundle-Blueprint: OSGI-INF/*.xml
```

This bundle is referred to as a Blueprint bundle because of the manifest header Bundle-Blueprint as boldfaced in the code above. This header refers to one or more Blueprint XML files, and these XML files are typically placed under a directory named OSGI-INF.

The Blueprint XML file is an XML file with <blueprint> as the top-level element. The Blueprint XML file is used to define components and their assembly using the Blueprint programming model. This XML file is crucial in instantiating components and wiring them together to form a running module. The Blueprint container instantiates and wires the components based on the information in the Blueprint XML file. The beans are POJOs, components declared using the <bean> element in the Blueprint XML file. The <bean> element will have an id for identifying the bean and the bean class implemented as a POJO as shown below:

```
<blueprint xmlns = "http://www.osgi.org/xmlns/blueprint/v1.0.0">
<bean id = "tableService"
  class = "codabook.pos.eosgi.postable.biz.TableBiz" >
</bean>
</blueprint>
```

In the example, the bean is identified as tableService and is implemented by a POJO called codabook.pos.eosgi.postable.biz.TableBiz. The Blueprint Container will instantiate the bean either using a constructor or using a static factory method or instance factory method. Beans can optionally declare properties using the <property> element.

The Blueprint XML file can have any name with an .xml extension. The Blueprint XML file contains bean declarations, registrations of services with the OSGi service registry, and references to the services registered in the OSGi service registry. A sample Blueprint XML file is shown below:

```
<blueprint xmlns = "http://www.osgi.org/xmlns/blueprint/v1.0.0">
<service ref = "tableService"
   interface = "codabook.pos.eosgi.postable.
                        biz.api.ITableBiz"/>
<bean id = "tableService"
   class = "codabook.pos.eosgi.postable.biz.TableBiz" >
</bean>
<bean id = "DAO"
   class = "codabook.pos.eosgi.postable.
               persistence.mySql.DAOFactory" >
     <property name = "dbService" ref = "DB"/>
</bean>
<reference id = "DB"
      interface = "codabook.pos.eosgi.dbService.
                              api.IDBService"/>
</blueprint>
```

In the example Blueprint XML file shown above, a bean component is declared using a <bean> element. There is also a <service> element that defines the registration of a service with the OSGi service registry. The <service> element has defined two attributes:

- *ref*—Refers to the bean id that provides the service object
- *interface*—Defines the interface under which the service is registered

In this example, the service name is tableService, which is provided by the bean with id tableService and bean implementation TableBiz. The service tableService is registered with the OSGi service registry under the interface ITableBiz, which is implemented by the bean.

Services in the OSGi service registry are referred using the <reference> element. In the example, there is a reference named DB, which is looked up in the registry. If a reference is found in the service registry it will be set to IDBService.

The Blueprint container specification is implemented by two well-known open source frameworks: *Eclipse Gemini Blueprint* and *Apache Aries*. The *Eclipse Gemini Blueprint* can be used by application developers for developing modular and dynamic applications. *Apache Aries* consists of pluggable Java components enabling an enterprise OSGi application programming model. Thus, in this section, we understood how business components (simple POJOs) can be exposed as services and can be registered with the OSGi service registry using the Blueprint specification.

9.6 JPA Service

The Enterprise OSGi specification defines the JPA service that defines how bundles can access and use Java Persistence API (JPA) in an application within an OSGi framework. JPA can be used within an OSGi framework through persistence bundles. JPA entities are packaged in the form of bundles and are referred to as OSGi persistence bundles or simply persistence bundles.

A persistence bundle is like any other OSGi bundle with the following additional features:

- Bundle manifest will have an additional header named `Meta-Persistence` in `MANIFEST.MF`. The value of this header attribute points to the JPA configuration file called `persistence.xml`.
- Bundle will have one or more configured JPA persistence units defined through the `persistence.xml`.
- Bundle will have one or more JPA entity classes included in the appropriate persistence units.

The manifest header is used to locate the JPA configuration file `persistence.xml`. Usually the `persistence.xml` file is placed under the `META-INF` folder where the `MANIFEST.MF` file is present. In this case, the header will have an empty value, which implicitly points to the default `persistence.xml` under the `META-INF` folder.

```
Meta-Persistence:
```

This is equivalent to

```
Meta-Persistence: META-INF/persistence.xml
```

If the `persistence.xml` is placed in a different location, the location is specified as a value for the manifest header as shown in the example below:

```
Meta-Persistence: persistence/persistence.xml
```

Let us look at the manifest file having the `Meta-Persistence` header:

```
Manifest-Version: 1.0
Bundle-ManifestVersion: 2
Bundle-Name: Model
Bundle-SymbolicName: codabook.pos.eosgi.model
Bundle-Version: 1.0.0.qualifier
Export-Package: codabook.pos.eosgi.model,
codabook.pos.eosgi.model.entities
Meta-Persistence:
Import-Package: com.mysql.jdbc.jdbc2.optional,
javax.persistence;jpa = "2.0",
javax.sql,
org.apache.openjpa.enhance;version = "2.0.0",
org.apache.openjpa.util;version = "2.0.0"
```

The `persistence.xml` in the default location under the `META-INF` folder, which defines persistence units and entities, is shown below:

```
<?xml version = "1.0" encoding = "UTF-8"?>
<persistence version = "2.0" xmlns = "http://java.sun.com/xml/ns/
    persistence" xmlns:xsi = "http://www.w3.org/2001/XMLSchema-
    instance"
    xsi:schemaLocation = "http://java.sun.com/xml/ns/persistence
        http://java.sun.com/xml/ns/persistence/persistence_2_0.
        xsd">
    <persistence-unit name = "codabook.pos.eosgi.posDB"
        transaction-type = "RESOURCE_LOCAL">
            <non-jta-data-source>osgi:service/javax.sql.DataSource/
                (osgi.jndi.service.name = jdbc/posdb)
                </non-jta-data-source>
        <class>codabook.pos.eosgi.model.entities.Food</class>
        <class>codabook.pos.eosgi.model.entities.
            TableConfig</class>
        <class>codabook.pos.eosgi.model.entities.Bill</class>
        <class>codabook.pos.eosgi.model.entities.
            BillLineItem</class>
        <class>codabook.pos.eosgi.model.entities.Gratuity
            </class>
        <exclude-unlisted-classes>true</exclude-unlisted-
            classes>
        <properties>
        <property name = "openjpa.RuntimeUnenhancedClasses"
            value = "supported"/>
        </properties>
    </persistence-unit>
</persistence>
```

Persistence units and the entities are declared using `<persistence-unit>` and `<class>` elements in the `persistence.xml` file. In this example, the persistence unit is `codabook.pos.eosgi.posDB`. The entities `Food`, `TableConfig`, `Bill`, `BillLineItem`, and `Gratuity` are mapped to the persistence unit `codabook.pos.eosgi.posDB`.

A persistence bundle having entities, `persistence.xml`, and manifest file is shown in Figure 9.4.

9.7 Enterprise CODA Using Enterprise OSGi—An Example

To understand the Enterprise OSGi services through an example, let us consider some of the components we introduced in the point-of-sale (POS) application in Chapter 4. In this section, we discuss the componentization of the POS example using Enterprise OSGi services. Let us take the example of the Guest Check-In use case that was discussed in the previous chapters using Java EE and Spring component

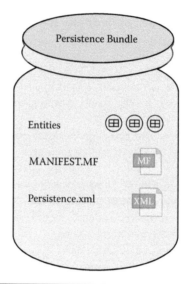

Figure 9.4   Persistence bundle.

models. Let us see how this use case can be realized using Enterprise OSGi services. As we know, this use case is invoked by the waiters whenever there is a new guest in the restaurant. In this use case, the application displays a list of empty tables; the waiter chooses an empty table and allocates this to a guest.

Table 9.1 discusses the various components that will be used as part of this use case using Enterprise OSGi services. The table also presents the details of several components used in different component models like Java EE and Spring discussed in earlier chapters for the Check-In use case.

As discussed earlier, an enterprise application is built using various bundles like Web application bundle, Blueprint bundle, and persistence bundle. The Web application bundle contains Web components like Servlet and Java Server Pages. The Blueprint bundle contains the business components, which are POJOs. The persistence bundle contains the JPA entities, persistence units, and persistence configuration file. Apache Aries is used as the Blueprint container specification implementation. The structures of the three bundles—Web application bundle, Blueprint bundle, and persistence bundle—used in building the enterprise application are shown in Figure 9.5.

9.7.1 Persistence Bundle

The persistence bundle consists of JPA entities, a JPA configuration file named `persistence.xml`, and bundle manifest information in `MANIFEST.MF`. There is a single JPA entity named `TableConfig` used for the Check-In use case. The entity is a POJO and is the same as the `TableConfig` entity used in the component models discussed in the earlier chapters. The `TableConfig` entity is shown below:

```
package codabook.pos.eosgi.model.entities;
//imports….
```

Table 9.1 Comparison of Implementation Components on Various Models

COMPONENT	COMPONENTS IN ENTERPRISE OSGI	COMPONENTS FROM POS APPLICATION	COMPONENTS IN JAVA EE PLATFORM	COMPONENTS IN SPRING MVC MODEL
Presentation tier	*Web application bundle (WAB)* `checkIn.jsp` (JSP views) `CheckIn.java` (servlet controller) `Table.java` (model)	`CheckInUI.java`, `CheckInCtrlr.java` `Table.java`	`checkIn.xhtml` (Facelets) `CheckInBean.java` (managed bean)	`checkIn.jsp`, `checkInSuccess.jsp` (JSP views) `CheckInController.java` (controller) `Table.java` (model)
Business tier	*Blueprint bundle* `TableBiz.java` (business component) `ITableBiz.java` (interface for the component registered with the registry)	`TableBiz.java`	`TableBean.java` (EJB component) `TableBeanRemote.java` (business interface) `Table.java` (helper class)	`TableService.java`
Persistence tier	*Persistence bundle* `TableConfig.java`	`TableConfigDAO.java`	`TableConfig.java` (entity class)	`TableConfig.java` `TableConfigDAO.java` `TableConfigDAOImpl.java`

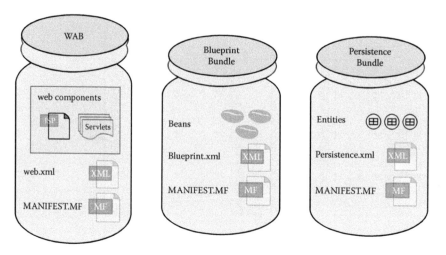

Figure 9.5   General structure of Enterprise OSGi application deployment.

```
@Entity
public class TableConfig{
        @Id
        @GeneratedValue(strategy = GenerationType.IDENTITY)
        private int tableConfigId;
        private int noOfTables;
        public TableConfig() {
        }
        public int getNoOfTables() {
                return noOfTables;
        }
        public void setNoOfTables(int noOfTables) {
                this.noOfTables = noOfTables;
        }
        public int getTableConfigId() {
                return tableConfigId;
        }
        public void setTableConfigId(int tableConfigId) {
                this.tableConfigId = tableConfigId;
        }
}
```

As discussed earlier, the persistence bundle manifest contains the header
Meta-Persistence, which is used to locate the JPA configuration file persis-
tence.xml. In this example, the persistence.xml file is placed in the default
location under the META-INF folder where the MANIFEST.MF file is present. So, the
manifest header will have an empty value as shown below:

```
Manifest-Version: 1.0
Bundle-ManifestVersion: 2
Bundle-Name: Model
```

```
Bundle-SymbolicName: codabook.pos.eosgi.model
Bundle-Version: 1.0.0.qualifier
Export-Package: codabook.pos.eosgi.model,
codabook.pos.eosgi.model.entities
Meta-Persistence:
Import-Package: com.mysql.jdbc.jdbc2.optional,
javax.persistence;jpa = "2.0",
javax.sql,
org.apache.openjpa.enhance;version = "2.0.0",
org.apache.openjpa.util;version = "2.0.0"
```

From the manifest headers, we can see that the persistence bundle imports the JPA-related bundles, driver bundles, and OpenJPA bundles. Apache OpenJPA is used as the JPA persistence provider. Apache OpenJPA provides container-managed persistence for the OSGi framework and provides excellent support for the Blueprint container. A persistence unit is defined for the entity `TableConfig` in the `persistence.xml` file. The `persistence.xml` with the persistence unit and entity is shown below:

```
<?xml version = "1.0" encoding = "UTF-8"?>
<persistence version = "2.0" …>
        <persistence-unit name = "codabook.pos.eosgi.posDB"
        transaction-type = "RESOURCE_LOCAL">
                <non-jta-data-source>osgi:service/javax.sql.
                DataSource/(osgi.jndi.service.name = jdbc/posdb)
                </non-jta-data-source>
                <class>codabook.pos.eosgi.model.entities.
                TableConfig</class>
                <exclude-unlisted-classes>
                   true
                </exclude-unlisted-classes>
                <properties>
                <property name = "openjpa.RuntimeUnenhancedClasses"
                value = "supported"/>
                </properties>
        </persistence-unit>
</persistence>
```

The persistence unit is `codabook.pos.eosgi.posDB`. The `TableConfig` entity is defined as part of the persistence unit. The data store has been made available as a service, and it is looked up in the service registry using `osgi.jndi.service.name = jdbc/posdb`. This is specified using the `<non-jta-data-source>` element, which is boldfaced in the text above. The data store is registered with the OSGi service registry through a separate blueprint bundle. The bundle provides data store details along with a name `jdbc/posdb` with which it is registered in the service registry. The persistence bundle provides a JPA service that will be used by the business components.

9.7.2 Blueprint Bundle

The business components in this example are POJOs, which are exposed as Blueprint services. A Blueprint bundle is defined for exposing the business functionality as services. The Blueprint bundle also consumes JPA services defined by the persistence bundle. The JPA services are automatically looked up in the service registry, and the Blueprint container takes the responsibility of wiring the component services and references. The Blueprint XML file is shown below:

```
<blueprint xmlns = "http://www.osgi.org/xmlns/blueprint/v1.0.0"
        xmlns:jpa = "http://aries.apache.org/xmlns/jpa/v1.0.0"
xmlns:tx = "http://aries.apache.org/xmlns/transactions/v1.0.0">
<service ref = "tableService"
   interface = "codabook.pos.eosgi.postable
                            .biz.api.ITableBiz"/>
<bean id = "tableService"
        class = "codabook.pos.eosgi.postable.biz.TableBiz"
        init-method = "initialise">
        <tx:transaction method = "*" value = "Required"/>
        <jpa:unit property = "entityManagerFactory"
                unitname = "codabook.pos.eosgi.posDB"/>
</bean>
</blueprint>
```

The bean component is registered as a Blueprint service `tableService` through the service element in the Blueprint XML file. The business component is `codabook.pos.eosgi.postable.biz.TableBiz`, which provides the business functionality. The `TableBiz` exposes functionality as Blueprint services through an interface `ITableBiz`, which is boldfaced in the Blueprint XML file shown above. The business component is in need of `EntityManagerFactory` provided by the persistence bundle. The JPA service is consumed in the Blueprint container by mentioning the persistence unit in the Blueprint XML file. The persistence unit is mentioned using the `<jpa:unit>` element as boldfaced in the example above.

The bean component is `TableBiz`, which contains the business logic of the application defined by the interface `ITableBiz`. This bean component is registered as a service with a name `tableService` with the OSGi service registry through the service element and the bean element in the Blueprint XML file. The container takes the responsibility of registering the `tableService` with the OSGi service registry. The interface `ITableBiz`, which is registered with the OSGi service registry as `tableService`, is shown below:

```
package codabook.pos.eosgi.postable.biz.api;
//imports
public interface ITableBiz {
        public abstract List<Table> getEmptyTables();
        List<Table> getTables();
```

```
                //Business logic methods....
}
```

The bean component `TableBiz` implementing the business methods defined in the interface is shown below:

```java
package codabook.pos.eosgi.postable.biz;
//imports....
public class TableBiz implements ITableBiz {
        public EntityManagerFactory entityManagerFactory;
        private EntityManager em;
        private TableConfig tableConfig;
        List<Table> tables = new ArrayList<Table>();
        public EntityManagerFactory getEntityManagerFactory() {
                return entityManagerFactory;
        }
        public void setEntityManagerFactory(EntityManagerFactory
           entityManagerFactory) {
                this.entityManagerFactory = entityManagerFactory;
        }
        public void initialise() {
                em = entityManagerFactory.createEntityManager();
                TypedQuery<TableConfig> query =
                   em.createQuery("SELECT t FROM TableConfig t",
                   TableConfig.class);
                //Business logic.....
        }
        @Override
        public List<Table> getEmptyTables() {
                List<Table> emptyTables = new ArrayList<Table>();
                for (Table table : tables) {
                        if (!table.isOccupied())
                                emptyTables.add(table);
                }
                return emptyTables;
        }
        @Override
        public List<Table> getTables() {
                return tables;
        }
        //Other Business methods.....
}
```

From the above example it is clear that the Blueprint container takes the responsibility of looking up the JPA service (`EntityManagerFactory`) defined as a persistence unit and binds the service reference automatically through the setter methods in the bean component. The bean implementation declares an object of `EntityManagerFactory` and defines setter methods for `EntityManagerFactory` through which the dependency injection happens. The wiring between the components is handled by the Blueprint container in a simplified way. Thus, consuming a JPA service is made simpler and easier by the Blueprint container.

9.7.3 Web Application Bundle

The Web application bundle consists of the Web components Servlet and Java Server Pages. The Web application is packaged as a WAB, and the context path is specified using the Web-ContextPath manifest header. Let us recall that WAB contains the same structure as that of a WAR file and has the MANIFEST.MF file under the META-INF directory. The manifest file is shown below:

```
Manifest-Version: 1.0
Bundle-ManifestVersion: 2
Bundle-Name: Codabook.pos.eOSGI.Web
Bundle-SymbolicName: codabook.pos.eosgi.web
Bundle-Version: 1.0.0.qualifier
Web-ContextPath:/codabook_pos
Import-Package: codabook.pos.eosgi.postable.biz.api,
codabook.pos.eosgi.model.entities,
codabook.pos.eosgi.model,
javax.el,
javax.naming,
javax.servlet;version = "2.5.0",
javax.servlet.http;version = "2.5.0",
javax.servlet.jsp,
javax.servlet.jsp.el,
Bundle-ActivationPolicy: lazy
```

The context path for this application is /codabook_pos, and the WAB imports bundles specific to Web components and the bundles having model components for transfer of data between tiers. A servlet component named CheckIn is used as a controller. This component requires the reference of the business component TableBiz. The business component should be looked up in the OSGi service registry. It is recommended to do this lookup when the WAB is initialized. A ServletContextListener is defined, which will look up for the tableService when the WAB is initialized. The service is looked up using a default prefix osgi:service/ as shown in the following code snippet:

```
//sce - ServletContextEvent
tableBiz = (ITableBiz) ctx.lookup("osgi:service/"+ITableBiz.class.
getName());
sce.getServletContext().setAttribute("tableBiz", tableBiz);
```

The reference of the service is set in the ServletContext so that Web components can get it as an attribute whenever it is required. Once the service reference is available, the business methods are invoked through the service reference. The CheckIn controller is shown below, which invokes the business methods and invokes the presentation component:

```
//imports
public class CheckIn extends HttpServlet {
        protected void doGet(HttpServletRequest request,
        HttpServletResponse response) throws ServletException,
        IOException {
                ITableBiz tableBiz = (ITableBiz)
                getServletContext().getAttribute("tableBiz");
                List<Table> emptyTables = tableBiz.
                        getEmptyTables();
                request.setAttribute("emptyTablesList",
                        emptyTables);
                RequestDispatcher r = request.
                getRequestDispatcher("checkIn.jsp");
                r.forward(request, response);
        }
        protected void doPost(HttpServletRequest request,
        HttpServletResponse response) throws ServletException,
        IOException {
        }
}
```

The presentation component is a JSP named checkIn.jsp that uses the controller attributes to display the value as shown below:

```
<html>
<body>
            <h2>POS CheckIn</h2>
            <form method = "post" action = "CheckInController">
                <tr>
                <td>TableNo</td>
                <td><select name = "tableNo" >
                <option value = "0">Choose Table No.</option>
                <%
                List<Table> emptyTablesList =
                    (ArrayList<Table>)request.
                            getAttribute("emptyTablesList");
                for(Table table : emptyTablesList) {
                %>
                <option value = "<% = table.getTableNo()%>">
                        <% = table.getTableNo()%>
                </option>
        <%}%>
                </select></td> </tr>
//code omitted for brevity….
</body>
</html>
```

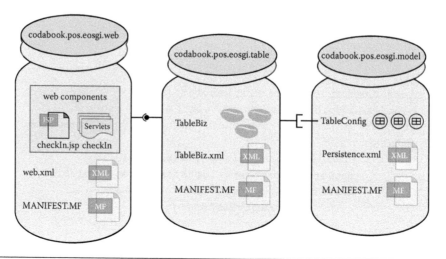

Figure 9.6   Enterprise OSGi application deployment of the POS Check-In use case.

The business component, controller, and JSP all use the `Table` model component for transferring the data across tiers. The `Table` is a POJO with the same setter and getter methods, which was discussed in Chapters 7 and 8. The Web components that access business components which in turn access JPA service are shown in Figure 9.6.

9.8 Summary

This chapter discussed the Enterprise OSGi specification. The Enterprise OSGi defines various specifications for OSGi-based services such as Web application service, JPA service, remote service, Blueprint container services, and declarative services. The *declarative services specification* provides dependency injection for services. It handles the life cycle dynamics by notifying the component or managing the component's life cycle. The *Blueprint container specification* is based on the Spring dynamic module, which provides a powerful dependency injection framework.

The Blueprint container specification provides Blueprint container, bundles, and XML files declaring components, services, and references. The components in Blueprint are POJOs declared as bean components. The Blueprint container is the runtime for the components using the Blueprint specification. A Blueprint bundle will have one or more associated Blueprint XML files.

Web Application Services define how Web components can be packaged and deployed in the OSGi framework. Web applications in OSGi are packaged as *Web application bundles (WABs)*. The JPA service defines how bundles can access and use a Java Persistence API (JPA) unit in an application within an OSGi framework. JPA units can be used within an OSGi framework as persistence bundles.

We discussed how an enterprise application can be built for the Check-In use case of the POS application. The application is built as a set of bundles. WABs contain the Web components, the business components are packaged as Blueprint bundles, and the persistence entities are packaged in the form of persistence bundles. The persistence bundle provides `EntityManagerFactory` as a service, which is consumed by the business components using dependency injection provided by the Blueprint container. The Blueprint container automatically provides the wiring between the components. It looks up for the required services and injects the services in the required components. The business components are accessed by the Web components by looking up for the services in the OSGi registry.

Review Questions

1. What is Enterprise OSGi?
2. What is declarative services and its significance in OSGi?
3. What is WAB?
4. What is the difference between WAR and WAB?
5. What is the Blueprint container specification?
6. What is the role of Spring in the Blueprint container specification?
7. Mention the services part of the Enterprise OSGi specification.
8. What is a Blueprint container?
9. How does a bundle become a Blueprint bundle?
10. What is a Blueprint XML file and its significance?
11. What are beans in Blueprint?
12. How is a persistence bundle different from regular OSGi bundles?
13. How is the JPA service used along with the Blueprint container?
14. How can services declared in a JPA service be referred using a Blueprint container specification?
15. How are Blueprint services exposed?

PART III

PARADIGM

Component Testing, Business Application Case Study, and Tools

10

TESTING COMPONENT-ORIENTED SOFTWARE

10.1 Introduction

In previous chapters we learned about component-oriented development and assembly principles, various component models available in Java, and how to design and architect a component-oriented software system. In this chapter, we learn about testing software components. Testing plays an important role in software quality assurance. The testing of software components is slightly different from traditional software testing as we discuss in this chapter.

10.2 Concepts in Software Testing

Like in all other walks in life, to err is human in software development as well. Without proper testing of the software, one cannot assume that the software produced by a team of developers is correct, complete, and of good quality. After software gets developed by the team of programmers, an independent group of testers conduct quality verification on the produced software. Testing reveals errors in implementation logic, features that have been missed out to be implemented, and any other quality issues. All these are logged as defects of the software. After one round of testing, the identified defects are fixed and the software product is subjected to the next round of testing. Software quality assurance may involve multiple rounds of software testing, fixing, and retesting until the defects are brought down to an acceptable level.

Different types of tests are carried out at different phases of the traditional software development life cycle. Some types of tests inspect the associated artifacts of the software development process rather than the software product itself. We focus on testing techniques that focus on the software rather than the artifacts.

During the course of development, as and when development of small units of software is completed, the developers conduct *unit testing* of the software produced. Unit testing involves verification of the developed software based on the knowledge of the internal implementation specification, and the actual implementation of the software. Such testing is known as *white-box testing*.

When individual developers complete the programming work assigned to them, the software produced by individuals is brought together and integrated. Tests are conducted to verify that the software units together interact and work as per the specification. The testing carried out in this phase of the software is known as *integration testing*. Typically, integration testing makes use of the white-box testing technique.

When the software for the complete system is ready, the system is tested against the requirements specifications. This phase of testing is known as *system testing*. Unlike the other two phases of testing, which employed white-box testing, system testing treats the whole system as a black box, with no assumption about the implementation contained within the box. The focus of black-box tests is to verify that the system provides all the functionality specified in the system requirements. Test cases are developed only with reference to requirements specifications, and not with reference to implementation specifications or the actual implementation. This type of testing is known as *black-box testing*.

10.3 Concepts in Component-Oriented Software Testing

The component-oriented software development life cycle is different from the traditional software development life cycle as discussed in Section 1.8. As explained in that section, components are provisioned either as readily built or newly developed before the components are assembled into a system. Either way, the components need to be tested before they are assembled. The scope of software component testing can be broadly divided into *functional testing* and *quality of service testing*.

The scope of functional testing includes:

- Validation of component interfaces
- Verification of component implementation—white-box testing
- Verification of component functionality—black-box testing

The scope of quality of service testing includes:

- Verification of component performance
- Verification of error handling of the component
- Verification of data accuracy of the component
- Verification of error recovery features of the component
- Verification of reusability of the component
- Verification of reliability of the component
- Assessment of the maintainability of the component

In the rest of this chapter we elaborate on the functional testing with examples. Quality of service testing is beyond the scope of this book. After the software components have been assembled together as a system, the system as a whole gets tested, similar to traditional system testing. The system testing scope and approach remain the same, irrespective of whether the system is component oriented or not.

10.4 Validation of Component Interfaces

In this validation, the tester validates that the component implementation provides the interfaces that were specified in the component design specifications. The validation can be done by using either the white-box testing technique or the black-box testing technique.

In the white-box testing technique, the tester inspects the component implementation code to validate that there exists implementation code that offers the interfaces defined in the component design specification.

In the black-box testing technique, the tester deploys the component in the component framework along with a test driver component. The test driver tries to consume the interface provided by the component under test. The test passes if the composition of the test driver component with the component under test is successful. We explain both techniques with the help of an example.

10.4.1 Example of White-Box Validation

Consider the `TableBiz` component from the POS example introduced in Chapter 4. We use the OSGi component model implementation of this component (refer to Section 5.8) to explain the testing technique. The `TableBiz` component design specifies that it is supposed to provide the `ITableBiz` interface shown below:

```
public interface ITableBiz {
        public abstract int getNoOfTables();
        public abstract List<Table> getOccupiedTables();
        public abstract List<Table> getEmptyTables();

        public abstract void occupyTable(Table table, int noOf-
           Guests, String waiter)
                        throws Exception;
        public abstract void unOccupyTable(Table table) throws
           Exception;
        public abstract void reconfigureTables(int newNoOfTables)
           throws Exception;
}
```

Let us use the white-box testing technique to validate that the `TableBiz` component provides the interface. In white-box testing, we inspect the source code of the implementation of the `TableBiz` component. We find from the source code that the component is implemented as an OSGi bundle, and the bundle contains a class by the name `TableBiz`. The `TableBiz` class implements the Java interface `ITableBiz`. We further notice that the OSGi bundle includes a declarative service definition, which declares the `TableBiz` class as a component class that provides the `ITableBiz` interface, as shown below:

```
<?xml version = "1.0" encoding = "UTF-8"?>
<scr:component xmlns:scr = "http://www.osgi.org/xmlns/scr/v1.1.0"
```

```
      name = "codabook.pos.table.biz">
<implementation class = "codabook.pos.table.biz.impl.TableBiz"/>
<service>
 <provide interface = "codabook.pos.table.biz.ifce.ITableBiz"/>
</service>
<reference bind = "bindEMF" cardinality = "1..1"
       interface = "javax.persistence.EntityManagerFactory" name =
       "EntityManagerFactory"
       policy = "static"/>
</scr:component>
```

Thus, by means of white-box inspection of the component implementation, we validated that the component implementation does provide the ITableBiz interface as defined in the specification. In the next section we demonstrate the black-box testing for which the validation of interfaces would be carried out.

10.4.2 Example of Black-Box Validation

Now consider the black-box testing technique by which we can establish that the component does provide the interface as per the specification. In black-box testing, we consider the given component implementation as a black box and assume no knowledge of its internal contents or implementation. We deploy the component in the OSGi component framework and validate its provided interface. In order to test that the deployed component provides the specified interface, we use a test driver component that would try to consume the provided interface. If the test driver component succeeded in the consumption of the provided interface, the validation is successful. If the test driver component did not succeed in the consumption of the interface, then the validation fails.

For validation of the TableBiz component, we need a test driver component that would consume the ITableBiz interface. We create a new OSGi bundle POS. Test.Table.Biz, which has a declarative service component that binds with the ITableBiz service. Code for the component implementation class is provided below:

```
public class TestTableBiz {

       private ITableBiz tableBiz;

       public void setTableBiz(ITableBiz tableBiz) {
               this.tableBiz = tableBiz;
       }

       public void activate() {
               if (tableBiz ! = null)
                       System.out.println("SUCCESS - Got
                           ITableBiz service");
```

```
        else
            System.out.println("FAIL - Could not get
                ITableBiz service");
    }
}
```

The component implementation class depends on the `ITableBiz` through the `tableBiz` member attribute. The dependency injection is enabled through the bold-faced method `setTableBiz()`. The component `activate()` method verifies that the reference was provided by the `TableBiz` component. The declarative service component definition for the `TestTableBiz` component is presented below:

```
<?xml version = "1.0" encoding = "UTF-8"?>
<scr:component xmlns:scr = "http://www.osgi.org/xmlns/scr/v1.1.0"
      name = "codabook.test.table.biz">
<implementation class = "codabook.pos.test.tablebiz.TestTableBiz"/>
<reference bind = "setTableBiz" cardinality = "1..1"
      interface = "codabook.pos.table.biz.ifce.ITableBiz" name =
      "ITableBiz" policy = "static"/>
</scr:component>
```

As boldfaced in the declarative service component definition, the component implementation class `TestTableBiz` has a dependency on the `ITableBiz` interface, and the dependency injection is through the binding method `setTableBiz()`. When we deploy this test driver component along with the `TableBiz` component and `POS.Data` bundle, it can be observed that the test driver component's `activate()` method prints out a successful composition message. Thus, we have verified that the `TableBiz` component has provided the `ITableBiz` interface as defined in the component design specification.

The black-box testing technique explained above is beneficial when acquiring third-party components whose source code is not available. The interface verification also reveals any type of incompatibilities that may exist between what is required and what is provided.

10.5 Verification of Component Implementation—White-Box Testing

While testing an implementation of a component, it is important to verify that the functionality is implemented properly. In traditional software testing, this kind of verification is carried out through white-box testing. Similar testing is done in the case of verification of the internal component implementation. This testing is carried out with full knowledge of the internal implementation details of a component. Knowing the implementation logic of each internal segment of the component, test cases are devised to check that the implementations are error free. The effectiveness of the test cases is measured by the amount of statement coverage, object coverage, object interaction coverage, branch coverage, and so on.

As an example, consider the `TableBiz` component that was validated in the last section. As already discussed, this component provides the `ITableBiz` interface. In the verification of internal implementation, one needs to test all the operations defined in the `ITableBiz` interface. For illustration purposes, we present the testing technique for one of the operations defined in the `ITableBiz` interface: the `occupyTable()` operation. This operation is implemented in the class `TableBiz`. The code snippet of the implementation is given below:

```
public void occupyTable(Table table, int noOfGuests, String
    waiter)
                throws Exception {

    if (table = = null) {
            throw new Exception("Cannot checkin -
                Invalid Table");
    }

    if (table.isOccupied()) {
            throw new Exception("Table is already
                occupied");
    }

    if (noOfGuests = = 0) {
            throw new Exception("Cannot checkin -
                Invalid number of guests");
    }

    if (waiter = = null) {
            throw new Exception("Cannot checkin -
                Invalid waiter name");
    }

    Order order = new Order();

    table.occupy(noOfGuests, waiter, order);
}
```

As we examine this implementation, we see that there are four conditional statements. White-box testing employs the boundary value testing technique to verify the conditional statements. The boundary value testing technique involves supplying a range of input values to the operation being tested and verifying that the behavior of the invoked operation is as per the specification for all the values. The input values are so chosen that they hover around the success and failure of the conditional statements covered. Values hovering around the conditional expressions are called *boundary values*. Based on this technique, we obtain the test data as tabulated in Table 10.1 to test the above implementation.

For example, to test the first conditional block of code boldfaced above, we have test cases 1 and 2 in Table 10.1. Test case 1 verifies that the implementation accepts

Table 10.1   Test Cases for White-Box Testing of `occupyTable()`

SR. NO.	TABLE	NUMBER OF GUESTS	WAITER NAME	EXPECTED BEHAVIOR
1.	`tableNo = 1` `occupied = false`	4	TestWaiter	Success
2.	`null`	4	TestWaiter	Failure; invalid table
3.	`tableNo = 1` `occupied = true`	4	TestWaiter	Failure; table is occupied
4.	`tableNo = 1` `occupied = false`	0	TestWaiter	Failure; invalid no. of guests
5.	`tableNo = 1` `occupied = false`	−1	TestWaiter	Failure; invalid no. of guests
6.	`tableNo = 1` `occupied = false`	2	*null*	Failure; invalid waiter

and processes the non-null table object whose state is not occupied. Test case 2 verifies that the implementation properly handles a null value for the table. The remaining test cases perform such verification on the remaining conditional blocks of the implementation.

To perform these tests, we need to deploy the `TableBiz` component and invoke the `occupyTable()` operation. We enhance the test driver component introduced in the last section so that we can invoke the `occupyTable()` operation with the set of test values above. The `activate()` method of the `TestTableBiz` class presented in the last section is enhanced as shown below:

```
public void activate() {
        if (tableBiz ! = null) {
                System.out.println("SUCCESS - Got ITableBiz
                service");
                testCase1();
                testCase2();
                testCase3();
                testCase4();
                testCase5();
                testCase6();
        }
        else
                System.out.println("FAIL - Could not get ITableBiz
                service");
}
```

As can be seen from the code above, the `activate()` method calls methods that invoke individual test cases by supplying appropriate test data. Consider for instance, the `testCase1()` method that tests the no. 1 test case in Table 10.1. The source code for this method is shown below:

```
private void testCase1() {

        System.out.println("\n— — — — — — — — — — -");
```

```
System.out.println("Executing Test Case 1");
Table table = new Table (1);
table.setOccupied(false);

System.out.println("Created an empty table");
printTableStatus(table);

String waiter = "TestWaiter";
int noOfGuests = 4;

System.out.println("Calling occupy table with TestWaiter
and 4 guests");

try {
        tableBiz.occupyTable(table, noOfGuests, waiter);
} catch (Exception e) {
        System.out.println("ERROR - " + e.getMessage());
} finally {
        printTableStatus(table);
        System.out.println("- - - - - - - - - - -\n");
    }
}
```

As boldfaced in the code above, the testCase1() method creates appropriate test data as per the test data defined in Table 10.1. After the preparation of the test data, it invokes the occupyTable() method which is being tested. Similar to this, other methods implement test cases as tabulated in Table 10.1. We deploy this TestTableBiz component along with the TableBiz component and the POSData OSGi bundle and execute the resultant assembly, and we observe the results shown in Table 10.2 for the test cases.

Table 10.2   Test Results for White-Box Testing of occupyTable()

SR. NO.	TABLE	NUMBER OF GUESTS	WAITER NAME	EXPECTED BEHAVIOR	RESULT AND ACTUAL BEHAVIOR
1.	tableNo = 1 occupied = false	4	TestWaiter	Success	Pass
2.	null	4	TestWaiter	Failure; invalid table	Pass
3.	tableNo = 1 occupied = true	4	TestWaiter	Failure; table is occupied	Pass
4.	tableNo = 1 occupied = false	0	TestWaiter	Failure; invalid no. of guests	Pass
5.	tableNo = 1 occupied = false	−1	TestWaiter	Failure; invalid no. of guests	Fail; implementation does not complain about wrong number of guests. It accepts the test value −1.
6.	tableNo = 1 occupied = false	2	*null*	Failure; invalid waiter	Pass

We observe that all test cases except test case no. 5 have failed. This test case expected the implementation to reject the no. of guests value less than 0. However, the implementation did not reject this value and accepted the value. When we look at the source code of `occupyTable()` method in the `TableBiz` component, we can see that this behavior is due to the following code segment:

```
if (noOfGuests = = 0) {
            throw new Exception("Cannot checkin - Invalid number
                of guests");
    }
```

To fix this defect and to make test case 5 pass, the following modification in the code is required:

```
if (noOfGuests < = 0) {
            throw new Exception("Cannot checkin - Invalid number
                of guests");
    }
```

When we deploy the modified code, we observe that test case 5 does pass.

10.6 Verification of Component Functionality—Black-Box Testing

The set of tests conducted in the last section focused on testing the component implementation with the full knowledge of the implementation specification and the actual implementation. This kind of testing is feasible when the component is being tested by the producer or developer of the component. However, the component gets consumed in the context of a system assembly, and the consumers of the component are only aware of the component's interface and its functional specification. They do not have access to the component's implementation or the implementation specification. It is important that the component gets tested before it is deployed and assembled in the system context. For such purposes, black-box testing at the component level is necessary to verify that it fulfills the functions as per its functional specification.

Black-box test cases rely on the functional specifications of the component's provided interface. Based on the functional specifications, test cases are devised to cover testing of all the operations in the interface. Multiple test cases may be needed for a single operation in order to test its functional behavior exhaustively across a spectrum of input values. In the following, we present the test cases and testing approach for the `TableBiz` component. The interface provided by the `TableBiz` component is presented below for ready reference:

```
public interface ITableBiz {

            public abstract int getNoOfTables();
            public abstract List<Table> getOccupiedTables();
```

Table 10.3   Functional Specifications of `ITableBiz` Interface

SR. NO.	OPERATION	FUNCTIONAL SPECIFICATION
1.	`getNoOfTables()`	Returns the total number of tables maintained by the `TableBiz` component
2.	`getOccupiedTables()`	Returns a list of tables that are occupied. If none of the tables is occupied, the list size would be 0.
3.	`getEmptyTables()`	Returns a list of tables that are empty. If none of the tables is empty, the list size would be 0.
4.	`occupyTable(table, noOfGuests, waiter)`	Marks the table as occupied if the following conditions are met: 1. Specified table is empty 2. `NoOfGuests` is more than 0 3. Waiter is not null If any of these conditions are not met, it throws an exception that contains the error message.
5.	`unOccupyTable(table)`	Empties the table if the following conditions are met: 1. Specified table is occupied 2. The order associated with the table is null, or has no order items in it If any of these conditions are not met, it throws an exception that contains the error message.
6.	`reconfigureTables()`	Changes the number of tables maintained by the `TableBiz` component

```
            public abstract List<Table> getEmptyTables();

            public abstract void occupyTable(Table table, int noOfGuests,
            String waiter)
                            throws Exception;
            public abstract void unOccupyTable(Table table) throws
            Exception;
            public abstract void reconfigureTables(int newNoOfTables)
            throws Exception;
    }
```

Functional specifications of all these operations are presented in Table 10.3.

Based on the functional specifications, test cases are developed to test all the operations of the interface. In the following sections, we present a few example test cases and procedures to execute them. These test cases are only a representative set and are not exhaustive enough to cover all the scenarios that need to be tested.

10.6.1 Test Case for the Number of Tables

In this test case, we want to verify the operations through which the number of tables in the `TableBiz` component is maintained. There are two methods responsible for this, and we test both these methods through the following sequence of operations:

1. Invoke `reconfigureTables()` with 20 number of tables
2. Call the `getNoOfTables()`

At the end of these sequences of operations, we expect to get 20 as a return value from the getNoOfTables() operation. To perform this test, we use a test driver component similar to those used in the last two sections. The test driver component's activate() method calls on the test case implementation methods. The test case implementation code for the current test case is presented below:

```
private void testCase1() {

        System.out.println("\n- - - - - - - - - -");
        System.out.println("Executing Test Case 1");

        try {
                System.out.println("Calling reconfigureTables(20)");
                tableBiz.reconfigureTables(20);
                System.out.println("Calling getNoOfTables() and it
                    returned " +
                        tableBiz.getNoOfTables());
        } catch (Exception e) {
                System.out.println("ERROR - " + e.getMessage());
        } finally {
                System.out.println("- - - - - - - - - -\n");
        }

}
```

As can be seen from this source code, the test driver first invokes the reconfig-ureTables() operation on the component. This is followed by an invocation of getNoOfTables(). If the test driver component is assembled with the TableBiz component and executed, we can verify that the output returned is as per the expected value of 20.

10.6.2 Test Case for the Occupy Table Functionality

In this test case, we want to verify the operations related to occupying the tables. We test these methods through the following sequence of operations:

1. Call occupyTable() for Table 5
2. Call occupyTable() for Table 10
3. Call getOccupiedTables()

At the end of the test case execution, we expect the getOccupiedTables() to return a list of two tables, Table 5 and Table 10. To execute this test case, we write one more method in the test driver component whose code is presented below:

```
private void testCase2() {

        System.out.println("Executing Test Case 2");
```

```
        try {

            List<Table> tables = tableBiz.getEmptyTables();
            Table table5 = null;
            Table table10 = null;
            for (Table table : tables) {
                if (table.getTableNo() = = 5)
                    table5 = table;
                if (table.getTableNo() = = 10)
                    table10 = table;
            }

            System.out.println("Calling occupy table for
                table 5");
            tableBiz.occupyTable(table5, 4, "waiter");

            System.out.println("Calling occupy table for
                table 10");
            tableBiz.occupyTable(table10, 4, "waiter");

            System.out.println("Calling getOccupiedTables()
                and it returned following
                    tables ");

            tables = tableBiz.getOccupiedTables();
            for (Table table : tables) {
                System.out.println("Table " + table.
                    getTableNo());
            }

        } catch (Exception e) {
                System.out.println("ERROR - " + e.
                    getMessage());
        } finally {
                System.out.println("- - - - - - - - - - -\n");
        }
    }
```

When we execute this test case, we find that the output is in line with the expected output of two tables: Table 5 and Table 10.

10.6.3 Test Case for the Empty Table Functionality

In this test case, we want to verify the operations related to emptying the tables. We test these methods through the following sequence of operations:

1. Call unOccupyTable() for Table 5
2. Call getOccupiedTables()

At the end of the test case execution, we expect the getOccupiedTables() to return a Table 10. To execute this test case, we write one more method in the test driver component whose code is presented below:

```
private void testCase3() {

        System.out.println("Executing Test Case 4");

        try {
                List<Table> tables = tableBiz.
                getOccupiedTables();
                Table table5 = null;

                for (Table table : tables) {
                        if (table.getTableNo() = = 5)
                                table5 = table;
                    break;
                }

                System.out.println("Calling unOccupy table for
                   table 5");
                tableBiz.unOccupyTable(table5);

                System.out.println("Calling getOccupiedTables()
                   and it returned following
                        tables ");

                tables = tableBiz.getOccupiedTables();
                for (Table table : tables) {
                        System.out.println("Table " + table.
                           getTableNo());
                }

        } catch (Exception e) {
                System.out.println("ERROR - " + e.
                   getMessage());
        } finally {
                System.out.println("- - - - - - - - - - -\n");
        }
    }
}
```

When we execute this test case, we find that the output is in line with the expected output of a single table: Table 10.

As mentioned earlier, the three test cases presented above are only an example set of test cases. A complete black-box component testing required many more test cases that cover a number of scenarios.

10.7 Summary

In this chapter, we introduced concepts of software testing and software component testing. We learned that software component testing involves validation of the software component's provided interfaces, verification of the internal implementation of software components through white-box testing, and the functional verification of component functionality using black-box testing. We presented examples to explain how these tests are conducted.

Review Questions

1. What is the difference between black-box testing and white-box testing?
2. What are the differences between unit testing, integration testing, and system testing?
3. Why is functional testing different from quality of service testing?
4. How does one validate a component implementation to its interface specification?
5. What is involved in verification of the internal implementation of software components?
6. Can white-box testing be carried out by a component consumer? Why or why not?
7. How does a component consumer verify if he or she got the right component?
8. What are tester components and how are they relevant in black-box and white-box testing contexts?

11

IMPLEMENTING A BUSINESS APPLICATION USING CODA—A CASE STUDY

11.1 Introduction

In our progression from the first chapter through the previous chapter, we learned the fundamental concepts of software components, component models, and component frameworks. We also learned about various standard component models available on the Java platform. In this chapter, we apply the knowledge gained to build an end-to-end business application using Component-Oriented Development and Assembly.

We begin the chapter with software requirements specifications of a real-life business application. The requirements are specified as a collection of use cases. We analyze the requirements and arrive at a general component-oriented design. Components identified in the design process are known as design components. Following the design, we perform software implementation of the design components using various Java component models and frameworks. The companion Web site of the book presents the complete source code for each of these implementations.

11.2 Case Study Problem—Point-of-Sale Application for Restaurants

Point-of-sale (POS) is a software application meant for tracking orders and payments in a restaurant. A restaurant operator can set up the POS application and customize it to his or her restaurant environment by configuring the number of tables available in the restaurant and various food items available for sale in the restaurant. A brief description of the POS business application was provided in Chapter 4. In this section we provide a detailed list of use cases for the POS application. The use cases to be supported by the POS application are described in brief below:

- *Configure Dining Tables*—The restaurant operator configures the number of dining tables in the restaurant.
- *Configure Menu Items*—The restaurant operator configures the items available from the restaurant. Each menu item has a name, category, price, and tax rate.
- *Guests Check-In*—Waiters select an empty table at which a new group of guests can be seated.

- *Place Order*—Waiters capture the orders placed from a table. Order details include the menu item and quantity ordered.
- *Modify/Cancel Order*—Upon request from the guests, waiters modify the quantity or cancel an order already placed.
- *Print Receipt*—When guests have finished dining, waiters print a receipt payable by the guests.
- *Guests Checkout*—When guests from a table leave, waiters check out the guests so that POS can mark the particular dining table as empty.

We elaborate on each use case in the sections below.

11.2.1 Use Case 1—Configure Dining Tables

Table 11.1 presents use case 1.

11.2.2 Use Case 2—Create New Menu Item

Table 11.2 presents use case 2.

11.2.3 Use Case 3—Modify/Remove Existing Menu Item

Use case 3 is presented in Table 11.3.

11.2.4 Use Case 4—Check-In Guests

Table 11.4 presents use case 4.

Table 11.1   Use Case 1—Configure Dining Tables

USE CASE	CONFIGURE DINING TABLES
Actors	Restaurant Operator
Precondition	1. The number of tables in the restaurant has changed. 2. Nobody is currently dining in the restaurant and all the dining tables are empty.
Postcondition	POS updated the number of dining tables in the restaurant.
Main flow	1. Restaurant operator asks the system to configure the dining tables. 2. POS checks that none of the tables are occupied at the moment. 3. POS presents the currently configured number of dining tables and prompts for the new number of dining tables. 4. The restaurant operator specifies the new number of dining tables. 5. POS verifies that the specified number of tables is a valid number. 6. If the verification succeeds, POS reconfigures the number of dining tables to the new value specified.
Alternative flow 1	2a. If any of the dining table is occupied at the moment, then POS throws an error message and aborts configuration.

Table 11.2 Use Case 2—Create New Menu Item

USE CASE	CREATE NEW MENU ITEM
Actors	Restaurant operator
Precondition	A new menu item is being introduced in the restaurant.
Postcondition	POS added the new menu item to the list of menu items available in the restaurant.
Main flow	1. Restaurant operator asks the system to add a new menu item. 2. POS prompts for the details of the menu item such as name, food category, price, and tax rate. The restaurant operator specifies the same. 3. POS verifies data entered are valid. 4. If the verification succeeds, POS creates a new menu item with the details provided and adds it to the list of available menu items.
Alternative flow 1	3a. Verification fails if there is an existing menu item with the same name.

Table 11.3 Use Case 3—Modify/Remove Existing Menu Item

USE CASE	MODIFY/REMOVE EXISTING MENU ITEM
Actors	Restaurant operator
Precondition	Any one of the details of an existing menu item such as the food category, price, or tax rate has changed. Or, a menu item is no longer offered.
Postcondition	The menu item details internally stored by the POS application are updated.
Main flow	1. Restaurant operator asks the system to modify existing menu item. 2. POS prompts the restaurant operator to choose an existing menu item, and the restaurant operator chooses one. 3. POS presents the details of the selected menu item to the restaurant operator. The restaurant operator either chooses to remove the menu item or specifies a new value for any one of the menu item details (i.e., food category, price, or tax rate). 4. POS verifies the new set of details is valid. 5. If the verification succeeds, POS modifies the menu item with the details provided. If the menu item was marked to be removed, then POS removes the menu item from the stored list of menu items.
Alternative flow 1	4a. If any of the new menu item details is invalid, POS prompts the user to correct the same.

Table 11.4 Use Case 4—Check-In Guests

USE CASE	CHECK-IN GUESTS
Actors	Waiter
Precondition	A group of new guests have arrived at the restaurant.
Postcondition	The guests have been allotted an empty dining table, and the POS application has updated the state of the dining table as occupied.
Main flow	1. Waiter asks the system to check in guests. 2. POS displays the list of empty dining tables. 3. Waiter selects a dining table and provides the number of guests and the identity of the waiter. 4. POS marks the selected dining table as occupied and stores the number of guests and waiter details against it.
Alternative flow 1	2a. If no empty tables are found, the check-in fails.

11.2.5 Use Case 5—Place Order

Use case 5 is presented in Table 11.5.

11.2.6 Use Case 6—Modify/Cancel Order

Use case 6 is presented in Table 11.6.

11.2.7 Use Case 7—Print Receipt

Table 11.7 presents use case 7.

11.2.8 Use Case 8—Guests Checkout

Use case 8 is presented in Table 11.8.

Table 11.5   Use Case 5—Place Order

USE CASE	PLACE ORDER
Actors	Waiter
Precondition	Guests from a table have placed their orders for food.
Postcondition	POS recorded the details of order—the table, menu item ordered, and quantity ordered.
Main flow	1. Waiter asks the system to record order details of a specific occupied table. 2. POS prompts the waiter to choose a menu item and specify the quantity ordered. Waiter provides the details. 3. POS stores the order details.

Table 11.6   Use Case 6—Modify/Cancel Order

USE CASE	MODIFY/CANCEL ORDER
Actors	Waiter
Precondition	Guests want to modify or cancel an order already placed.
Postcondition	POS recorded the changes to the details of the order.
Main flow	1. Waiter asks the system to modify existing order of a specific occupied table. 2. POS prompts the waiter to choose a particular order by listing all the current orders from that table. Waiter chooses an order. 3. POS prompts for new order quantity. Waiter provides a new quantity if modification is required, or 0 if order is to be cancelled. 4. POS stores the modified details on the order.

Table 11.7   Use Case 7—Print Receipt

USE CASE	PRINT RECEIPT
Actors	Waiter
Precondition	Guests finished dining and are ready to pay.
Postcondition	POS printed receipt and cleared all current orders on the table.
Main flow	1. Waiter asks the system to print receipt for a specific occupied table. 2. POS prints a receipt based on all the current orders on the table. If the number of guests is equal to or more than 8, then a gratuity amount of 10% should be added to the bill. Once receipt is printed, POS clears all the current bills on the table.

Table 11.8   Use Case 8—Guests Checkout

USE CASE	GUESTS CHECKOUT
Actors	Waiter
Precondition	Guests have paid and are ready to vacate a table.
Postcondition	POS marked the table as empty.
Main flow	1. Waiter asks the system to checkout guests from a specific occupied table. 2. POS verifies there are no current orders pending on the table. 3. If the verification is successful, POS marks the dining table to be empty and available.
Alternative flow 1	2a. If there are orders pending on the selected table, checkout fails.

11.3 Component-Oriented Design of POS

We first identify a suitable high-level architecture for the POS application. We then drill into each architectural element to arrive at a low-level design.

11.3.1 POS Architecture

Based on the success of a multitiered architecture in various business applications that are similar to the POS application, we choose a three-tier architecture for the POS application. Figure 11.1 illustrates the three-tier architecture of the POS application.

The three-tier architecture is based on the principle of separation of concerns. Concerns related to presentation and user interactions are handled by the *presentation tier*. Core business logic and rules are handled by the *business tier*. Persistence of data is handled by the *persistence tier*. Each tier depends on the interfaces provided by the tier below. Multiple components are present within a tier. Components within a tier collaborate with one another and depend on the components from the lower tiers. The UI tier components depend on business tier components, and business tier components depend on persistence tier components.

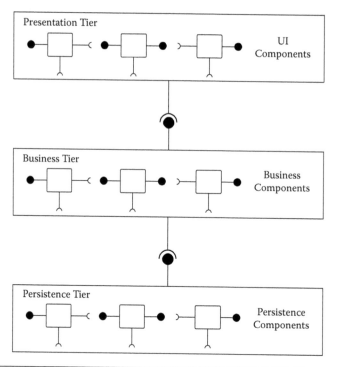

Figure 11.1   POS application architecture.

11.3.2 Domain Model Design

In order to facilitate business data communication among components, it is essential to have a common business domain data vocabulary. A set of software objects that can carry business data forms such a domain vocabulary. These data-carrying software objects are called *domain objects* or *model objects*. After analysis of the POS problem domain, we come up with the model objects illustrated in Figure 11.2. In the following, we elaborate on each model object identified.

In the model objects, we have a Table object that represents a dining table in the restaurant. Each dining table has a unique tableNo attribute associated with it. The dining table can be either occupied or empty. The occupied status is captured in the occupied state variable. An occupied dining table has a definite number of guests seated on it, as captured by the noOfGuests attribute. The name of the waiter who attends to these guests is captured in the waiter state variable. The number of tables in the restaurant is stored in the TableConfig object.

A food item being sold in the restaurant is represented by a Food object. Food has a name. Unit price for a serving portion of the food is captured in the price attribute. If any tax is to be charged, applicable tax rate information is captured in the taxRate member variable. There can be many categories of food such as starter, main course, dessert, and so on. The category of a food item is captured in its category attribute.

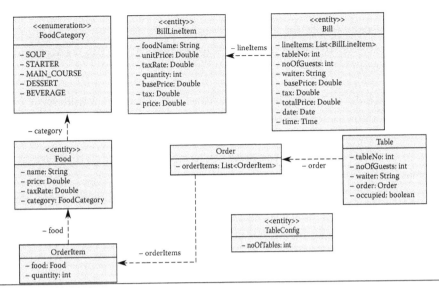

Figure 11.2 Model objects.

Guests seated at a dining table order food. An `OrderItem` represents the order placed by the guests for a specific food item. The `food` attribute captures the specific food item ordered. The `quantity` attribute captures the number of portions ordered.

During their stay in the restaurant, guests keep placing orders for different food items at different times. An `Order` object maintains a collection of `OrderItem` objects. All of the order items maintained in an order object belong to a specific set of guests seated at a particular table. The `Order` object is associated with the `Table` object through the `order` attribute of the table.

After the guests have finished dining, a bill is printed for the table. The `Bill` model object has a collection of `BillLineItem`. A bill line item corresponds to an `OrderLineItem`. The bill line item captures the name of the food ordered through the `foodName` attribute. The quantity of the order is captured through the `quantity` attribute. The price of the food is copied to the `unitPrice` attribute. The tax rate applicable for the food is copied to the `taxRate` attribute. Using all these values, the price payable for the bill line item is calculated. The bill sums all the bill line item prices to arrive at the total amount payable.

11.3.3 Presentation Tier Design

Having identified the model objects that would serve as vehicles of data communication across the components, we perform the design of the presentation tier. We need to identify the UI components that would be present in this tier. For the identified UI component, we must also determine the business interface that it requires. The component and interfaces can be determined through use case realizations. We present individual use case realizations below.

11.3.3.1 Realization of UC1—Configure Dining Tables   Let us call the UI component that is primarily responsible for all user interactions in this use case as the `Table AdminUI` component. The sequence of operations involved in the realization of this use case is as below:

1. User invokes the use case. The `TableAdminUI` component asks some business component to provide the currently configured number of tables. Let us call this operation `getNoOfTables()`.
2. `TableAdminUI` presents the currently configured number of tables to the user and collects a new configuration value from him.
3. `TableAdminUI` passes the new configuration value to some business component. Let us call this operation `reconfigureTables(int noOfTables)`. The business component is supposed to act on this newly configured value and change the number of tables in the restaurant.

In order to carry out the UI responsibility, the `TableAdminUI` component needs support from the business tier for the following two operations:

- `getNoOfTables()`
- `reconfigureTables(int noOfTables)`

Services required by a component are captured in a required interface. Hence, we can club these two operations into a required interface of this component. Let us call this required interface `ITableBiz`. Figure 11.3 illustrates the identified component and its required interface.

11.3.3.2 Realization of UC2—Create Menu Item and UC3—Modify/Remove Menu Item   Let us call the UI component which is primarily responsible for all user interactions in these two use cases as the `FoodAdminUI` component. The sequence of operations involved in the realization of these use cases is as below:

1. User invokes the use case. The `FoodAdminUI` component asks some business component to provide the currently available list of `Food` items. Let us call this operation `findAllFoods()`.
2. `FoodAdminUI` presents the list of food items to the user and asks the user to choose an item to edit/delete, or create a new item (depending on whether UC2 or UC3 was invoked).

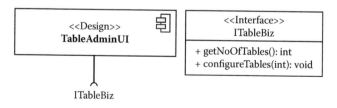

Figure 11.3   Design of the `TableAdminUI` component.

3. FoodAdminUI passes the appropriate inputs collected from the user to some business component. Let us call these operations as below:

- createNewFood(String name, double price, double
                         taxRate, FoodCategory category)
- modifyFood(String foodName, Food modifiedFood)
- deleteFood(Food food)

4. The business component is supposed to act on these operations appropriately.

From the above, we can derive that the FoodAdminUI component depends on a business interface that provides all the business operations identified above. Call this required interface of this component IFoodBiz. Figure 11.4 illustrates the identified component and its required interface.

11.3.3.3 Realization of UC4—Check-In Guests Let us call the UI component that is primarily responsible for all user interactions in this use case as the CheckInUI component. The sequence of operations involved in the realization of this use case is as shown below:

1. User invokes the use case. The CheckInUI component asks some business component to provide the currently available list of empty Tables. Let us call this operation getEmptyTables().
2. CheckInUI presents the list of available tables to the user and asks the user to choose a table along with details of the number of guests and waiter name.
3. CheckInUI passes the appropriate inputs collected from the user to some business component. Call this operation occupyTable(Table table, int noOfGuests, String waiter).
4. The business component is supposed to mark the table as occupied along with other details.

From the above, we can derive that the CheckInUI component depends on a business interface that provides the business operations getEmptyTables() and occupyTable(). Since these business operations relate to the administration of tables in the restaurant, add these operations to the ITableBiz interface identified in Figure 11.3. The modified version of the ITableBiz interface along with the CheckInUI component is shown in Figure 11.5.

Figure 11.4 Design of the FoodAdminUI component.

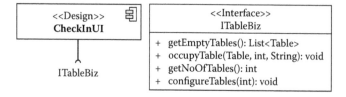

Figure 11.5 Design of the CheckInUI component.

11.3.3.4 Realization of UC5—Place Order   Let us call the UI component that is primarily responsible for all user interactions in this use case as the OrderUI component. The sequence of operations involved in the realization of this use case is as below:

1. User invokes the use case. OrderUI component asks some business component to provide the currently occupied list of Tables. Call this operation getOccupiedTables().
2. OrderUI presents the list of occupied tables to the user and asks the user to choose a table from which to place orders.
3. OrderUI component asks some business component to provide the list of Food items available in the restaurant. Call this operation findAllFoods().
4. OrderUI presents the list of Food items to the user and asks the user to select the ordered food and quantity.
5. OrderUI passes the inputs collected from the user to some business component to place the order. Let us call this operation placeOrder(Table table, Food food, int quantity).
6. The business component is supposed to add an OrderItem to the Order associated with the table.

From the above, we can derive that the CheckInUI component depends on a business interface that provides the business operations getOccupiedTables(), findAllFoods(), and placeOrder(). Of these, findAllFoods() is already defined in the business interface IFoodBiz shown in Figure 11.4. The getOccupiedTables() operation seems to go well with the ITableBiz interface. Let us assign the placeOrder() operation to a required interface called IOrderBiz. The UI component and all the required interfaces are illustrated in Figure 11.6.

11.3.3.5 Realization of UC6—Modify/Cancel Order   Let the OrderUI component identified in the last use case be primarily responsible for all user interactions in this use case. The sequence of operations involved in the realization of this use case is as below:

1. User invokes the use case. The OrderUI component asks some business component to provide the list of currently occupied Tables. This can be achieved with getOccupiedTables() already defined on the ITableBiz interface.
2. OrderUI presents the list of occupied tables to the user and asks the user to choose a table whose orders are to be modified/cancelled. User selects the table.

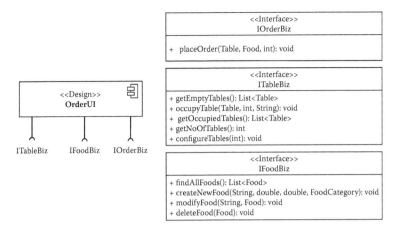

Figure 11.6 Design of the `OrderUI` component.

3. `OrderUI` asks some business component to provide the current list of items ordered from the table. Let us call this operation `getOrderItems(Table table)`.

4. `OrderUI` presents the list of `OrderItems` to the user and asks the user to select the item to modify/cancel.

5. `OrderUI` passes the inputs collected from the user to some business component to modify the `Order`. Call this operation `modifyOrder(Table table, OrderItem orderItem, int newQuantity)`. For cancelling the `OrderItem`, we define the operation as `cancelOrder(Table table, OrderItem orderItem)`.

6. The business component is supposed to act on this operation appropriately.

From the above, we can derive that the `OrderUI` component depends on a business interface that provides the business operations `getOrderItems()`, `modifyOrderItem()`, and `cancelOrderItem()`. These three operations seem to fit appropriately in the `IOrderBiz` interface already presented in Figure 11.6. In addition to these, the `OrderUI` component depends on the `ITableBiz` interface for `getOccupiedTables()`. We incrementally add these changes on top of the `OrderUI` design presented in Figure 11.6 to arrive at Figure 11.7.

11.3.3.6 Realization of UC7—Print Receipt Let us call the UI component that is primarily responsible for all user interactions in this use case the `BillUI` component. The sequence of operations involved in the realization of this use case is as below:

1. The user invokes the use case. The `BillUI` component asks some business component to provide the list of currently occupied `Tables`. This can be achieved through the `getOccupiedTables()` operation already defined for the `ITableBiz` interface.

2. `BillUI` presents the list of occupied tables to the user and asks the user to choose a table whose receipt is to be printed. User selects the table.

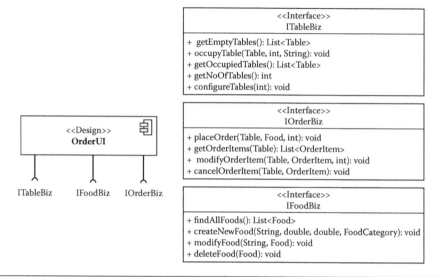

Figure 11.7   Updated design of the OrderUI component.

3. BillUI passes the Table information to some business component asking it to print the receipt. Call this operation payBill(Table table).

4. The business component generates a Bill object corresponding to the Order object associated with the Table and returns it. The BillUI component displays the bill based on the details present in the Bill object.

From the above, we can derive that the BillUI component depends on a business interface that provides the business operation payBill(). Assign the payBill() operation to a new business interface called IBillBiz. The design of the BillUI component along with the required interfaces is presented in Figure 11.8.

11.3.3.7 Realization of UC8—Guest Check-Out   Let us call the UI component that is primarily responsible for all user interactions in this use case as the CheckOutUI component. The sequence of operations involved in the realization of this use case is shown below:

1. User invokes the use case. The CheckOutUI component asks some business component to provide the list of currently occupied Tables. This operation is already defined in the ITableBiz interface as getOccupiedTables().

2. CheckOutUI presents the list of occupied tables to the user and asks the user to choose a table. The user selects the table.

3. CheckOutUI passes the Table information to some business component asking it to mark the table as unoccupied. Let us call this operation unOccupyTable(Table table).

From the above, we can derive that the CheckOutUI component depends on a business interface that provides the business operation and unOccupyTable().

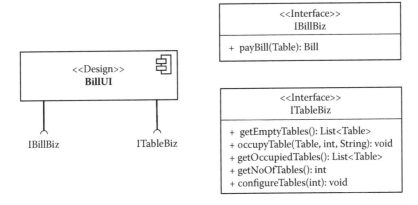

Figure 11.8   Design of the `BillUI` component.

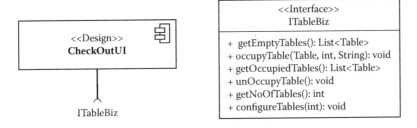

Figure 11.9   Design of the `CheckOutUI` component.

The operation `unOccupyTable()` is best fit within the `ITableBiz` interface. The updated `ITableBiz` and the design of the `CheckOutUI` component are presented in Figure 11.9.

The consolidated design of all the UI components and the business interfaces that they depend on is presented in Figure 11.10.

11.3.4 Business Tier Design

In the last section we identified a number of UI components and a set of business interfaces that these components require. Components in the business tier must provide the interfaces required by the UI components in the presentation tier. Based on the business interfaces determined in the last section, we decide to have four business components: `TableBiz`, `BillBiz`, `OrderBiz`, and `FoodBiz`. Each business component provides one business interface as shown in Figure 11.11.

Based on the use case realization descriptions we provided in the last section while identifying the UI components, we have a fair idea of what is required to be done by the business component offering an interface. We provide a brief description of the business logic to be implemented for each of the interface operations in the following.

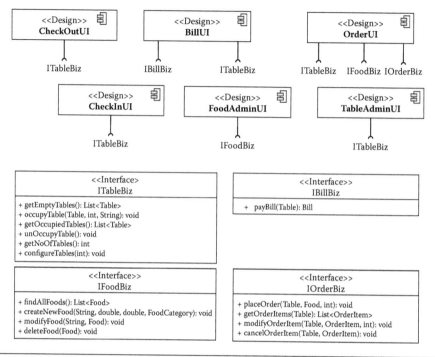

Figure 11.10 Consolidated presentation of tier design.

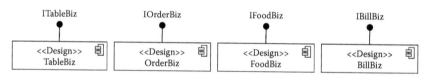

Figure 11.11 Design of business components and interfaces.

11.3.4.1 Design of the TableBiz Component The `TableBiz` component provides the `ITableBiz` interface as shown in Figure 11.12. This component is responsible for managing the states of dining tables in the restaurant. It stores the number of tables in the restaurant in the `TableConfig` object (refer to model diagram in Figure 11.2). Whenever the number of tables in the restaurant is configured through invocation of the `reconfigureTables()` operation, the implementation of the method updates the `noOfTables` attribute of the `TableConfig` object. In addition, the `TableConfig` object is stored in a persistent data store so that the configured value will be in effect even when the application is restarted. The persistent storage is achieved by invoking the services of the persistence tier. This is shown through the required interface `ITableConfigPersistence` in Figure 11.12. When the `getNoOfTables()` call is invoked, the implementation would return the value of `noOfTables` attribute of the `TableConfig` object.

When the application starts, the `TableBiz` component retrieves the `TableConfig` object from the persistence tier. Based on the `noOfTables` attribute value, the component instantiates as many `Table` objects. The implementation of the

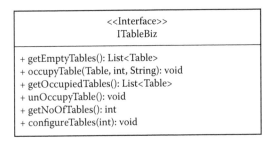

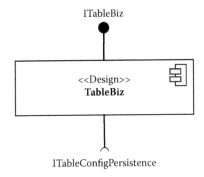

Figure 11.12 Design of the `TableBiz` component.

`occupyTable()` method updates the status of the `occupied` state variable of the specified `Table` object to `true`. In addition, it stores the values of `noOfGuests` and `waiter` attributes of the `Table` object based on the parameters passed in the call. The `unOccupyTable()` method implementation marks the `occupied` status to `false` and resets the values of `noOfGuests` and `waiter` attributes of the `Table` object.

When the `getOccupiesTables()` method is invoked, the `TableBiz` component scans through the list of `Table` objects and collects the subset of this collection whose `occupied` state is `true`. The set of occupied `Table` objects is returned back to the caller of the operation. Similarly, when the `getEmptyTables()` method is invoked, the set of `Table` objects that are not occupied is returned.

11.3.4.2 Design of the FoodBiz Component The `FoodBiz` component provides the `IFoodBiz` interface as shown in Figure 11.13. This component is responsible for managing the list of food items available in the restaurant. Whenever a new food item is added to the menu through invocation of the `createNewFood()` operation, the implementation creates a `Food` object based on the parameters passed and persists it in the data store. For the persistence operation the component requires an `IFoodPersistence` interface as shown in Figure 11.13.

When the `findAllFoods()` operation is invoked, the implementation fetches all the `Food` items from the data store and returns the collection. When the `modifyFood()` operation is invoked, the attributes of the specified `Food` object are modified as per the parameters passed in the operation, and the `Food` object stored in

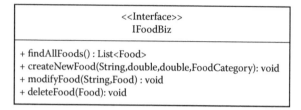

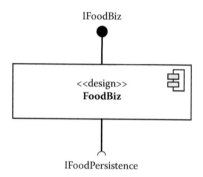

Figure 11.13   Design of the FoodBiz component.

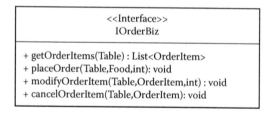

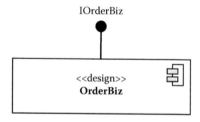

Figure 11.14   Design of the OrderBiz component.

the data store is updated as well. When the deleteFood() operation is invoked, the specified Food object is removed from the persistent data store.

11.3.4.3 Design of the OrderBiz Component   The OrderBiz component provides the IOrderBiz interface as shown in Figure 11.14. This component is responsible for managing orders made from guests seated at various tables. When a Table is occupied by guests, an Order object is created and stored in the order attribute of the Table. The newly created Order item has an empty list of orderItems attribute.

When the placeOrder() method is invoked, an OrderItem object is created as per the parameters of the method and added to the orderItems list of the Order object on the specified Table. Similarly, when the modifyOrderItem() operation is invoked, the orderItems list in the Order object corresponding to the specified Table is updated. When the deleteOrderItem() is invoked, the specified item is removed from the list of orderItems in the Order object corresponding to the specified Table object. The operation getOrderItems() returns the list of OrderItem objects found under the orderItems attribute of the Order corresponding to the specified Table object. Notice that the OrderBiz component does not persist any data; hence, it does not have any dependency on the persistence layer.

11.3.4.4 Design of the BillBiz Component The BillBiz component provides the IBillBiz interface as shown in Figure 11.15. This component is responsible for creating a bill for a table based on food items consumed by the guests at that table. When the payBill() operation is invoked, the implementation retrieves the Order object associated with the Table object. This is achieved by calling the accessor method for the order attribute of the Table object. A new Bill object is created. For each OrderItem object found in the orderItems attribute of the retrieved Order object, a BillLineItem object is created and added to the list of billLineItems attribute in the created Bill object. The method returns the created Bill object after persisting it in the data store. For the persistence operation, the component requires an IBillPersistence interface as shown in Figure 11.15.

11.3.4.5 Consolidated Design A consolidated design of all the UI components and business components identified so far is shown in Figure 11.16.

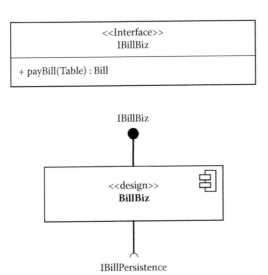

Figure 11.15 Design of the BillBiz component.

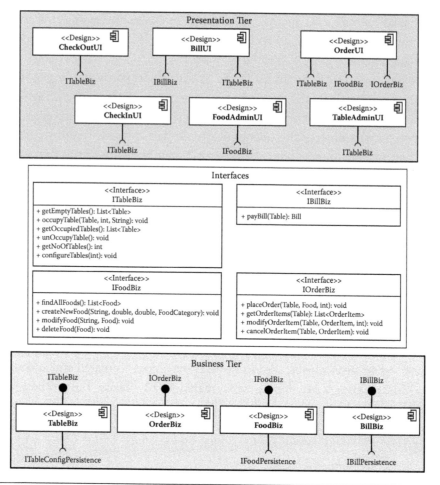

Figure 11.16 Consolidated design of UI and business components.

11.3.5 Persistence Tier Design

In the business components design that was performed in the last section, we identified that all business components except the `OrderBiz` component require the services of a persistence layer. Specifically, these components required the persistence of the objects of type `TableConfig`, `Food`, and `Bill`. When `Bill` objects are persisted, the `BillLineItem` objects contained in them are also required to be persisted. If we use a relational database to store these objects, we can persist these objects with the help of the relational database schema shown in Figure 11.17.

In order to consume the services of the data store from the business tier, we use the standardized JPA (Java Persistence API). The objects that need to be persisted are annotated with the JPA annotation `@Entity`. JPA implementations provide an `EntityManager` that manages the persistence of objects marked for persistence. Through the `EntityManager` API object, business components can consume the services of the persistence tier. If you refer back to Figure 11.2, in the model class diagram, all objects to be persisted are marked with a stereotype `Entity`.

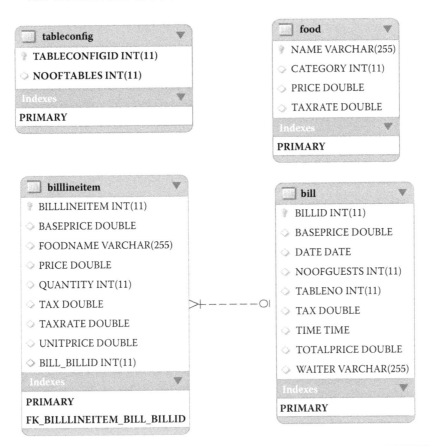

Figure 11.17   Database schema.

11.4 Implementation of the POS Application Using the OSGi Component Framework

In this section, we present details of how to implement the POS application using the OSGi component framework (discussed in Chapter 5) as per the component-based design derived in the last section. Component-based development in OSGi is based on the following principles with which we are familiar:

- Components are packaged as OSGi bundles
- OSGi bundles can house one or more components; provided interfaces of a component are to be registered with the OSGi service registry. The registration process can be automated using OSGi declarative services or OSGi Blueprint.
- The OSGi bundle can expose parts of its internals selectively using the `export-package`.
- The OSGi bundle can declare dependency on the types declared in the other bundles using the `import-package`.
- OSGi runtime will autowire the *export-package* from one bundle to the *import-package* from other bundles; similarly, a declarative service or Blueprint service container will autowire the *provided interface* of one bundle to the *required interface* of other bundles.

Based on the above principles, we implement a console UI-based POS application. Following the design developed in the last section, we need to create a bundle that exposes the model objects. This bundle will form the basic lingua franca for all other components of the application. So we implement a model bundle named POS.Model as shown in Figure 11.18. This bundle exposes all the model objects as an *export-package*.

We had identified six different design components in the presentation tier design in the last section. We implement these components using four OSGi bundles, which are tabulated in Table 11.9.

We elaborate on the implementation of the POS.Admin.UI bundle below. The implementations of other bundles are similar.

This bundle implements the TableAdminUI and FoodAdminUI components from the POS design. Internally, this bundle consists of three components as shown in Figure 11.19. Apart from the TableAdminUI and FoodAdminUI components from the design specifications, the AdminUI component has been added in

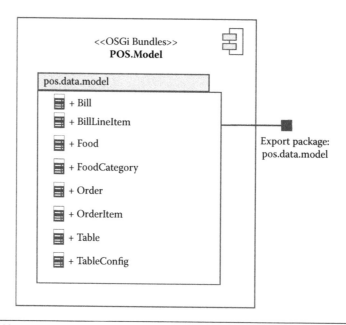

Figure 11.18 POS model OSGi bundle.

Table 11.9 UI Design Components to OSGi Implementation Bundle Mapping

NUMBER	DESIGN COMPONENT	OSGI BUNDLE
1	TableConfigUI	POS.Admin.UI
2	FoodAdminUI	
3	CheckInUI	POS.Table.UI
4	CheckOutUI	
5	BillUI	POS.Bill.UI
6	OrderUI	POS.Order.UI

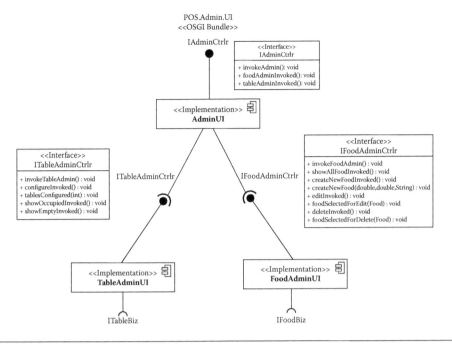

Figure 11.19 OSGi implementation—POS.Admin.UI bundle.

the implementation as a convenience component that provides a single Restaurant Administration UI. Depending upon the user selection, one of the FoodAdminUI or TableAdminUI component services is invoked by the AdminUI component.

Internal implementation of each of these three components consists of views and controller objects as per the model-view-controller (MVC) design pattern. The internal class diagram of the TableAdminUI component is presented in Figure 11.20. The internal structures of other components are similar. Note that one of the implementation classes, the TableAdminCtrlr, requires ITableBiz. This required interface is specified in the declarative service specification of this component.

We have covered the implementation of all the UI components for the POS application using the OSGi framework. We now present details of the business components implementation. There are four design components in the business tier. Each business component is implemented as an OSGi bundle. Each OSGi bundle contains one OSGi declarative service component, which registers an OSGi service corresponding to the interface provided by the component. The details of the bundles along with the services they register are tabulated in Table 11.10.

We present details of the POS.Food.Biz bundle in the following. All other business bundles follow a similar pattern of implementation. The POS.Food.Biz bundle implements the FoodBiz design component. Internally, this bundle consists of a single component as shown in Figure 11.21. The component has dependency on the EntityManagerFactory data persistence interface (from JPA). The component provides the business interface IFoodBiz.

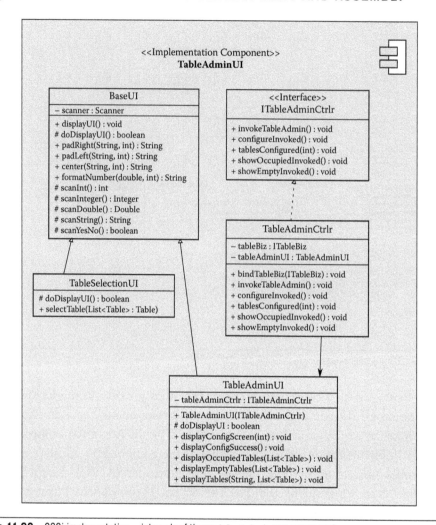

Figure 11.20   OSGi implementation—internals of the `TableAdminUI` component.

Table 11.10   Business Design Components to OSGi Implementation Bundle Mapping

NUMBER	DESIGN COMPONENT	OSGI BUNDLE	PROVIDED SERVICE
1	TableBiz	POS.Table.Biz	ITableBiz
2	FoodBiz	POS.Food.Biz	IFoodBiz
3	BillBiz	POS.Bill.Biz	IBillBiz
4	OrderBiz	POS.Order.Biz	IOrderBiz

Note that an internal implementation class `FoodBiz` has a reference to the JPA `EntityManager` interface. There is also a `bindEMF()` method that takes the JPA `EntityManagerFactory` object as a parameter. The dependency on the persistence layer is specified through the OSGi declarative service specification, in which the required interface `EntityManagerFactory` is specified. The OSGi declarative service runtime calls back the `bindEMF()` method with an instance

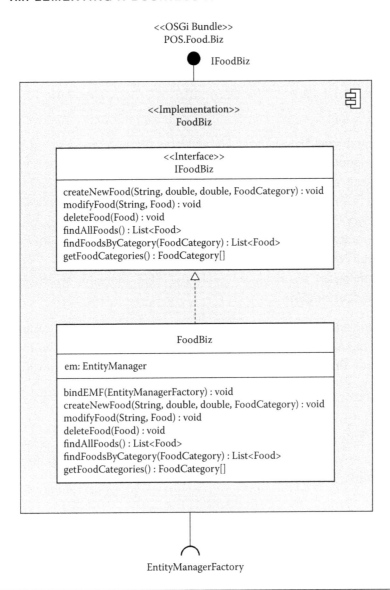

Figure 11.21 OSGi implementation—POS.Food.Biz bundle.

of the EntityManagerFactory available from the runtime environment. The EntityManagerFactory is provided by the JPA provider. We have used Eclipse Gemini JPA as the provider in the implementation source code provided in the companion Web site.

As detailed in the design section, persistence components are implemented as JPA entities. The model objects that are to be persisted—TableConfig, Food, Bill, and BillLineItem—are annotated with the @Entity JPA annotation. All these objects are present within the POS.Model bundle shown in Figure 11.18. The POS.Model bundle defines the JPA persistence unit using the persistence.xml file, which is parsed by the JPA provider to expose the persistence service through the EntityManagerFactory.

11.5 Implementation of the POS Application—Using Service Component Architecture

In this section we elaborate on the implementation of a textual UI-based POS application implementation using Service Component Architecture (SCA), which was discussed in Chapter 6. To recapitulate the SCA principles of component implementation:

- SCA components expose provided interfaces through services
- SCA components specify required interfaces through references
- Components are defined and wired using composite files
- Multiple SCA components can be composed together to form a composite
- Certain services offered by the SCA components within the SCA composite can be promoted to the level of SCA composites, so that applications from outside can consume these services
- SCA composites are deployed onto the SCA domain, which hosts the components at runtime

The SCA implementation of a POS application consists of a SCA composite called POS. This composite consists of all the UI components and the business components identified. The composite diagram in SCA notation is shown in Figure 11.22.

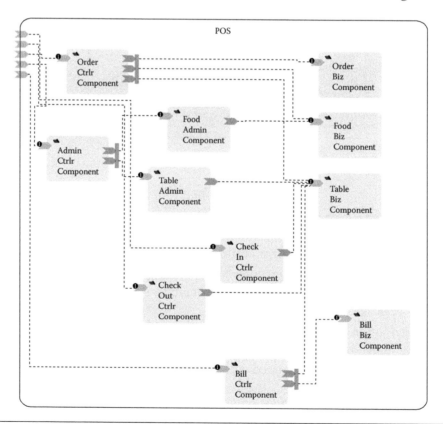

Figure 11.22   SCA implementation of the POS application.

Table 11.11   UI Design Components to SCA Implementation Components
Mapping

NUMBER	DESIGN COMPONENT	SCA IMPLEMENTATION COMPONENT
1	TableAdminUI	TableAdminComponent
2	FoodAdminUI	FoodAdminComponent
3	CheckInUI	CheckInCtrlrComponent
4	CheckOutUI	CheckOutCtrlrComponent
5	OrderUI	OrderCtrlrComponent
6	BillUI	BillCtrlrComponent

The SCA implementation components corresponding to the six UI components are tabulated in Table 11.11.

Each of the UI components has one or more controllers and associated views as per the MVC design pattern. The internals of the UI components are similar to the implementation of the `TableUI` component illustrated in Figure 11.20. Apart from the six components shown in Table 11.11, there is an `AdminCtrlr` Component that presents a single restaurant admin UI combining the table admin and food admin UI screens. Depending on the functionality invoked from the restaurant admin screen, the control flows to `TableAdminComponent` or `FoodAdminComponent`. From the presentation tier components, the following five services have been promoted to be visible at the composite level. The implementation consists of a main program that consumes these promoted services to show a menu-based text-driven console to the users:

- `IAdminCtrlr`
- `ICheckInCtrlr`
- `ICheckOutCtrlr`
- `IPayBillCtrlr`
- `IOrderCtrlr`

The UI components have dependency on the business components. These dependencies are specified through SCA references to the required business interfaces. For example, the `CheckInCtrlrComponent` specifies an SCA reference for the `ITableBiz` interface. The `TableBizComponent` declares `ITableBiz` as an SCA service that it provides. In the composite diagram shown in Figure 11.22, you can see that the SCA reference of the `CheckInCtrlrComponent` has been wired to the SCA service declared by the `TableBizComponent`. Other UI components are wired to appropriate business components in a similar manner. Table 11.12 presents the list of implementation business components against the design components.

Each business component exposes an SCA service corresponding to the provided interface in the design component. The internal implementation of business components is similar to the implementation presented in Figure 11.21.

Table 11.12 Business Design Components to SCA Implementation Component Mapping

NUMBER	DESIGN COMPONENT	SCA IMPLEMENTATION COMPONENT
1	`TableBiz`	`TableBizComponent`
2	`FoodBiz`	`FoodBizComponent`
3	`OrderBiz`	`OrderBizComponent`
4	`BillBiz`	`BillBizComponent`

Persistence components are implemented using JPA entities. All the objects in the model shown in Figure 11.2 are deployed as a JAR library in the CLASSPATH. The objects required to be persisted—`TableConfig`, `Food`, `Bill`, and `BillLineItem`—are annotated with the JPA annotation `@Entity`. In addition, a `persistence.xml` file in the model JAR library specifies the JPA persistence unit. The JPA provider library is deployed along with the rest of the application, and the business components load the JPA API objects from the CLASSPATH. In the companion code, the Open JPA implementation from Apache is used as the JPA provider.

11.6 Implementation of the POS Application—Using the Enterprise OSGi Component Framework

Chapter 9 on Enterprise OSGi introduced the general structure of an enterprise application built using the Enterprise OSGi framework. In this section, we elaborate on how the POS application can be implemented with a Web front-end using the Enterprise OSGi component framework. Based on the Enterprise OSGi application development principles in Chapter 9, the implementation of the POS Web application involves the following:

- Implementation of UI layer as a Web application bundle (WAB)
- Implementation of business tier components as OSGi bundles that provide business interfaces using OSGi services; OSGi services can be registered using declarative services or Blueprint
- Implementation of persistence bundle; OSGi JPA service uses this bundle to expose persistence service
- Deployment of all the bundles in an Enterprise OSGi runtime environment; deployment environment used in the companion implementation is Apache Aries

The overall structure of the Enterprise OSGi implementation of the POS application is presented in Figure 11.23.

The presentation tier is implemented using JSP pages as views and servlets as controllers. All the views and controllers are bundled together as a Web application bundle (WAB) that can be deployed in an Enterprise OSGi container (Apache Aries in our companion implementation). The mapping of the UI design components to the implementation components is tabulated in Table 11.13.

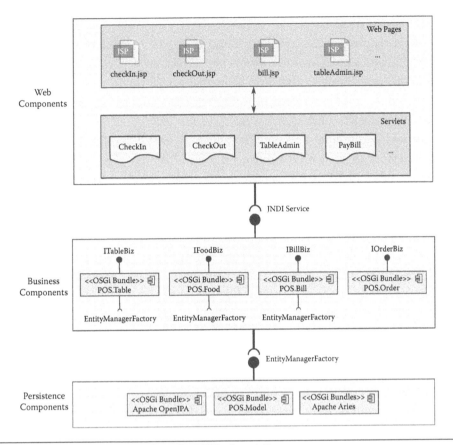

Figure 11.23   POS Web application—Enterprise OSGi implementation.

Table 11.13   UI Design Components to Enterprise OSGi Implementation Component Mapping

NUMBER	DESIGN COMPONENT	ENTERPRISE OSGI IMPLEMENTATION COMPONENT	
		VIEWS	CONTROLLERS
1	TableAdminUI	tableAdmin.jsp	TableAdminController
2	FoodAdminUI	foodItems.jsp	FoodAdminController
3	CheckInUI	checkIn.jsp	CheckInController
4	CheckOutUI	checkOut.jsp	CheckOutController
5	OrderUI	orderItems.jsp	OrdersController
6	BillUI	bill.jsp	PayBillController

The business components are implemented as POJO classes and are split into four OSGi bundles, similar to the bundles shown in Table 11.10. OSGi Blueprint is used for specifying the provided interface of each of the business components. A OSGi Blueprint container registers the provided interfaces with the OSGi service registry at runtime. Apache Aries exposes these OSGi services registered by the business components as JNDI services. This enables the UI layer to look up the business layer components using a JNDI query. In the presentation layer, a `ServletContextListener` is implemented to get references of business components during startup or initialization.

The `ServletContextListener` performs a JNDI lookup for each of the four business interfaces required—`ITableBiz`, `IFoodBiz`, `IOrderBiz`, and `IBillBiz`. The `ServletContextListener` stores the object references as attributes of the `ServletContext` object so that it is accessible across the application. All the UI controller components (the servlets) pick the references to business components from the `ServletContext` object.

The business components are implemented as OSGi bundles, which provide business interfaces as an OSGi service. The bundles and the provided interfaces are shown in Table 11.10. Services provided by these bundles are exposed through Blueprint specification. This is done with the help of the `blueprint.xml` file in each bundle.

All the model objects shown in Figure 11.2 are packaged in the `POS.Data` bundle. The `POS.Data` bundle is a persistence bundle (it has a `Meta-Persistence` manifest header, as well as a `persistence.xml` file). The model objects that are to be persisted—`TableConfig`, `Food`, `Bill`, and `BillLineItem`—are annotated with the `@Entity` JPA annotation. The `persistence.xml` file is parsed by the JPA provider to expose the persistence service through the `EntityManagerFactory`. Apache Aries OSGi JPA service implementation is used in the companion implementation.

The business components that require persistence service—`TableBiz`, `FoodBiz`, and `BillBiz`—express their dependency on the persistence layer by specifying a required interface of type `EntityManagerFactory`. This is specified through Blueprint using the `blueprint.xml` file. The Blueprint container wires the `EntityManagerFactory` from the JPA provider to these business components at runtime.

11.7 Implementation of the POS Application—Using the Spring Component Framework

In this section, we elaborate on how to implement a Web-based POS application using the Spring component framework that was discussed in Chapter 8. As discussed in Chapter 8, we have the following underlying principles that we can use to build a Spring-based component-oriented application:

- Spring framework includes support for MVC design pattern; controllers can be written as POJOs rather than servlets; views can be written as JSP pages; views and controllers can be joined by means of Spring annotations on the POJO controller implementations, and additionally through the Spring configuration file
- Business components can be implemented as Spring beans; UI components can consume the business components through Spring dependency injection
- Business components can consume persistence services through Spring dependency injection

The overall structure of the Spring framework–based implementation of the POS application is presented in Figure 11.24.

All the view components are implemented as Java Server Pages (JSPs). All the controllers are implemented as POJOs with a Spring `@Controller` annotation. The controllers declare their dependency on business components through the `@Autowired` Spring annotation. Table 11.14 provides a mapping of a UI design component to the Spring UI implementation components.

The business components are implemented as Spring beans, which are POJOs. Mapping of the Spring beans to the business design components is shown in Table 11.15.

The implementations of these POJO classes are similar to the implementation illustrated in Figure 11.21. The only difference is that the Spring beans do not implement any interfaces. The implementation class itself is exposed as a bean that is visible to the UI component by the bean class name. The UI components declare the dependency on a specific business component using the `@Autowired` annotation. The Spring dependency injection module wires the business bean instance to the UI component at runtime.

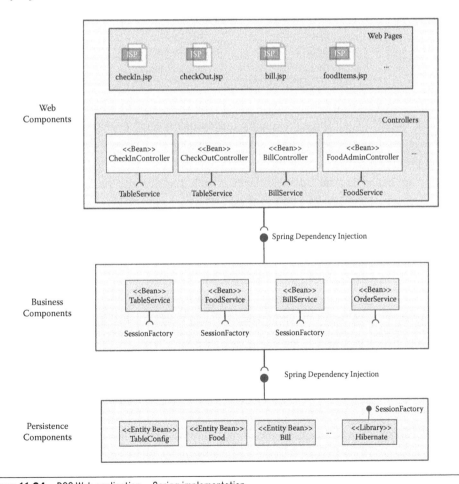

Figure 11.24 POS Web application—Spring implementation.

Table 11.14   UI Design Components to Spring Implementation Component Mapping

NUMBER	DESIGN COMPONENT	ENTERPRISE OSGI IMPLEMENTATION COMPONENT	
		VIEWS	CONTROLLERS
1	TableAdminUI	tableAdmin.jsp tableConfig.jsp	TableAdminController
2	FoodAdminUI	foodItems.jsp	FoodAdminController
3	CheckInUI	checkIn.jsp emptyTables.jsp	CheckInController
4	CheckOutUI	checkOut.jsp occupiedTables.jsp	CheckOutController
5	OrderUI	orderItem.jsp occupiedTables.jsp orderUpdateSuccess.jsp	OrderItemController
6	BillUI	occupiedTables.jsp bill.jsp	PayBillController

Table 11.15   Business Design Components to Spring Implementation Component Mapping

NUMBER	DESIGN COMPONENT	SCA IMPLEMENTATION COMPONENT
1	TableBiz	TableService
2	FoodBiz	FoodService
3	OrderBiz	OrderService
4	BillBiz	BillService

Persistence layer components are implemented as Spring entity beans, which are nothing but POJOs. These beans are annotated with the @Entity annotation. Hibernate is used as the persistence service provider that parses through the entity beans and provides persistence service.

The Spring beans in the business layer which require the persistence service—TableService, FoodService, and BillService—declare a dependency on the Hibernate SessionFactory object using the @Autowired annotation. The database connection parameter details are provided in the Web configuration file. Using this configuration, the Spring framework initializes the Hibernate framework and injects the SessionFactory object to all requiring business beans.

11.8 Implementation of the POS Application—Using the Java EE Framework

In this section, we elaborate on how to implement a Web-based POS application using the Java EE component framework. As discussed in Chapter 7, we have the following underlying principles we can use to build a Java EE–based component-oriented application:

- Java EE provides a component-based model for the presentation tier called Java Server Faces (JSF). JSF uses facelets as views in the MVC pattern and POJO-based managed beans as the model. The JSF programming model facilitates easy binding of UI elements in the facelets to the properties of managed beans.

- Business components are implemented as Enterprise Java Beans (EJB). EJBs are injected to the model managed beans in the UI layer by the EJB container dependency injection.
- Persistence is implemented using JPA. EJBs leverage JPA to access persistence. Persistence management is handled by the application or by the EJB container.

The overall structure of the Java EE framework–based implementation of the POS application is presented in Figure 11.25.

The Java EE implementation of a POS Web application includes a number of JSF components at the presentation tier. The mapping of the JSF components to UI design components is tabulated in Table 11.16. Each JSF component consists of an XHTML-based view and a managed bean model object. View elements are automatically bound

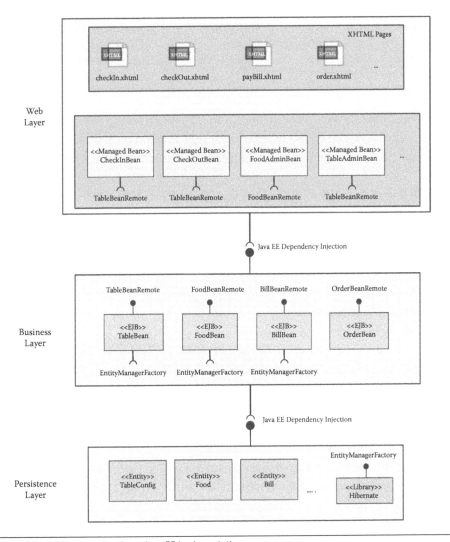

Figure 11.25 POS Web application—Java EE implementation.

Table 11.16 UI Design Components to Java EE Implementation Component Mapping

NUMBER	DESIGN COMPONENT	ENTERPRISE OSGI IMPLEMENTATION COMPONENT	
		VIEWS	MANAGED BEAN
1	TableAdminUI	tableAdminBean. xhtml	TableAdminBean
2	FoodAdminUI	foodAdmin.xhtml	FoodAdminBean
3	CheckInUI	checkIn.xhtml	CheckInBean
4	CheckOutUI	checkOut.xhtml	CheckOutBean
5	OrderUI	order.xhtml	OrderManagedBean
6	BillUI	payBill.xhtml	BillPaymentBean

Table 11.17 Business Design Components to Java EE implementation Component Mapping

NUMBER	DESIGN COMPONENT	JAVA EE EJB COMPONENT	EJB REMOTE INTERFACE
1	TableBiz	TableBean	TableBeanRemote
2	FoodBiz	FoodBean	FoodBeanRemote
3	OrderBiz	OrderBean	OrderBeanRemote
4	BillBiz	BillBean	BillBeanRemote

to attributes of the managed bean. Hence, the UI programming is made simple in the JSF model. The managed bean Java classes in turn depend on EJB for business logic. They declare their dependency on EJB business components through the @EJB Java EE annotation.

Business components are implemented as EJBs. Each EJB implements operations specified in a EJB remote interface. The EJB implementation component corresponding to each business design component is tabulated in Table 11.17.

Implementation of the business component is similar to the implementation illustrated in Figure 11.21. Each business component implements the EJB remote interface that it provides. The UI components declare @EJB dependency over the EJB remote interface. The application server runtime wires the appropriate EJB instance to the UI component.

All the model objects shown in Figure 11.2 are implemented as POJOs. Among these POJOs, TableConfig, Food, Bill, and BillLineItem are annotated using the JPA @Entity annotation. These JPA entity objects implement the persistence components. All the persistence unit details are specified through a persistence. xml file. The JPA provider makes use of the file details to provide the persistence of entity objects. The JPA provider exposes an EntityManagerFactory JPA interface object. The EJBs that require persistence support—TableBean, FoodBean, and BillBean—make use of JPA to obtain an instance of the EntityManager Factory. Using the EntityManagerFactory, the EJBs manage the persistence of the entity objects as per business logic requirement. The companion implementation uses the Glassfish application server for deployment.

11.9 Summary

In this case study, we presented a detailed business problem, a component-oriented design to cater to the requirements specified in the problem, and various implementations of the component-oriented design. We presented textual UI-based implementation using OSGi and SCA component frameworks. This was followed by Web UI–based implementation using the Enterprise OSGi framework, the Spring framework, and the Java EE framework. The companion Web site of the book carries the source code of all the implementations. We hope readers are able to appreciate the methodology for component-oriented design and the nuances associated with implementation in different component frameworks.

CODA Tools—A Fictitious CODA Workbench

12.1 Introduction

We have covered the fundamentals of Component-Oriented Development and Assembly (CODA) using various component models in the earlier part of the book. In the previous chapter we provided a real-life case study problem using the point-of-sale (POS) application and solved it using CODA. CODA practice can be made easier and simpler with the help of tools like development tools, component storage and retrieval tools, assembly tools, and testing tools. The assembly phase of CODA can especially benefit by using the tools. For example, one needs to choose the right set of components for assembly. This can be made easier with an automated search for compatible components for a given component. The tool can further support visual assembly; the user can choose one of the suggested compatible components and build the assembly iteratively. For the purpose of demonstration of the usefulness of such a tool, we developed a fictitious tool called *CODA Workbench*. This tool is built using the OSGi component model, and the tool supports components developed using the OSGi component model. We present the usefulness of the tool through a visual assembly of the POS application in this chapter.

12.2 CODA Workbench—The Features

The CODA Workbench provides the following high-level features:

- Storing and retrieving OSGi components from a repository
- Visualizing the properties (exported and imported packages, declarative services) of OSGi components
- Assembling the OSGi components in a common assembly area by drag and drop
- Suggesting compatible components for assembly
- Executing tests of the assembly

In the following sections, we demonstrate these features with the help of software components developed for the point-of-sale (POS) case study application in Chapter 11.

12.3 CODA Workbench—User Interface

The CODA Workbench has a graphical user interface with the main screen as shown in Figure 12.1.

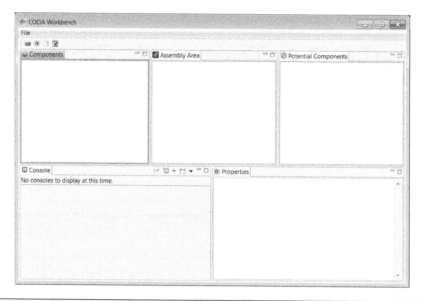

Figure 12.1   CODA Workbench main screen.

The main screen has five visual sections:

- *Components Section*—This section provides a tree view of all the components that are present in the repository.
- *Assembly Area Section*—This section is the area in which components can be assembled together to form an application. Components can be dragged and dropped from other sections.
- *Potential Components Section*—This section presents the components that can potentially fulfill the required services of the assembly found in the assembly area.
- *Properties Section*—This section presents the description of the selected component. The description is part of the OSGi header information in the component.
- *Console Section*—This section provides input and output from the application to the user. When the assembled application is being test executed, the console section displays the output and collects the input.

12.4 Viewing Repository—Components Section and Properties Section

OSGi components can be archived in a file system folder. The folder serves as a common repository. Using the open repository operation of the workbench, one can load the list of components in the repository to the *Components Section* of the main screen. The open repository operation can be invoked either through the menu or through the toolbar icon. The open repository operation is demonstrated in Figure 12.2.

Once the repository folder is specified, the workbench provides a tree view of all the components in the repository folder in the *Components Section* of the main screen.

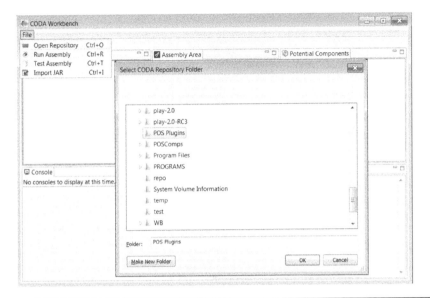

Figure 12.2 Open repository operation.

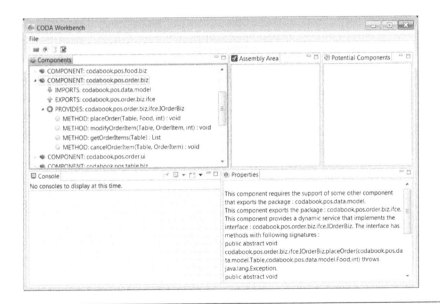

Figure 12.3 View of components in the repository.

Each component can be expanded in the tree view, and the list of exported and imported packages of the component can be seen. In addition, any declarative service that is provided or required by the component can also be seen. This is illustrated in Figure 12.3.

In Figure 12.3, the *Components Section* of the screen lists all the OSGi components found in the repository folder. If a particular component is selected and drilled down, the details of imported packages, exported packages, provided and required interfaces, and the method signatures of the interfaces can be seen. For instance, in Figure 12.3, the POS.OrderBiz component has been chosen. As seen in the expanded tree nodes below this selected node, the component exports the codabook.pos.order.biz. ifce package, and it imports the codabook.pos.data.model package. The component provides the interface IOrderBiz as a declarative service. The methods present in the provided interface can also be seen below the provided interface node. In addition to the visual details seen in the *Components Section*, a textual description about the component is provided in the *Properties Section* of the main screen.

12.5 Assembling Components into Application—Assembly Area and Potential Components Sections

Components can be dragged from the repository displayed in the *Components Section* into the *Assembly Area Section*. Let us try to build the POS application using the components. Drag and drop the POS.App component from the repository into the *Assembly Area Section* to start the assembly process. The result of dragging this component is illustrated in Figure 12.4.

In Figure 12.4, the POS.APP component has been dragged into the *Assembly Area*. The triangular warning symbol next to it indicates that this component is not satisfied within the assembly. If we expand the component, we can further drill down into aspects of the component which are not fulfilled. For example, the component imports four different packages (admin.ui.ifce, bill.ui.ifce, order.ui.ifce, and table.ui.ifce), which are not available in the assembly. Similarly, the component requires five different interfaces (IAdminCtrlr, ICheckInCtrlr, ICheckOutCtrlr, IOrderCtrlr, and IPayBillCtrlr), which are not being provided by any other component in the assembly.

If we select any one of the unfulfilled aspects of the component in the assembly area (like a missing import package or a missing required interface), the workbench

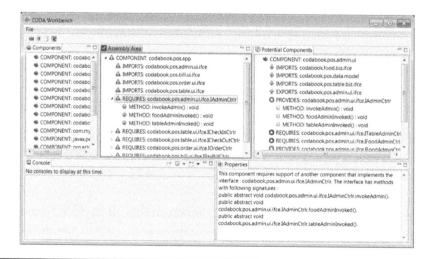

Figure 12.4 Assembling components.

searches for a possible component from the repository which can fulfill this particular aspect and display that component in the *Potential Components Section*. For example, in Figure 12.4, we selected the required interface IAdminCtrlr, which is not fulfilled. Upon selection of this interface, the workbench highlights that Admin. UI component is a potential component that can provide this interface. This component is displayed in the Potential Components section of Figure 12.4. When we expand this potential component, we find that it provides an interface that matches the required interface of the POS.APP component in the assembly area. We can drag this potential component from the *Potential Components Section* into the *Assembly Area Section*. Once we do that, we can see that the IAdminCtrlr required interface is marked as fulfilled, by means of a tick mark to its left. As a side effect, the admin.ui.ifce import package requirement is also fulfilled. This is illustrated in Figure 12.5.

We notice from Figure 12.5 that the newly added Admin.UI component in the assembly area is not fulfilled. Some of its required interfaces and import packages are not satisfied by the other components in the assembly. If we select this component from the *Assembly Area Section*, we see that three potential components are displayed in the *Potential Components Section*. This is illustrated in Figure 12.6.

We drag and drop all these suggested components into the assembly area. Once we introduce more components into the assembly area, we find that they have further dependencies. By selecting each of the unfulfilled components and dragging the suggested components from the potential area, we can build a complete application assembly iteratively. Such an iterative assembly leads to a final set of components in the assembly area as illustrated in Figure 12.7. It can be noticed that all the components are marked as fulfilled with a tick mark against each of them.

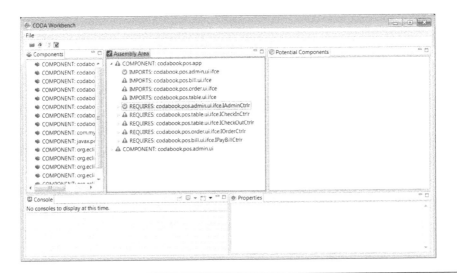

Figure 12.5   Component dragged from potential components to assembly.

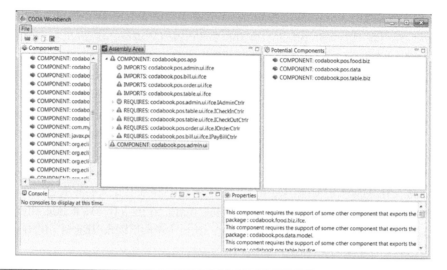

Figure 12.6   Potential components for the unfulfilled `Admin.UI` component.

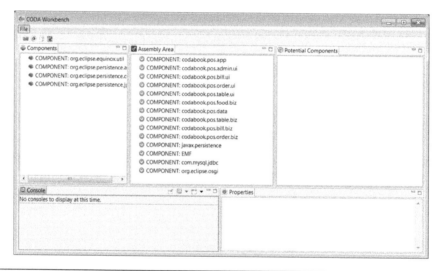

Figure 12.7   Completed assembly of the POS application.

12.6 Test Execution of Assembled Application—Console Section

Having completed the assembly process of the POS application, we can use the workbench to test-run the assembled application. The test execution can be invoked either through the menu or through the toolbar icon. When we run the application, the *Console Section* of the workbench performs the user interface input and output. Figure 12.8 provides a screenshot of the test execution output.

In Figure 12.8, we can see that on execution, the POS application provides a textual menu output. The user can provide the input by typing the user's selection inside the *Console Section*. In the example operation shown in Figure 12.8, the user has chosen menu option 1 to perform check-in. Subsequently, the application has prompted

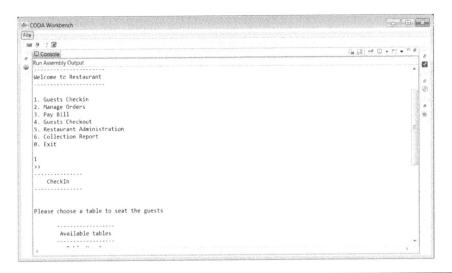

Figure 12.8 Test execution of the POS application assembly.

the user to choose a table from the list of unoccupied tables. The user interaction thus continues using the *Console Section*.

12.7 Summary

An appropriate tool can ease the difficulties perceived by the novice practitioner of CODA. In this chapter, we presented a fictitious, minimalistic tool support for graphical assembly of OSGi components. The CODA Workbench tool provided the following features:

- Repository feature to store and retrieve components
- Assembly feature to assemble components into an application
- Potential components feature to suggest compatible components to assemble
- Test execution feature to run the assembled application
- Textual description feature to describe the capabilities of the component

While the CODA Workbench tool supported the OSGi component model, it is possible to build universal tools that can support multiple component models. With rapid advancement in tooling and technology, the day is not far off when CODA practitioners search for components from the Internet and assemble them over the Cloud to create new software applications.

Index

Milton Keynes UK
Ingram Content Group UK Ltd.
UKHW020823141024
449569UK00008B/526